**Prefab Housing
and the Future of Building:
Product to Process**

An 'R4' project by R.HOUSE. Located on
the Isle of Skye in Scotland, R.HOUSE was
founded to offer affordable architectural
houses.

Prefab Housing and the Future of Building: Product to Process

Mathew Aitchison, Toktam Bashirzadeh Tabrizi,
Anne Beim, Rachel Couper, Robert Doe, Dan Engström,
Ivana Kuzmanovska, Helena Lidelöw, Duncan Maxwell,
John Macarthur, Jonathan Nelson, Masa Noguchi,
Marc Norman, Martin Rudberg, Ivan Rupnik,
Ryan Smith, Lars Stehn and Jose Torero Cullen

LUND
HUMPHRIES

First published in 2018 by Lund Humphries
Office 3, Book House
261A City Road
London
EC1V 1JX
UK

www.lundhumphries.com

Copyright © 2018, Mathew Aitchison

ISBN 978-1-84822-218-2

A Cataloguing-in-Publication record for this
book is available from the British Library.

Designed by Mark Thomson
Printed in Slovenia

Contents

Preface and Acknowledgements 7

1 **Introduction** 11

2 **Foundations in Literature** 20

3 **Utilitarian Prefab, Conceptual Prefab, or a Third Way** 37

4 **Barriers to the Uptake and Success of Prefab Housing** 61

5 **A Problem-solving Approach for Industrialised House Building** 97

6 **Prefab Housing and the Future of Building** 118

Conclusion 147

Notes 148
Notes for Text Boxes 153
Illustration Credits 158
Index 159

Thematic Text Boxes

Assembly and Construction Methods for Industrialised House Building 24

Digital and Automated Fabrication 33

USA 39

The Platform Approach 48

Business Models and Industrialised Construction 57

Case Study USA: Simplex Homes 66

Computational Design 75

Integrated Building Performance 84

Japan 93

Construction Logistics and Supply Chain Management 98

Design for Disassembly 106

Case Study Japan: Sekisui House 115

Sweden 120

Affordability and Industrialised House Building 127

Case Study Sweden: BoKlok 133

Environmental Systems 139

Life Cycle Analysis 143

Preface and Acknowledgements

When I began research on prefab housing, I thought it would be easy. Our team started working with companies and tried to help them marry great design with more efficient and flexible production systems. We saw enormous potential not only to raise quality and efficiency, but to do it with building practices that were more sustainable and that could be flexible enough to adapt to homeowners' needs and desires. Unknown to me, I had stepped on to a very well-trodden path. At the end of that path was architecture's 'Holy Grail' – the promise of finally turning our hands to the provision of housing, not just for wealthy patrons but for the masses.

What seemed like a straight path at first became more and more convoluted. Prefab must be more efficient than conventional building, we thought. Surely it is possible to have design, efficient production and flexibility. Costs should be lower. But they weren't, at least not always. Like many other well-intentioned teams before us, we realised that although the path we had embarked on may have been well-trodden, it was still perilous.

This book recounts the problems we encountered on this journey and tries to equip the reader with the lessons to understand this complex and, at times, unruly field. We also outline the opportunities that appeared along the way, which we hope will provide the reader with ideas and tools to map their own path.

It is not common to have a book with eighteen authors, less common still that those authors hail from ten different countries. It is, perhaps, rather a reflection of the new reality in the field of industrialised housing and a statement about what is needed to move knowledge beyond the confines of the individual and the institution to a mode of engagement that is closer to the challenges in industry and the needs of the end user.

As our work on prefab housing in recent years progressed, our team's skills and knowledge have expanded beyond those typical for architects and engineers and they continue to grow. This range and diversity is hardwired into this book and evidenced by our collaboration, the variety of disciplinary knowledge we have assembled, and the enormous cultural and geographical spread represented by our book's contributors.

Finally, the book's title was derived in part from a collaborative design workshop in early 2015. We were discussing the disjoint between the modes of working as architects and engineers. The architect-designers in our team were very focused on the outcome, the product. The engineer-analysts in the team were very focused on the parameters, the methodology and the process. It was then that Jose Torero Cullen, a civil engineer by training, admonished us 'Process not Product' and the maxim stuck.

The focus on process in this book is intended to make readers aware of the myriad constraints and particularities of housing (particularly industrialised housing), which, if they are not taken into account, can derail ventures. Our book suggests not only a new way of working together on the challenges of industrialised house building, but also placing more value on starting with the process and ending with the product. This might sound straightforward, but it is remarkable how often we have been confronted with the reverse.

Acknowledgements

It would be impossible to list all the companies we have studied and visited in the lead-up to the production of the book, only a fraction of which are directly referenced on the following pages. Rather, and perhaps to spare them being inundated with requests for tours and visits, I express our deepest gratitude on behalf of the entire team (you know who you are). I am continually struck by the generosity and hospitality of the individuals and companies we have met with around the world, who take the time and energy to discuss their business and research with us.

I speak on behalf of the whole team when I say that the risks taken and commitments made by these companies is more than any amount of ink or words can approach. This extends to our industry partners with whom we undertake our respective research projects. Without these companies and our partners, there would be no industry to speak of and we would not have been able to make this book.

The eighteen authors who have contributed to this book are listed on the cover page alphabetically, and it is to them that the greatest thanks are owed. It is more than coincidental that my name is first, as the book was conceptualised and directed by me. However the final result would not have been possible without the collaboration and generosity of the whole group. While each section of the book had an original lead author, each text then underwent a deep review and collaborative editing process. It should be pointed out that not every view or opinion expressed in the following pages is held by all. Yet, the whole – we hope – is more than the sum of the parts.

The original lead authors are as follows: Chapters 1–6, Mathew Aitchison; Life Cycle Analysis, Toktam Bashirzadeh Tabrizi; Design for Disassembly, Anne Beim; Computational Design, Robert Doe; Assembly and Construction Methods for Industrialised House Building, Dan Engström; Sweden, Helena Lidelöw; The Platform Approach and Case Study Sweden: BoKlok, Duncan Maxwell; Digital and Automated Fabrication, Jonathan Nelson; Japan, Case Study Japan: Sekisui House and Environmental Systems, Masa Noguchi; Affordability and Industrialised House Building, Marc Norman; Construction Logistics and Supply Chain Management, Martin Rudberg; USA and Case Study USA: Simplex Homes, Ivan Rupnik and Ryan E. Smith; Business Models and Industrialised Construction, Lars Stehn; and Integrated Building Performance, Jose Torero Cullen.

Standing behind these lead authors has been the inner circle of the book's production, without whom this book could not have been published. John Macarthur has been a key collaborator on the main body text and an intellectual 'Godfather' to me and an entire generation of Australian researchers. Rachel Couper managed the intense process of peer review and editing, and together Rachel and Ivana Kuzmanovska are responsible for the curation of the book's fine visual content, essential to any work attempting to bridge disciplinary and institutional boundaries in design and building. Duncan Maxwell, in addition to his own text contributions and being a constant sounding board, provided tireless (and unflinching) research assistance for the entire project. Justine Clark provided high-level editorial advice on the book, making sure we spoke clearly and directly to our audience. Thanks to David Kelly who carefully edited our final text.

I would also like to thank the Lund Humphries team, whose patience and latitude allowed this book to become more than we could have first anticipated. In particular, I thank our commissioning editor Val Rose, and Nigel Farrow for his support. I would also like to thank the Lund Humphries production team: Sarah Thorowgood for managing the book's production, Jacqui Cornish for her thorough copy editing, and Mark Thomson for layout and design.

Many groups and institutions have been instrumental in getting this project off the ground. Sincerest thanks to my colleagues and supporters at the University of Sydney's School of Architecture, Design and Planning, in particular Dean John Redmond and Associate Dean for Research Robyn Dowling who have supported the endeavours of the Innovation in Applied Design Lab at every turn. The work towards this book originally stemmed from a generous research grant from the Australian Research Council's 'Linkage' scheme, which funds industry–university research. As our group has grown, so too has the list of granting bodies through whom some of the research published in this book was carried out. These include the Queensland Government's 'Accelerate Partnerships' programme, and the Australian Government, Department of Industry, Innovation and Science's 'Cooperative Research Centres Programme'.

I would also like to thank the industry bodies prefabAUS (Australia) and PrefabNZ (New Zealand) for their generosity and collegiality. Also, the undergraduate and graduate students of the 'Prefab Architecture' course at the University of Sydney – through which we have developed and tested some of the materials used in this book.

Finally, on behalf of the whole group, I want to thank the families, friends and partners of our book's contributors, for borrowing the requisite weekends and nights that inevitably come into play in any big collaborative venture. At a personal level, I want to thank my extended family – the Aitchisons and the Hirsts. To Angela and Oliver, you are always with me.

Mathew Aitchison, May, 2017
Innovation in Applied Design Lab
The University of Sydney

1.1 Japanese company, Muji's 'Vertical House', suited to urban in-fill projects, has an aesthetic in keeping with their minimalist, no-brand policy.

1   Introduction

This book is about the promise of prefabricated housing. It explores the promise that new modes of housing design and production and a more industrialised approach to building might hold for the future, and provides a deeper understanding of the unmet promises of the past and the lessons we can draw from them. The book is a guide for those who wish to understand the complex and unruly field of prefab housing – its contradictions, idiosyncrasies and paradoxes – and also for those who wish to cut a path through this thicket.

Historically, prefab never quite lived up to its promise. This book is underpinned by the observation that the conditions for a more industrialised approach to housing have rarely been better. Changing consumer expectations, rising design literacy and increasing demand for interaction with services and products have resulted in strong potential markets. The industry is well placed to take advantage of this with new thinking and opportunities in the structure and management of business ventures, the rise of computational design tools, new material science and manufacturing capabilities, and rapidly developing digital and automated fabrication technologies. Prefab housing can also offer a means to respond to worrying urban and environmental shifts such as international housing shortages and affordability crises, concerns around environmental impact and sustainability and the emerging demographic and design challenges associated with population growth and instability, and rapid urbanisation.

These changing conditions set the scene for prefab to become a potential disruptor in the conservative and slow-moving construction sector. If these new circumstances can be correctly understood, and the lessons drawn from them appropriately applied, we think that prefab may finally fulfil its promise and unlock some of the industry's millennial claims.

Prefab and other industrialised approaches to housing might be timely, but why – especially in light of past failures – should we put our faith in them? We think that a more industrialised approach to house building has the potential to respond directly to contemporary challenges by asserting smarter, more efficient, and high-quality design of housing. This will not only give users more flexibility and higher quality houses, but also bring down costs and raise productivity. We propose a more integrated and holistic approach to design and production that can respond more deeply to people's needs but do so in a more sustainable, less wasteful and ecologically friendly way. Contemporary industry can respond positively to the challenges brought about by technology and its impact on construction labour by making meaningful work, better conditions, and providing a longer-term outlook for the workforce. Finally, in today's advanced capitalist society and globalised market, we think that an industrialised approach to housing not only *will* be more profitable for companies embarking on this path, but *must* be profitable for these ideas and our objectives to succeed.

The bulk of the book is devoted to understanding these contemporary and historical challenges, determining correct application of the solutions to them, and making this material accessible to a wide, general audience. This can be distilled into three key observations:

1 Prefab looks simple on the outside, but it is really very complicated. This paradox has led many ventures astray. This book shows a more complicated picture, a certain unruliness, that must be taken into account if prefab is to reach its promise. The book shows it is possible to understand and visualise this complexity as a pattern that, once seen, is very hard to *un-see*.

2 There is no *single* right way to do prefab but *many* possibilities. The move towards a greater industrialisation of housing is not linear or exclusive. There is room for many players – big and small, slow and fast – and many, many different approaches. The path to overcoming past failures and generating appropriate solutions in the future will be founded on an integrated and holistic view of the complexity and constraints of housing.

3 Fresh and balanced thinking is required for prefab to be successful. The history of prefab is one of extremes – utilitarian *or* conceptual versions of prefab. The future will be one of mediation and calculated trade-offs. It will involve a balancing of design value *and* efficient production systems. This will lead to the determination of appropriate solutions rather than a *solutions-in-search-of-problems* approach. Our emphasis will shift to process rather than product, favouring imperfect application over conceptual purity, commercial viability over ideology, substance over style, and innovation over pure invention.

Our view of the future is optimistic, despite the long history of hyperbole and failure. The many streams of knowledge, interest and circumstance in contemporary industry and society are coalescing in a way that suggests we are on the cusp of a deep restructuring of the housing and construction industries. Nevertheless, the reader should be wary and cautious (as are we) of such grand claims, particularly in light of all that has come before.

1.2 Conventional construction practices and materials have remained much the same for over a century. A timber-framed house under construction at Long Island, NY.

The Promise of Prefab

Prefab has been a recurring idea in housing and construction culture from the nineteenth century to the present day. It has cast a cyclical 'spell' over many in the industry: each successive generation to redis-cover prefab applies prodigious amounts of energy to it, only to encounter similar problems and mistakes. Protagonists have been lured to prefab by its trans-formative potential and core promises – these include better quality, shorter build times, lower cost and special solutions. Recently, these promises have been joined by the potential of more sustainable and indi-vidualised solutions. Yet, many disregard such basic advantages, showing that the promise of prefab is a complex jumble of concepts and approaches, which we seek to untangle.

At a time of rapid technological advancement, building design and construction has remained much the same.[1] Consumer electronics, computing and mobile telecommunications, which were niche concerns only 50 years ago, are now an essential part of modern life, and have changed the very essence of our social, cultural and economic practices. In contrast, the mainstream construction industry embodies little of this dynamism and seems largely immune to the creative force of technological dis-ruption. The construction industry moves slowly and – for very good reason – is deeply averse to risk.

Today, there is increased pressure to make build-ings that are more responsive to their users' needs and desires, that achieve a higher and more consist-ent quality, and that are made in a way that reduces both their energy consumption during construction and operation, and consequently their lifetime carbon footprint. Most significantly, contemporary designers and producers of the built environment need to find ways to achieve all these goals in the context of the major challenges of our time: climate change, unprecedented population growth, and the ensuing mobility and urbanisation of these populations.

Within the professional circles charged with the design and production of the built environment, there is now an overwhelming expectation that the industry will change dramatically in coming years if it is to meet the challenges of the twenty-first century. While this mood for change is widespread, there is little consensus about how this future will appear. It is here that the enthusiasm for the trans-formative potential of prefab finds fertile ground.

This interest is far from new. The project of the 'prefab house' has entranced numerous professions – architects, designers, inventors, engineers, builders, developers and entrepreneurs. Taken by the seem-ingly boundless expansion of automotive manufac-turing, time and again, individuals and companies were struck with what the historian Gilbert Herbert called 'The Henry Ford Syndrome'. Herbert sums up the condition, channelling the thoughts of its suffer-ers: 'Why can't we mass-produce houses – standard, well-designed, at low cost – in the same way Ford mass-produced cars?'[2]

In recent decades, fundamental changes to the conditions in which housing and construction oper-ate have led to an increased interest, even a rediscov-ery, of a range of approaches, ranging from prefab and modular housing to off-site and industrialised building. Again, we might ask: what is the promise of prefab?

The core promise of prefab can be condensed to better quality, shorter build times, lower cost and special solutions for difficult or unusual problems. A range of added advantages are often cited on top of these foundational claims: less waste, reduced risk (worker safety, financial exposure and time delays due to inclement weather), increased efficiency and greater productivity. More recently, prefab has also promised improved environmental performance. These 'green' benefits are derived from higher quality, better thermal performance, less waste, more recycling, and generally more environmental systems and technologies which can be layered into prefab housing because of the extensive planning required (see Life Cycle Analysis and Environmental Systems boxes, pp.143 and 139). Recently, prefab has also become the standard-bearer for a more flexible and custo-misable mode of building, responding to new design requirements under the banner of 'mass customisation'.

1.3 Here, 'A Portable Town for Australia' shows the buildings ordered by the Bishop of Melbourne in 1853, which were to be fabricated in Bristol, UK and sent to Australia.

These core promises have been there from the beginning of the prefab endeavour. They were present as early as 1910, when Walter Gropius pitched his idea for a new industrialised house building company to Emil Rathenau, the then president of the German industrial giant AEG:

> The new Company intends to offer its clients not only inexpensive, well-built and practical houses and in addition a guarantee of good taste, but also take into consideration individual wishes without sacrificing to them the principle of industrial consistency.[3]

Increased interest in prefab has also been marked by external demands: shortages of housing, materials or labour scarcity, and unique or difficult locations where prefab provides solutions where no other method would work. In the early- to mid-nineteenth century, this was about new colonial settlements, or remote and frontier mining sites. In the years immediately after World War II it was about the governments of almost all industrialised countries launching large-scale house-building schemes. In the twenty-first century, the same logic is at play with futuristic modular housing for Mars.

Understanding these different streams of prefab, and the problems and opportunities that attend each, is important for identifying paths forward. In Chapter 3 we will return to this problem, teasing apart the different types of prefab and reasons for pursuing its promises.

1.4 Future housing pods on Mars. These images, along with others depicting space colonisation, demonstrate the same core promises of prefab since the mid-nineteenth century.

The core promises of prefab (quality, cost, and timeliness) are rational and quantifiable. A further, less rational promise is revealed by the popular media focus on a very narrow band of application – that is, the expensive, one-of-a-kind houses we typically see in trade magazines such as *Dwell* (see Fig. 2.4). In Chapter 2 we discuss this popular literature in greater detail. Here, it is important to note that such houses are likely to fail on the cost and timeliness promises and would arguably be easier to build using conventional methods. So why pursue prefab in such a context? The promise such houses contain is *aspirational*, and they also propagate a belief in the transformative capacity of prefab.

This aspirational promise has led many designers and entrepreneurs down a questionable path. But misplaced aspiration is not the only reason prefab has not fulfilled its promise to deliver mass housing. Other issues have also come into play. The tendency in twentieth-century prefab ventures to place a high value on inventiveness has often been at the expense of innovation, uptake and application. This is compounded by a lack of historical understanding within building culture about previous attempts at prefabrication and the mistakes that were made. Also, there has too often been scant regard for the very conditions and core promises that make prefabrication of interest to the market in the first place. Lastly, the twentieth century also revealed a tendency to place an inordinate amount of effort into applying technology or systems that are derived from analogous construction industries – in car, ship and aerospace manufacturing, for example. These companies have been caught up in a race with a questionable version of progress – Herbert's 'Henry Ford Syndrome'. These barriers and problems, in all their range and diversity, are discussed in Chapter 4.

How to Define Prefab

'Prefab' means many things to many groups. In this book, we refer to a range of terms and approaches interchangeably including: prefab, prefabrication, modular, off-site and industrialised house building.

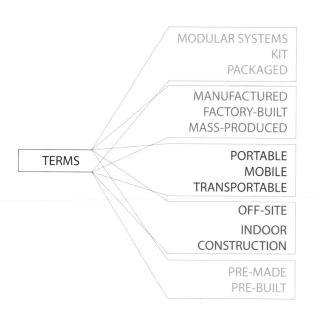

1.5 A broad range of terms exist to describe the industrialisation of the construction industry. By no means exhaustive, this list describes a few of the major categories of terms. Terms and definitions of prefab vary greatly from country to country and company to company.

There are numerous terms associated with industrialised building techniques in circulation, which change from country to country. Each of these terms can represent slightly different methods, techniques or traditions. Modular, systems, kit or packaged homes point towards the flexible nature of prefabrication (see Assembly and Construction Methods for Industrialised House Building box, p.24). Today, we also hear the terms volumetric (3D volumes), or flat-packed (2D elements) broadly used to denote if the building components are brought to site as volume to be racked and stacked, or as elements to be assembled on site like IKEA furniture. Offsite or indoor construction refers to how and where the components are made. Pre-made and pre-built are simply synonyms of prefabrication. Portable, mobile and transportable housing highlight the moveable nature of these buildings. And finally, manufactured, factory-built, mass-produced and mass-customised are all references to scale and level of industrialisation involved.

Previous studies have attempted to fine-tune nomenclature in the area. In 1951 Burnham Kelly pointed out that the definition of prefabrication was a question of *degree*, not an absolute, and that 'the distinction between prefabricated and conventional construction may well become meaningless within the next few decades'.[4] This did not occur to the extent Kelly forecast; the burgeoning list of terms used in the field indicates that the nuances around the term 'prefabrication' have actually grown. In 2010, 60 years after Kelly, Ryan E. Smith's *Prefab Architecture* concurs with Kelly's idea of 'degree':

> ... "prefabrication", "offsite fabrication", and "offsite production" are used interchangeably to mean elements intended for building construction that are produced offsite to a greater degree of finish and assembled onsite.[5]

Revisiting the historic and contemporary usage of the term 'prefabrication' and its short form 'prefab' can tell us much about where we came from, where we are now, and what the future might hold. In Chapter 4 we also discuss usage outside English-language countries to show how this can undo some of the confusion surrounding the meaning and definition of prefab. We think it is more helpful to think about prefab and its associated terms with their commonalities and intended outcomes in mind, rather than attempting, once and for all, to reach consensus around terminology and definition.

Part of the confusion around the term 'prefab' stems from its different uses in the various professional cultures that make up the construction industry. In current architectural discourses, Chris Knapp provocatively called for 'The End of Prefabrication', because he felt 'there is not another word in the current lexicon of architecture that more erroneously asserts positive change'.[6] Knapp is not alone in thinking that the problems that have coalesced around the term are an outcome of the

hubris associated with its 'special' status within architect-led attempts. Allison Arieff's 2002 book *Prefab* carries a warning to the reader regarding 'our definition of PREFAB', noting that 'Many of the houses presented ... are not prefabricated in the strictest sense of the word.'[7] A decade later in an article entitled 'Prefab Lives!' Arieff avoids describing the projects as prefabricated altogether, referring to the construction techniques as 'modular building'.[8]

It might seem relatively simple to denote the difference as between buildings that have been predominantly fabricated off-site and others predominantly in situ. But this definition does not take into account that in contemporary building – with very few exceptions – the overwhelming majority of building components are fabricated off-site and merely assembled in situ. There is a strong argument that a large portion of housing construction in industrialised countries is an industry of *assembly*, and not the artisan, craft-based industry of bespoke, climatically and regionally adapted building that we might think of when invoking, say, vernacular housing examples. These vernacular buildings are almost always examples of manifestly in situ building, built from local materials, labour, techniques and traditions.

The Path to Prefab

This book is conceived as a guidebook to help navigate a path towards industrialised building. It outlines the complexity of prefab housing and shows its broader pattern of operations. It argues that we require a new approach to collaborative, interdisciplinary knowledge production that connects existing knowledge in new and productive ways. The book is also a plea to industry to adopt a new approach to problem solving, one that places greater value on 'the ends' and less on 'the means' to achieving industrialisation.

As a guide to the unruly and complex landscape of prefab, this book describes the path to an industrialised approach to housing. Along the way, we point to some of the major landmarks in the field, the opportunities and potential, along with the pitfalls and problems. The path outlined is not singular, rather it comprises multiple routes leading in a general direction. Depending on the equipment, experience and capability of those involved, and depending on where they began, the journey may be slower or faster, involve more or less risk, mean different things to different groups, and finish with different outcomes.

This book aims to reveal the complexities of prefab and industrialised housing and put those lessons into action. It seeks to assist the reader to grasp, and then navigate, the multifactorial interdependencies at play in the field.

A successful path to prefab is one of collaboration, which requires teamwork and a broad set of complementary skills and knowledge (see Integrated Building Performance box, p.84). The contributors to this book comprise such a multidisciplinary team. All have spent time working directly with or in industry and examining the broad range of problems and opportunities from varying perspectives. Our approach incorporates scholarship from the humanities, the sciences (in particular, engineering) and the social sciences. A uniting feature of all the researchers who have contributed to this book is that although we may have begun the journey as historians, architects, planners, engineers, or construction managers, the work on industrialised building has blurred the boundaries of our disciplines, and led us to a new, emerging plane of operations.

Our research work with industry pertains not only to the actual findings of the R&D undertaken – that is, the *knowledge* produced – but also the *structure* of that knowledge and the approach to *knowledge production* that lies behind it. In Chapter 5 we mount a case for a new approach to problem solving that is appropriate to industrialised housing ventures. We argue that much work has been done of a fundamental and primary kind across a range of areas: material science, construction management, IT integration, business modelling, management and development, construction technology, architectural and engineering design and analysis, logistics and supply chain management, to name but a few. The increasing specialisation of contemporary disciplines, along with the explosion of knowledge production and its ready dissemination, has resulted in

an unusual challenge for contemporary R&D endeavours. Our experiences in the construction industry have shown that research in some corners has proceeded far in advance of the capacity of industry, not only to be aware of the latest developments or tools, but also to be able to incorporate them into their everyday practices. Similarly, the speed of building development, the episodic nature of its 'projects', and the rapidly changing circumstances of business in complex networked economies, provide further barriers against industry absorbing the latest thinking.

In charting a path to prefab, this book brings together high-level expertise and insight from a range of disciplines and subject areas in a way that will lead to better outcomes for end users. The book is not about the production of fundamentally *new knowledge*, rather it brings together and organises existing knowledge in an accessible way for those seeking to apply it in practice. It will allow the reader to make new and productive connections between existing knowledge – to 'join the dots', as it were.

Avoiding the Problems of the Past

The problems and failures of the past have not been fully understood and continue to provide a barrier to the future of industrialised housing ventures. Through a combination of scholarship, hands-on experience, interviews, case studies, speculation, design and prototyping, risk-taking and trial and error, this book outlines lessons that seek to correct these deficiencies. There is a pattern at work in prefab housing, and this book aims to bring its shape into clear focus. By revealing this pattern and the meta-structure that governs the success and failure of earlier ventures, we hope to prevent the repetition of past strategic errors.

To escape the cyclical re-emergence of prefab as a perennial 'good idea' that ultimately leads to disappointment, this book is also something of a plea to adopt a new mindset and acknowledge past failures. It is a plea to value the process over the product, strategy over tactics, content over form, and substance over style. It proposes an approach that

1.6   Over the past two decades Resolution:
4 Architecture have developed a flexible,
modular construction system, shown here
at The Fisher Island House, New York.
This system allows highly customised,
architect-designed houses to be built off-
site. Resolution: 4 Architecture draw on
a network of established manufacturers
in the north-eastern states of the USA to
realise their projects.

favours service over branding, data over assumptions, results over posturing, and imperfect application over conceptual purity. The trail of wreckage left in the wake of the grand schemes, monumental claims and high-minded disdain for anything but perfection should not only check the ambitions of many prefab housing ventures but lead us to value historical awareness and instil a scepticism for the sparkle of the new that has bedazzled so many efforts in the past.

A fresh approach to these issues demands a critical analysis of why prefab has never lived up to its promise. Of course there are key countries and companies (some of which we review in this book) that have achieved success. But why has this success not spread? The answer, we believe, can be found in a sober reflection on the achievements of the past, and a calmer, more moderate view of the challenges and opportunities of the present. The track record of failure and unfulfilled promises is, in our opinion, not just a mistake, an accident, or misunderstanding, and it is also not solely the result of poor timing or a lack of judgment. It can be traced to underlying contextual, structural, philosophical and attitudinal problems at work in complex ways. We discuss and illustrate these on the pages that follow.

The promise of prefab has wielded a strange power on those under its spell, often leading to an over-determined view of technology, an under-valuing of the 'market' and its desires, and a lack of measure between design concept and technical aspects on the one hand, and the business and operational aspects on the other. To continue the guidebook analogy, many have mistakenly thought that 'prefab' was the destination. Once prefabrication had been achieved – so the thinking went – success would follow. Our work aims to avoid continuing a widespread tendency in the industry to create yet more *solutions-in-search-of-problems*. Instead, we suggest that we need to train ourselves to identify the significant problems of our time and then set about finding the appropriate solutions for them. Contrary to some in the industry, we believe that industrialised building does not have intrinsic value in and of itself. Put more simply – prefab is a means, not an end.

How to Use This Book

In this book we advocate fresh thinking, a deeper historical awareness and a new approach to problem solving that is fit for the challenges facing contemporary industrialised housing ventures. Similarly, the structure of this book is conceived in novel terms, which has demanded a new way of working and allows for a different way of reading. Our book is neither a classic monograph, nor an edited book. While each part has an original author, this writing has been subjected to deep review and has thus become a hybrid of sorts.

The main text is conceived as a long essay divided into six chapters to provide a discursive background, a long tour onto which a series of thematic information 'boxes' are added, providing concise and more detailed day trips. These thematic boxes are dispersed throughout the body text and cover three major areas of prefab housing and industrialised building, which we think are essential to a guidebook. These are: a) geographical case studies; b) contemporary concepts, problems and opportunities; and c) case studies of key prefab housing companies. The 'boxes' provide different perspectives on these same questions raised in the main text. Some discuss technical issues, describing the 'how', 'when' and 'what' of the field. Others canvas the countries that have played significant roles in developing substantial or interesting ventures.

Each chapter of the main text represents a thematic pass of its subject. With each successive pass, the reader can go deeper and deeper into the material, or not. Each chapter or box can be read independently and readers with specific questions or interests can refer directly to the relevant parts. Each chapter is prefaced with an overview text and each major section and text box begins with a short summary. This, we hope, will allow our book to be read in 10 minutes or 10 hours, allowing each reader to customise their own path.

2   Foundations in Literature

There are two broad groups of literature on prefab housing: popular and specialist works. This book does not seek to provide a comprehensive overview of this material; the specialist works reviewed below can do that much better. Rather, we have framed the material in this chapter with the aim of providing an overview of the field. A more complete understanding of this literature can tell us much about how we got where we are and help to build the foundations on which we will build our future approach.

Studying these works also raises a core paradox: many of the observations and criticism of the industry raised over 60 years ago are just as pertinent today. Why have these studies and their lessons not cut through? Why does the industry, its researchers, developers and its supporters continue to make the same – in some cases, *exactly* the same – mistakes of the 1950s? A better understanding of these issues is essential if we are to move beyond the patterns of the past.

In an attempt to reinforce the novelty and aspirations of prefab many popular works suppress the complexities and problems we alluded to in the introduction and which we will cover in greater depth in Chapter 4.

Specialist works are more diverse in format and content. In print, these range from monographs and edited books to journal and magazine articles. Such works include detailed historical and technical accounts, introductory handbooks, critical essays, polemical articles, or survey works and

some of these are covered in more depth in the case studies of Chapter 3.

This book positions itself between the popular and the specialist, between the laudatory 'coffee table' books and the technical, historical and critical academic accounts. This, we hope, will cut across the borders that separate the academy, industry and the public, and blur the boundaries often marked by the highly codified expert language of the disciplines and professions.

Popular Works

Popular works keep alive an image of prefab as novel and aspirational. These works play an important role in educating the general public but they also suppress the complexities and problems in the field. Such works include: large-format picture books (see Fig. 2.2), *magazines* (see Fig. 2.4), *television, newspapers, and industry websites* (see Fig. 2.1). *Mostly, they carry popular, topical or evangelical accounts of the beauty, novelty and utility of prefab.*

It is easy to disparage the popular literature around prefab. An uncharitable view might say these works propagate a shallow and uncritical view of industrialised building, or frame the industry's automatic ascendency to become either the standard-bearer of 'good taste' or a placeholder for 'the future'. Yet, it is largely through these popular books and media that the public imagination is captured. They play a large part in keeping the 'dream' of the factory-made house alive, but fail to acknowledge the shortcomings of the examples chosen or why an idea that seemed so 'explosive' or 'common-sense' may not have fulfilled expectations.

These popular works and sites are often compelling, and might include impressive time-lapse videos of buildings being erected to improbable deadlines, or photography depicting the uncanny situation of a whole or part building hovering somewhere incongruous – in mid-air, on a truck, or in a factory. There is often an episodic pattern at play in the emergence of these works. 'Prefab' appears to be a go-to option when journalists and trade writers are confronted with the appearance of a disaster scenario, a shipping container student complex, or, in the search for 'fresh' solutions to a housing affordability crisis. Here, prefab is routinely rolled out as the symbol of change or innovation, poised to rescue the day, or at least give the impression of action.

The popular books and media capture the public imagination and play a crucial role in setting the expectations of the general public, educating them on the diversity of approaches available. In particular, television programs such as *Grand Designs* have featured 'prefab' options and made a great popular impact.[1] But what does this media and literature show about prefab? We see prototypes that are technologically articulate, formally innovative, and attractive to wealthy, design-literate readers and viewers. The buildings – which are typically stand-alone houses or bungalows – inevitably express their technique and technology in a demonstrable way, and rehearse the idea that prefab is much like a designer commodity, to be owned and displayed as a treasured object and be a demonstration of good taste (not to mention an exercise in conspicuous expenditure).

Taken as a plan for action, such associations of prefab are symptoms of the 'solution-in-search-of-a-problem' approach we discuss in greater detail in Chapter 4. Nevertheless, we should not overlook, nor fail to value, the social and cultural implications of an interest in housing that takes a commodity form and which is explicitly novel.

2.1 Architectural news sites, such as those above, do much to promulgate the dream of prefab.

2.2 Cover images of richly illustrated, large-format high-volume books which have played their part in popularising and promoting prefabricated construction as a distinct form of architecture.

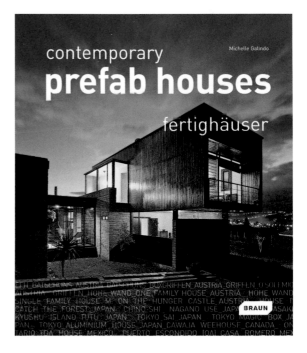

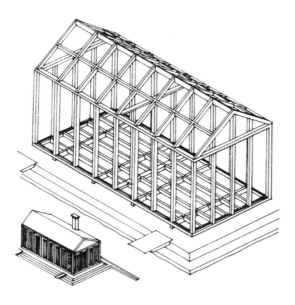

2.3   The Manning Portable Colonial Cottage, one of the mostly widely regarded examples of 19th-century colonial prefabricated house building.

2.4   *Dwell* magazine has done a great deal to popularise and disseminate the idea of a contemporary architectural prefab movement and its aspirational promise.

Two large-format, high-volume picture books stand out among popular works in this area: Taschen's *Prefab Houses* (2010) and Loft's *Prefab Architecture* (2012), both of which cement the role of prefabricated housing in the minds of the public and industry – or at least on their coffee tables.[2] *Prefab Houses* includes an historical narrative showing a progression from John Manning's prefabricated Colonial Settlers hut of the mid-nineteenth century to the latest designs, often from famous designers from around the world. *Prefab Architecture* has a narrower time frame but a much wider range of contemporary projects, carrying less descriptive text and thereby resembling more a large bound magazine.

Another way to consider these publications is by thinking about what we *do not* see. We do not see the volume factory-made housing of Northern Europe (see Fig. 6.11) and Japan (see Fig. L.1, p.115), or the manufactured-home industry of the United States (see Fig. 6.2).[3] Such case studies would provide examples that meet the needs of their markets by supplying staid familiar housing forms at low prices; but this would dilute the transformational promise of prefab that is at the core of these books. This sentiment taps into deeply held desires and the emotive impact of buildings, and to their attendant creativity or ingenuity – the 'first touch' of the gifted designer, the mad engineer or the megalomaniacal entrepreneur.

Projects selected for inclusion in this popular literature have a strong connection with the individual and with singular authorship. It also helps if the examples are the first, the new, the only. Such striking examples of design provide an aspirational view of the future, which is clearly a more glamorous vision than the undifferentiated sameness and banality of contemporary tract housing developments, from which such popular works keep a calculated distance.

Perhaps more than any other popular media form, the high-end architectural, interiors, and design magazine *Dwell* has led the charge towards an edgy, luxurious and architecturally striking view of what prefab can be. This is very much the world of aspirational lifestyle culture and the accoutrements of large amounts of disposable income. In 2003, under the aegis of editor and author Allison Arieff, the magazine staged a design competition and invited 16 architects to design a *Dwell* 'Home Design Invitational'.[4] The competition winners Resolution: 4 Architecture (see Case Study USA: Simplex Homes box, p.66) designed and built the winning entry.[5] Since then, *Dwell* has regularly featured high-design versions of their prefab houses. What is striking about *Dwell*'s consistent efforts to promote the value of prefab is the distance from the 'ends' part of why prefabrication or industrialised building is pursued in the first place. Lowering the cost of building is usually thought to be one of the major selling points for prefab (see Affordability and Industrialised House Building box, p.127), yet most of the houses previewed follow the format of expensive one-of-a-kind designer houses, a format that *Dwell* helped to generate. These houses are often prototypes and (arguably) would have been equally served by traditional building approaches. *Dwell*'s initiatives raise a question we will discuss at great length in Chapters 3 and 4: why use prefab? What does prefab offer in such a context that traditional building does not?

Specialist Works

Specialist works on prefab are mostly produced by universities and research institutions. They are more diverse in form and content than popular works and include: monographs, edited books, journals and magazine articles (digital and print). The treatment of prefab in specialist works ranges from detailed historical and technical accounts, introductory handbooks, critical essays and polemical articles. Historically, this literature is dominated by English-language publications. An introduction to key Japanese and Swedish works can offset this imbalance.

If prefabricated housing in the twentieth century mostly remained a dream recurring every ten to twenty years, then historical understanding of prefabricated housing and the challenges it has faced evidences a kind of amnesia. Despite a string of excellent studies stretching back to the 1950s there remains a distinct lack of historical awareness around the subject of prefabrication in broader construction culture.[6] Each new generation, it seems, holds on to the dream, but reinvents it from scratch.

The most significant problem in the specialist literature on prefab is the lack of awareness of works from non-English language authors. Owing to the language barrier, many such authors are little known outside their own national discourse. This is particularly the case for Northern European and Japanese works, which both have the most widespread and successful industries today (see Sweden and Japan boxes, pp.120 and 93). Much of the polemic, shadow boxing and drama in the debates about the acceptance and uptake of prefab can be seen to play out in English-language countries and literature.

Sweden, in particular, has benefited from a co-ordinated approach to industrial and academic research collaboration. Swedish academic research outputs have had a wide-ranging, and strongly technical focus. In Sweden, discourse has emphasised high-level concerns, such as establishing a base definition for industrialised house building, as well as the role that business models and strategies play in their effective delivery (see Business Models and Industrialised Construction box, p.57).[7] Other avenues of investigation concern more detailed issues, such as the planning and control of processes, production systems and design tools (see The Platform Approach box, p.48).[8]

Taking a broader view, the publication of the manifesto *Acceptera* (To Accept) by Swedish modernist architects in 1931, together with the Stockholm Exhibition of 1930, opened the door to the functionalist movement in Scandinavia.[9] *Acceptera* was a plea by the authors for a heightened engagement with production methods and for design to respond in a functional manner for the benefit of society and the individual; in many ways it set the tone for the pursuit of industrialised housing in Sweden across the twentieth century. Following World War II, the Swedish government's engagement with the industrialisation of construction was pursued through *Miljonprogrammet* (The Million Homes Program) (see Sweden box, p.120). Carl Ekbrant in *Miljonprogrammet i bostadsbyggandet, fortsättningen på 1946 års program* (The program to build a million homes, continuation of the 1946 program) provides a factual summary of the program.[10] Recently, a more holistic view of industrialised construction has emerged with *Industriellt Husbyggande* (Industrial House Building), a co-authored book by leading researchers and practitioners working in the field, many of whom are co-authors of the present study.[11] Industriellt Husbyggande summarises a range of important factors, critical to the success of industrialised house production: planning and control of the process, building systems, prefabrication, long-term relationships, logistics, ICT tools, customer and market focus, and experience feedback.

In the German-language context, Kurt Junghanns' *Das Haus für alle: Zur Geschichte der Vorfertigung in Deutschland* (The House for All: The History of Prefabrication in Germany) studies the history of housing construction in Germany until 1945.[12] Junghanns' account deals with the diversity of systems that were developed in Germany, arising from the social and political contexts of the early twentieth century.

Access to Japanese accounts of industrialised house building faces a greater language barrier than those from Northern Europe (see Japan box, p.93). As with Sweden, industry-led R&D is communicated in Japanese, while academic accounts are sometimes in English, leading to a dual-level discourse. Literature of a specialised nature considering Japanese house builders typically focuses on quality of production as well as quality of performance, emphasising lean production and efficiency, and on issues regarding customisation and the benefits of a customer-focused business.[13] Important contributions to Japanese industrialised construction discourse emerged in the 1970s with Ikebe Yo's *Product Development of Housing Industry*, which introduced concepts such as cost performance, and the 'unitisation' of the housing industry.[14] Understanding of the Japanese prefabricated

Assembly and Construction Methods for Industrialised House Building

There are many, varied approaches to the assembly and construction of industrialised housing; many permutations between the extremes of fully finished volumetric units and conventional site-building practices. No one material or system leads the industry – different countries and companies use different (and sometimes competing) systems and materials. Industrialised house-building companies must choose the system and materials best suited to their particular circumstances, and which best achieves the balance they require.

Addressing the requirements of each site is inherent to most architectural design processes and, from this perspective, each building is a unique response. However, from a production viewpoint, most – if not all – activities are the same for most buildings. This is the origin and aim of industrialised house building: to identify what buildings have in common and to develop these activities towards perfection.

Building prefabrication has a long history stretching back to the nineteenth century (see Fig. 2.3), but the main roots of contemporary industrialised housing building are found in the Modern Movement of the early twentieth century. Modernism proposed new, universally applied truths and principles that easily accommodated industrial processes. The 'machine aesthetic' was partly based on repetition, with recurring elements such as windows and doors, and very few ornaments. Louis Sullivan's credo 'Form follows function' echoed across architecture and construction, while Le Corbusier pronounced 'The house is a machine for living in'.[1]

In contemporary industrialised house building the balance between distinctiveness and commonality is usually a more practical concern and less a matter of architectural ideology. The choice of assembly method in prefabricated housing is strategic and should address a combination of issues: value-chain flow, production pace and safety, delivery precision and predictability, material and labour cost, and residential layout opportunities. Key decisions in choosing any industrial system revolve around the scope of the desired market and how much variability the customer is willing to pay for. 'Distinctiveness' provides an important value for many customers, but 'commonality' is usually where production savings are made (see The Platform Approach box, p.48).[2] The key to profitability is to strike the perfect balance between these two factors. This balance, once decided on, determines how early the customer can be brought into the production process and how much work can be carried out off-site. From there, a production method can be chosen. A high degree of commonality means less flexibility and more repetition and standardisation. Distinctiveness – the opportunity for the client to choose and customise, or a unique design by an architect – brings significant production costs. It is important to decide on this balance early, as many systems have failed because of path dependency – that is, current options and decision-making are limited by decisions already made in the past (see Business Models and Industrialised Construction box, p.57). For example, in projects led by contractors, development might start with the production method, technology or processes that the contractors are used to, with market considerations only entering in the second or third round of the development process, as by then some options will have been closed off due to earlier decisions.

When choosing a production strategy a key consideration should be the particular balance required between commonality and distinctiveness. Every system developer will interpret that context differently to arrive at a preferred balance, along with the most relevant production strategy to achieve it.

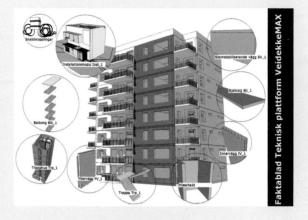

A.1   VeidekkeMAX is a typical example of how the production strategy leads to choices of standard methods and components. VeidekkeMAX employs a hybrid strategy of flat-packed walls, in situ concrete and volumetric bathroom systems.

A.2   Production of wall elements intended for assembly into volumetric housing units, produced at the Lindbäcks factory in Piteå, Sweden.

A.3   Swedish company NCC employs an insulated concrete sandwich panel, elements cast off-site and assembled at Kvillebäcken, Gothenburg, Sweden.

The practical upshot is that there is no clear 'best practice' for industrialised house building. There are a handful of dominant approaches but also myriad permutations for hybrid systems between them. The most common methods are as follows:

Flat-pack

• 'Flat-pack' is a broad umbrella covering systems that are typically '2D' and built and transported as largely flat elements: walls, floor cartridges, roof cassettes.[3] This is the staple method for timber buildings and infill walls as well as floor slabs for concrete buildings. Components are made in the factory, transported to the site, lifted into place and assembled. Merits include efficient transportation, flexible apartment layouts and relatively fast assembly. There are two major systems for concrete flat-pack:

• Semi-produced flat concrete base with infill wall

A traditional construction method for low- and medium-rise apartment buildings. Floors consist of a thin prefabricated concrete base supported by temporary shorings. This surface doubles as a temporary work floor for adding reinforcement and HVAC installations before a concrete floor is cast on site. The walls are most often prefabricated from stud-frame elements with steel studs. The advantage is a significant degree of flexibility in layouts and time frames. The disadvantages include shorings, health and safety and a long production time, often exposed to the weather.

• Free-bearing floor elements and load-bearing walls

A common combination, where installations are run under the floor or above a partition ceiling. The merits of this method are fast-paced production and no need for shorings; and, most of the frame supplements can be made indoors. But there is little opportunity for late changes because of the production time needed for the slabs.

Volumetric building

• In this method entire volumetric modules are built off site, including internal and exterior finishes, then transported to site where they are connected to services and other systems. This approach can be used for an entire house or for the bathrooms. The most usual material is timber or light gauge steel studs. The production pace is very fast and the desired finish quality is easily achieved. However, apartment layouts are limited by what can be produced and transported as a three-dimensional volume. Bathroom pods can be light or heavy and used with almost any construction system.

Hybrids

• Systems that rely on multiple production methods, typically both flat-pack and volumetric systems. For example, the VeidekkeMAX system (see Fig. A.1) uses volumetric bathroom pods in a flat-pack system of wall and floor components. Advantages and disadvantages are similar to those for the individual systems.

Beam-column systems

• A staple method for commercial buildings, this system is less often used for prefabricated homes. The German Huf Haus system is an exception allowing for large space, mezzanine internal spaces and large amounts of external glazing if required.

These systems are just a sample of the full range in the marketplace. Different materials each have their market niche and interact dynamically with different production strategies. For example, timber lends itself to the industrialisation of single-family dwellings, while medium-rise apartment buildings are more likely to be built in concrete. These material preferences are the outcome of an array of influences, including tradition, practicalities and regulatory environments. Market niches are not static, however, and material selections can shift in response to changes in context.

Timber suits the construction of individual houses for a number of reasons. On-site adaptability is high and can be accomplished with light hand-tools, while on-site transportation and assembly

A.4　Bathroom or service pods, increasingly popular for fast-tracked multi-residential development projects, shown here built in controlled factory conditions in Sweden for VeidekkeMAX.

A.5　Installation of timber-framed volumetric modules at a Lindbäcks construction site in Sweden.

A.6 Huf Haus, Poing, Germany.
A pre-cut timber post-and-beam
construction system which allows a high
level of design flexibility and large amount
of glazing on perimeter walls. The system
is delivered to site for rapid assembly.

can often be done with a lorry-sized crane. There is much existing knowledge within the industry as timber is the traditional material for single-family dwellings in many countries. These are also substantial opportunities to build on commonality and the industrialisation of single-family homes has brought many standard house products to the market.

Using timber to leverage commonality is fast and predictable for individual dwellings, but it does not lend itself well to producing multi-family homes, which need more site adaptation and have a larger urban impact. This has led to the development of open building systems, which combine material technology, modular coordination and new production technologies.[4] An open building system is an agreement between several suppliers to produce products with certain design methods, in certain sizes, to be combined through standardised interfaces. Competition between the suppliers keeps prices at a reasonable level. An example is concrete hollow decks, which come in pre-set size ranges with pre-engineered load-carrying capacity. From a structural point of view, such modular components enable open building for many different types of medium-rise residential projects, including houses.

Regulations also impact material choices. In recent decades the strict fire safety regulations restricting the use of timber in multi-residential buildings have been progressively wound back

around the world, and are increasingly substituted by performance-based design criteria. This has opened up the possibility of using timber building systems to construct taller buildings in Sweden, Canada and Australia. The introduction of functional requirements (for example, the Eurocodes) has strengthened the development of timber medium-rise buildings in the Nordic countries, where they are also supported by political incentives for timber-based construction. High-rise timber buildings are also under development using cross-laminated timber technology introduced from Austria, Switzerland and Southern Germany.

The difference in maturity of timber-based and concrete-based medium-rise building systems means that production costs of timber frames are still typically slightly higher than those for concrete. There are exceptions to this rule; for example, Lindbäcks Bygg AB in Piteå, Sweden, successfully builds medium-rise apartment buildings with timber-framed volumetric elements. The secret to their success is largely their patience in developing and implementing their approach to lean production.

Such careful exploration of material options, combined with a considered approach to selecting the most suitable production system to address the particulars of a market, is essential to the development of any effective industrialised building system.

housing industry has also been advanced by a number of comparative studies, especially from the United Kingdom.[15]

Moving back to English-language specialist literature, we are met with a diverse group of formats and content. There is a divide between works which are more laudatory and evangelical – such as those by Allison Arieff, Sheri Koones and Robert Kronenburg[16] – and those that offer more nuanced and critical accounts, commonly tackling the issue from a more specific standpoint.[17] Stephen Kieran and James Timberlake's *Refabricating Architecture* (2004), provides an insightful account of how new fabrication and manufacturing technologies and techniques will transform future building design and construction, and, to this extent, have much in common with this study.[18]

It is in this specialist group that we find the more technologist reviews of the subject. These works place great stock in technology and the role it will have in underpinning the future of construction.[19] Another group of works include the more technical accounts and the 'how-to' books which are instructive around particular practice problems and provide technical solutions and overviews.[20]

We also point the reader toward the vast number of local and national studies of prefabrication.[21] These tend to focus on particular projects or companies and provide detailed accounts of the experiences gained in working on or reviewing such projects. These studies often incorporate policy and economic issues. The final type of prefab literature comes in the form of the report.[22] These are of two main kinds: industry-led reports, commonly produced to provide information or act as lobbying tools to government; and those which are commissioned by government or publicly funded bodies, typically to assist and disseminate information to industry.

Landmark Studies

There is a vast amount of high-quality scholarship that commands a very low level of public and industry awareness. These publications go largely unacknowledged in the popular material introduced above. The 'landmark' works have been limited to six standout books from English language authors. These books are considered landmarks because they not only offer deep and erudite treatments of the subject, but because they are comprehensive and widely known. Together, these works have provided the foundations for our approach.

Burnham Kelly's *The Prefabrication of Houses* (1951) stands at the head of a stream of erudite literature that attempts to capture the full range of problems and opportunities of prefab in mid-twentieth century USA.[23] It is perhaps a better acknowledgement of Kelly's work to say that it was the culmination of two decades of study begun by the industrialist Albert Farwell Bemis and John Ely Burchard at MIT, who co-authored the three-volume series *The Evolving House* (1936).[24] In many ways, Kelly's book is fascinating for its treatment of a range of problems that are in complete accord with our contemporary experiences. One could easily be forgiven for thinking Kelly is writing for our own age and not that of the American post-World War II housing context.

Kelly's book is also remarkable for its breadth, its even-handed approach to treating the full scope of history and contemporary situation on the one hand, and its detailed reporting from technical studies, surveys and industry data on the other. In many regards, Kelly's philosophy and objectives are closely aligned with that of our study, including his admonition that the prefabrication of houses must be treated 'as a complete *pattern of operations* of which management, design, procurement, production, and marketing are the major subdivisions'.[25]

In 1969, again at MIT, Arthur D. Bernhardt set up a large-scale housing study focused on mobile and manufactured homes. His *Building Tomorrow: The Mobile/Manufactured Housing Industry*, first published in 1980, was a vastly compressed book from the original five-volume report to the Department of Housing and Urban Development (HUD), but

2.5 Arthur D. Bernhardt's diagram
showing the interactions involved in the
mobile home industry. This industry
involves the production, distribution
and park systems, drawing interactions
from their supporting and regulatory
environments.

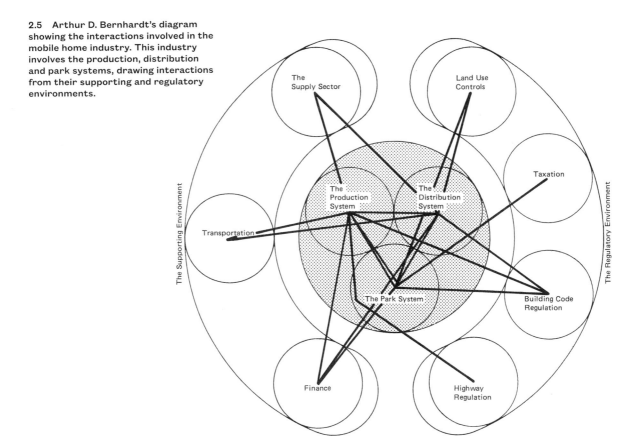

still extended to a hefty 523 pages.[26] Bernhardt's research was a broadly conceived, multidisciplinary study that included representatives not only from construction, design, engineering, management and property, as Kelly had previously done, but also drew input from researchers in economics, finance, political science, sociology and law. Bernhardt concluded that the mobile home industry – often viewed as an unloved outcome of attempts to prefabricate or industrialise housing – was actually 'the world's most efficient building industry because it has thoroughly and strategically manipulated virtually all the important functions that operate in or affect the larger building industry … .'[27]

Bernhardt's identification of the mobile/manufactured home industry as the crowning achievement of the modular housing industry led him to recommend scholars and officials to learn why this was so. His report and advocacy work aimed to show how the lessons from this highly efficient and unassuming industry might be applied to mainstream housing to break the deadlock of the housing crisis of his own day.[28] Of particular interest to our book is Bernhardt's multifactorial diagram (Fig. 2.5) that explains industrial organisation for housing production, to which we will return at the end of Chapter 3 and Chapter 5.

Gilbert Herbert is perhaps the foremost historian of twentieth-century prefab, and his two major books, *Pioneers of Prefabrication: The British Contribution in the Nineteenth Century* (1978) and *The Dream of the Factory-Made House: Walter Gropius and Konrad Wachsmann* (1984), set a high standard for all studies that followed.[29] *The Dream of the Factory-Made House* provides an excellent historical account of the experiences gained from one of the most crucial (and infamous) attempts to industrialise house building. The book charts the prehistory and the rise and fall of The General Panel Company and its chief product, 'The Packaged House' (see Fig. 3.12). Designed by émigré architects Walter Gropius and Konrad Wachsmann, this project had some of the best preconditions for success of any large-scale attempt to industrialise housing. The wider argument of Herbert's book is an extremely convincing account of why this thinking and the

mid-century experiments largely failed to materialise as a sustainable (or extensive) industry in the USA. It is also a key reference for this study because it provides an historical interrogation of the various barriers to success for prefab companies, and will be the subject of a longer, more detailed treatment in Chapter 3.

Colin Davies' compact, though wordy, volume *The Prefabricated Home* (2005) provides the best overview and examination of the role that prefabricated housing has played in the discipline of architecture and its curious relationship with the avant garde.[30] It is also a biting critique of many of the individual efforts (particularly by architects) to industrialise housing. Much like Bernhardt and Herbert before him, Davies' ultimate position acknowledges the achievements of the mobile/manufactured home in the USA (see Fig. 6.2) and sees it as a model worthy of further investigation. He describes in great detail how such exemplars are scorned not only by architects but by the wider public, evidenced by labels such as 'trailer trash' and the more recent 'tornado bait'. But Davies also praises the leading role of this industry for providing low-cost housing for emerging design requirements, advances made in construction techniques and efficiency, and changes it successfully brought about in the regulatory environment, which had historically provided a barrier to many architect-led ventures.[31] Davies' study of the bifurcation of the prefabricated housing industry between high end design-led and low-end mass-housing has been important for subsequent studies and for our proposal of conceptual and utilitarian prefab outlined in Chapter 3.

More than any other work of the last decade, MoMA's bold exhibition and catalogue *Home Delivery: Fabricating the Modern Dwelling* (2008) has done an enormous amount to recapture the public and specialist imagination around prefabricated housing.[32] The exhibition and catalogue was curated and co-edited by Barry Bergdoll. It not only carried a detailed historical survey of previous efforts but commissioned five full-size prototypes on an adjacent lot that were open to the general public, alongside four smaller partial-prototypes in the gallery proper. Unlike the popular works introduced above,

Home Delivery avoided the pitfalls of merely point-ing to the novelty or topicality of prefab through its rigorous, erudite and critical historical overview, in no small part because it was directed by Bergdoll, who is also Professor of Art History at Columbia University. Many of the works that appeared drew greatly on Kieran and Timberlake's admonition to incorporate manufacturing methodologies more widely into building design and production. Bergdoll's own essay in the catalogue points to the limits of design value in the prefab industry, drawing on Davies' critique of the high/low divide in contemporary prefab housing.[33]

The final major work to be introduced from the English-language specialist literature is Ryan E. Smith's *Prefab Architecture: A Guide to Modular Design and Construction* (2010).[34] Smith's volume is intended as a reference volume and covers an impressive range of topics spanning from historical origins to contemporary design and production technologies and techniques. His account shows off-site con-struction as part of a wider continuum of fabri-cation techniques that do not neatly stop or start with volumetric prefabricated housing modules, or with systems building, but includes examples of construction involving varying degrees of industrial-isation and prefabrication. Smith's work is particu-larly valuable for this book in so far as it provides an updated account of the field from a researcher who is active in R&D enterprises with industry and is, therefore, cognisant of the concerns and issues facing industry. This, as we have seen, is an element missing from Bernhardt's, Herbert's, and Davies' studies and provides Smith's book with a practical as well as theoretical grounding.

Why is the Understanding of Prefab so Poor?

Surveying these works might prompt the reader to ask: If we have such quality literature on the subject, why is general knowledge so poor? This gap between specialist and general knowledge, we speculate, can be traced to a few recurring factors. First, we can point to the limited education of graduates in built-environment fields. Second, is the growing divide between the academy and industry. And finally, there is the reductive and superficial approach of the popular studies above. As John Burchard framed the prefab scene in 1951 in his preface to Kelly's book:

> There are *blageurs* who are more interested in personal publicity than in a successful house and who, therefore, propose preposterous but fasci-nating fantasies. These take the eyes of publishers who have magazines rather than realities to retail, and they serve as interesting table conversation among the *avant garde*; unfortunately, they also raise hopes, only to shatter them again. This has been going on for a long time – too long.[35]

The date of this passage shows us that such posturing and the intermittent dabbling of the avant garde has indeed been going on a long time. But this alone cannot account for the scale of the prefab 'amnesia' at play. The spell of prefab previewed above has led many a venture on a path of self-deception. This leads to a fourth explanation of the gap between leading scholarly works and general knowledge: it appears that prefab fulfils a crucial role in the public imagination. If prefab is some-thing of a 'dream' or 'holy grail' for many involved in the construction industry, for the general public it represents a kind of science fiction, an opportunity to rehearse ideas about the future and what it might hold.

Digital and Automated Fabrication

Recent decades have seen the rapid advance of digital and automated fabrication technologies and techniques in the construction industry, which has occurred hand-in-hand with developments in Computational Design (see box, p.75). Although it is not yet clear how these technologies and techniques will impact the design and construction of buildings in the future, recent advances suggest that applications to pragmatic problems, such as those found in industrialised house building, will offer valuable solutions enabling a move beyond the early focus on formal and material inventiveness. Digital and automated fabrication also change the skills and knowledge required by professionals in the construction industry and have the potential to change the way the industry is structured altogether.

In 1910 the French artist Villemard produced a series of postcards exploring what life might be like in the year 2000. One of these, *En L'An 2000 – Chantier de construction électrique* (In the Year 2000 – Electric Construction Site), depicts the architect as a sort of puppeteer, choreographing a variety of robots, each performing its own specialised task on a construction site. Although the image is not without its anachronisms, it does accurately predict the trajectory of building construction in two critical areas: the newly contracted space between design and construction (file-to-factory processes), and the means and methods of construction itself (digital fabrication and automation). For example, the integration of advanced CAD/CAM software with Computer Numeric Controlled (CNC) and robotic equipment now allows data generated in the design to be used in fabrication and assembly, thereby facilitating more fluid processes.[1]

Stemming from military work in the 1950s, current digital and automated fabrication techniques and equipment have been effectively used in manufacturing small equipment and in maritime, automotive, industrial and aerospace applications for some time.[2] By the 1970s, computational design pioneer and architect William Mitchell thought that these technologies could become an integrating force throughout the architecture, engineering and construction industry (AEC).[3] The 1990s saw early successful builder-driven experiments such as the Shimizu SMART system, an automated on-site factory that completed a 30-storey tower in 1994.[4] In this same decade architects began rapid development and research in the field, with very different ambitions and outcomes. Spurred on by the work of pioneers such as Greg Lynn and Frank Gehry, architects such as Kieran Timberlake, Foster and Partners and Zaha Hadid Architects all worked to advance the technological capacity of architecture and construction.[5]

Countries such as Japan and Sweden have mature prefabrication industries with highly digital and automated workflows (see Japan and Sweden boxes, pp.93 and 120). Digital and automated fabrication techniques are also being used more widely across the construction industry, mostly by specialist fabricators and subcontractors operating on very specific aspects of projects, for example, structural steel, facade components and joinery.

As equipment becomes increasingly affordable and software workflows continually improve, architects and other building professionals are learning new skills and innovating at a greatly increased rate. The rise of Building Information Modelling (BIM), integrated with Computer Aided Manufacturing (CAM) software, allows unprecedented ability to prototype and fabricate on common equipment such as CNC routers and mills, 3D printers, laser and plasma cutters.

B.1 Villemard's *En L'An 2000 – Chantier de construction électrique* from 1910 depicts a vision of the future with the architect controlling an automated construction site.

The benefits of such approaches include strategies for simplifying the building of complex projects and complex geometries (resulting in higher capability and fewer errors) and greater productivity across the entire industry. More specifically, digital and automated fabrication offers the potential to overcome pervasive issues of jobsite safety, skills shortage, risk and cost, and of course quality.

More advanced robotics, typically taken from other industrial sectors, are also being used in the off-site construction of buildings. However, the majority of robotic systems for on-site work currently in late-development or early-consumer phases are replacements for simple, repetitive labour and rely on prescribed and highly controlled conditions.

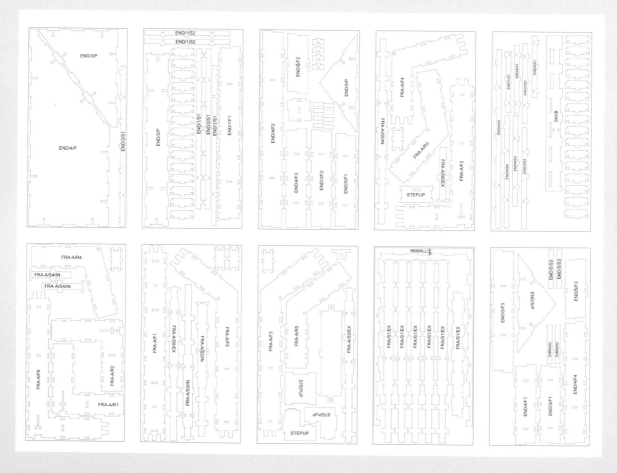

B.2 CNC cutting files (such as those used here by WikiHouse) utilise scripting to efficiently arrange and nest items for cutting on sheet material, creating a streamlined digital file-to-factory workflow.

B.3   An industrial robot carving custom
architectural detailing from foam.

The continued uptake of digital fabrication and automation strategies in construction is not without challenges, both real and perceived.[6] Economic concerns, relating to both automation costs and the displacement of traditional labour, are frequently voiced and at increasing volume. Overall equipment and plant costs are decreasing to suit integration, much like other industries with high degrees of automation such as the maritime and automotive industries. The displacement of labour is gradual, going through intermediary phases including skills transfer periods, human augmentation and robotic collaboration.[7]

Another important barrier is that of skills. This has two aspects – the question of how to automate or emulate the work of highly skilled and nuanced craftspeople in construction, and the availability of new skills that will be required in automation/robotics/software workflows. The former is the subject of much research in the area of skills transfer; the latter may be solved by integrating digital fabrication and computational design skills into many universities and technical colleges, not to mention the recent 'maker' culture boom.[8]

Finally, there are gaps in the maturity, development and adaptability of technology applied to construction work, which include hardware, software and workflow issues.

Fast progression in the industry is indicated by the uptake of digital fabrication methods within architectural firms such as NADAA (Boston), Snøhetta (Oslo) and SHoP (New York), who are increasingly capable of both design and production. The latter developed its own internal construction arm (SHoP Constructions) to facilitate large-scale integrated innovation pipelines such as for the façade to the Barclay Center in New York City, on which they served as both architect and fabrication consultant.

New specialised consultancy firms – such as designtoproduction, Gehry Technologies, AR-MA, and the former Case Inc. (now part of WeWork) – span design and construction and typically include architects, engineers, fabricators and computer scientists. This new generation of consultancy is invaluable in helping the construction industry to innovate by bridging the gaps in the design-to-construction process, by assisting designers to achieve design outcomes and providing expert advice to builders on highly complex projects.

At the residential scale, prefabrication companies such as Facit Homes (UK) and Blu Homes (USA) have invested in the development of proprietary fabrication systems that are integral to the construction yet permit relative flexibility in design, offering digital fabrication on-site (Facit) (see Figs 6.9 and 6.10) and off (Blu Homes) (see Fig. 4.1).

The field of robotics is another area of rapid development and expansion. Robotic equipment is extremely flexible, capable of performing complex tasks and integrating multiple systems such as sensors that allow machines to 'see' and react to their environment. Current technological development ranges widely, from large-scale additive manufacturing such as the Contour Crafting process developed at the University of Southern California (which promises the 3D printing of buildings) to coordinated on-site robotic assembly (helping to smooth the transition from human labour to mechanical).[9] Researchers are also working on skills-transfer methodologies whereby skilled tradespeople can 'teach' robots how to perform nuanced and highly skilled trades, for example, a project at Carnegie-Mellon University has expert plasterers teaching robots how to ply their trade (Fig. B.3).

Overall, technology has matured greatly in recent years as a result of the increasing proliferation of digital fabrication skills, continued research and development, and rapidly lowering cost of equipment. It is now feasible for construction projects of all scales to implement digital and automated technology at some level. The recent proliferation of skills in digital fabrication is also helping to blur the distinctions among the traditional roles of architects, engineers, fabricators and builders.

Nonetheless, automated fabrication techniques are still the exception rather than the rule in construction – often the domain of specialist subcontractors and consultants – or are resorted to when more traditional solutions are overly cumbersome. If we are to fully realise the potential of new technologies, we must also refine the procedural side of construction.

There are high expectations of digital and automated fabrication technologies. In many architecturally driven projects, the emphasis has been on testing formal, material and structural boundaries, and on the symbolic, experimental or fantastical potential of these technologies. In coming decades we are likely to see more pragmatic applications of technique and technology, as are beginning to emerge in the field of industrialised house building.

3 Utilitarian Prefab, Conceptual Prefab, or a Third Way

Our survey of past attempts at prefab housing reveals two broad types: the utilitarian and the conceptual. In each of these types, the 'promises of prefab' are manifest in different ways. Utilitarian prefab attempts to solve clear functional problems by tapping prefab's core advantages of cost, speed, quality, as well as on unique applications. Conceptual prefab appeals to different, less explicit objectives, often serving aspirational, rhetorical and polemical causes.

Making this distinction helps to explain why different companies and individuals have pursued prefab and for what reasons. In between the utilitarian and conceptual extremes is a wide space – a spectrum – that has become increasingly populated since the mid-twentieth century. It is from this 'Third Way' and its newer cohort of mid-range companies that our book takes its lessons for the future. Key case studies are explored below for their contribution to understanding the value of this third way.

3.1 Remote mining camps, such as this example from Fleetwood in Western Australia, demonstrate the utilitarian prefab at its most practical and functional. Sites such as this are often laid out in geometric patterns of repetitive identical units.

Utilitarian Prefab

Utilitarian prefab is an almost perfect reflection of the core benefits of prefab: quality, cost and timeliness, and special solutions. It provides shelter quickly, efficiently and effectively (for short or long periods), and responds to basic needs pertaining to time savings, strange or remote sites, shortages of material and labour, and cost efficiency. Utilitarian prefab is an example of a problem-oriented *approach: there is an immediate, identifiable problem, and prefab offers an appropriate and convenient solution. The development of utilitarian prefab is much easier to account for, as its metrics are logical, rational and easily quantifiable.*

Key historical examples of utilitarian prefab are found in colonial settlements, industrial applications such as mining and oil rigs, military camps, emergency and disaster relief housing, and remote or problematic sites such as lighthouses. Mobile/manufactured homes are also on the fringe of this category, because they are for many people the only affordable choice and fulfil a concrete and tangible need.

Much has been written about early prefabrication and its reliance on the development of new materials, technology and technique.[1] Almost all colonial endeavours had an element of prefab: Australia, New Zealand and North America provide many examples. The shortages of material and skilled labour explain the reliance on such solutions, along with the facility for easy transportation and assembly.

3.2 An Australian mining camp by Fleetwood, temporary, functional and quick to erect.

Similarly, the early twenty-first century mining and resource operations have drawn on prefab to meet the need for temporary mass housing, usually (but not always) in remote locations where no other solution is viable.[2] Examples include the Australian 'Donga' camps, and the so-called 'Man Camps' of North America. The logic of such applications is very similar to the prefabrication of the mid-nineteenth century gold rushes of Northwestern America and Australia, and they demonstrate a continuity of purpose in utilitarian prefab.

Utilitarian prefab is suited to anticipating need as well as responding to it. In Australia, for example, the state of New South Wales has a 'fleet' of around 6,500 demountable school classrooms, which it deploys as a convenient, semi-permanent solution for local schools that have outgrown their facilities.[3] In a context where many remote and regional towns are shrinking, or where demographic shifts have led to schools downsizing or closing, these buildings can also be refurbished and moved to new locations. The school 'demountables' are not designed with attention to appearance uppermost; however, since their introduction in the 1960s and subsequent modification in the 1980s, they continue to provide a valuable and appropriate solution to problems around cost, speed and reuse, and can be deployed with minimum interruption.

Finally, the core benefits of prefab are the reason for the revived interest in highly regular and repetitive modular 'pods' for future housing on Mars (see Fig. 1.4). Such solutions echo responses devised for other extreme sites like the polar regions. The logistical challenges of moving such enclosures to another planet, the premium placed on weight and space, and the requirement for high performance materials, all combine to recommend what has become a familiar set of solutions.

USA

The modular housing industry in the USA presents a complex and highly variable case study that complements ones looking at other highly industrialised countries such as Sweden and Japan (see Sweden and Japan boxes, pp.120 and 93). The diversity of climates, modes and methods of building, different states and jurisdictions, and parallel approaches to the industry make for a multi-faceted case study. On the one hand this ranges from a widely established (though largely unsophisticated) industry reliant on traditional timber building, and new companies (both large and small) attempting to enter the market both through novel methods, materials and building types. The USA is also the main site of the development of the mobile/manufactured home industry, which is governed by a separate code and is more widespread than any other country.

Light timber-framed construction has dominated housing construction in the USA since the mid-nineteenth century. With its high degree of standardisation and effective use of prefabrication, this system served the diverse geographic and climatic conditions well. In North America, the timber frame draws on ample resources and fits the market preference for low-rise typologies. The 2 × 4 inch stud continues to rule, in some cases preventing more advanced systems, such as panellised or kit-of-parts systems, from appearing in this market. Even in off-site production, the two largest prefabricated products and processes relate to light timber-framed construction. Operation Breakthrough, a heavily

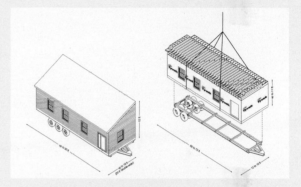

C.1   The USA has a large manufactured house building industry, these dwellings are constructed on their own transportable chassis (left) while the bulk of other prefabricated house building in the USA exists as 'modular' or volumetric construction (right) for installation as a permanent dwelling.

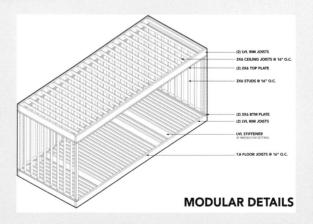

MODULAR DETAILS

C.2   Typical timber-framed volumetric structure.

funded federal program that attempted to replace this system with panellised and three-dimensional reinforced concrete systems during the 1970s, resulted instead in the world's largest mobile and manufactured home industry.[1]

In this context an entire new manufacturing industry emerged – the modular construction industry. The Modular Building Institute (MBI) defines modular construction as the use of 'three-dimensional building modules that are prefabricated off site and transported to the site to make up the entire building'.[2] Permanent modular construction (PMC) is distinct from relocatable modular construction (such as construction site trailers, man camps, mobile homes and classroom pods), as it typically complies with the North American International Building Code (IBC) Type V (wood frame, combustible). This limits height to a maximum of four stories; however, a small number of manufacturers fabricate modules in accordance with IBC Type II construction (steel, concrete, non-combustible), allowing for taller structures.[3] The most discernible differences between modular construction and typical Type II and V construction is the fabrication of a platform or frame in the factory, and the use of temporary structural reinforcement, both designed specifically for manoeuvring within the facility and to the construction site.

The size of building modules in North America is determined by the dimensional limitations of trucking. There is little standardisation across the continent, but the dimensions of loads that can travel on highways are aggregated in the Specialised Carriers & Rigging Association (SCRA) Oversize/Overweight Permit Manual. Modules under 8-feet wide require no special permits or delivery protocols, while the widest module (16 feet) requires specific permits and protocols. Some states or provinces do not allow modules over 14 feet, making this the default industry norm. Module heights (from 11 to 13 feet) and lengths (from 40 to a maximum 70 feet) are also directly informed by the SCRA Manual.[4]

Modular manufacturing in North America uses either in-line or stationary production platforms. The difference is whether the fabrication work is

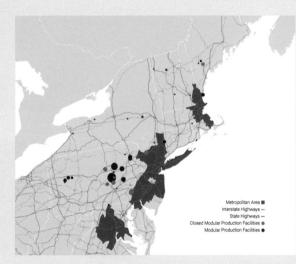

C.3   The North-East USA is home to a large number of volumetric house builders.

repetitively mass produced (high volume, low margin) or more bespoke (low volume, high margin). Few factories do both. Certification processes vary from state to state and may occur in the factory or on site. Modules leave the factory 60–90 per cent complete, with the facade and some interior finishes often being completed on-site, usually by a builder with whom the modular housing manufacturer has an established relationship.

A typical modular housing manufacturer is likely to offer services ranging from design and engineering to assistance with transportation to the construction site and, in some cases, construction management services on site. The general contractor is usually responsible for module assembly, finishes and site work as well as seeing the project through to final site inspection. Larger modular housing manufacturers employ full-time architectural and engineering staff, with most offering standard unit configurations to potential buyers.

The North American modular industry has three tiers: manufacturers, manufacturer-direct and dealers. Manufacturers produce modules to service general contractors or modular dealers. Manufacturer-direct may also contract directly with owners to provide modular solutions, acting as a general contractor. Both manufacturers and manufacturer-direct organisations may be specifically focused on a particular building type, for example residential or commercial, or focus on relocatable and/or permanent construction. Increasingly, however, manufacturers are becoming knowledgeable and skilled across the array of building types, markets and industry segments.

The permanent modular industry developed out of the larger mobile/manufactured housing industry during the late 1970s, with the first trade association, the Modular Home Builders Association (MBHA), founded in 1977 and the MBI founded in 1983. MBHA has focused on single-family housing, while MBI has focused on commercial modular construction, including multi-family, educational, office and administration, health and retail. The federally regulated manufactured housing industry's percentage of the overall US housing market hovers at around 10 per cent of new construction

over the last decade; data regarding the modular industry is more difficult to access and analyse.[5]

It is estimated that 200 modular construction manufacturers exist in North America, only 70 of which are members of MBI, with even fewer undertaking the association's annual survey.[6] In 2016, MBI estimated that the modular industry constituted 3 per cent of new construction in North America, and projected an increase to as much as 5 per cent by the end of the decade.[7] Work is distributed throughout North America, with a significant concentration in the northeast, particularly Pennsylvania. MBI estimates that the modular manufactured component is 55 per cent of a building project's overall cost. Over the past four years, a typical manufacturer's annual production was 330 modules, 680 square feet in size, and employed 100 to 200 workers. While a few companies operate multiple facilities, most MBI members own and operate a single facility focused on a single market, usually within a 500-mile radius.[8] Architects working with modular manufacturers report challenges with the lack of sophistication of this relatively new industry.[9]

The majority of the industry has optimised fabrication processes around the delivery of light timber-framed single-family housing; however, the last decade has seen a growing number of experiments that extend the scope. Resolution: 4 Architecture developed Modern Modular (see Fig. 1.6), a design methodology informed by the modular industry (see Country Study USA: Simplex Homes box, p.66).[10] First designed for a 2003 competition run by *Dwell Magazine*, this has evolved through over 30 residential commissions, leading to a close collaboration with Pennsylvania-based modular manufacturer Simplex Homes. In 2007 Blu Homes (see Fig. 4.1), founded by Bill Haney and Maura McCarthy, began developing folding technology to allow steel-framed (and subsequently timber) modules to be shipped at nearly 50 per cent of their final erection size. Blu Homes fabricated 28 homes before moving production from Massachusetts to a new facility in the San Francisco Bay Area in 2011. They have since patented their folding technology in the United States and in the European Union.[11] In 2010, architects Jared Levy and Gordon Stott established Connect Homes,

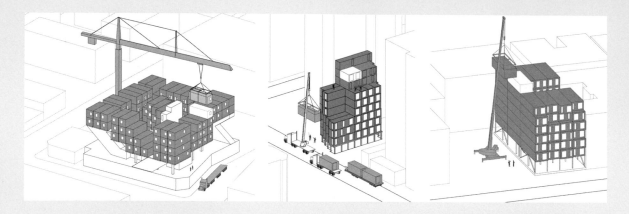

C.4   Organisation of on-site installation
of volumetric modules at (L–R) Star
Apartments, Los Angeles; My Micro, New
York; and The Stack, New York.

based in Los Angeles, and submitted a patent for
a modular system developed around an 8-foot-wide
steel frame that utilises standard shipping container dimensions and connections while allowing
for a high degree of customisation and off-site
fabrication.[12]

These innovations are paralleled by experiments
in multi-unit construction, a key industry growth
area. In 1996, New York-based Nehemiah Housing
Development Fund Company Inc. commissioned
hundreds of units of affordable housing from
Capsys Corp, a modular construction manufacturer
then based in Brooklyn's Navy Yard. Capsys also
fabricated nARCHITECTS' My Micro NY – ten stories
of steel modules stacked on a plinth completed in
2015 (see Cover Image). My Micro NY (now Carmel
Place) replaced the 2013 Stack project, by Peter Gluck
Architects and Deluxe Building Systems, as the tallest multi-unit modular construction project in New
York City. During the same period, Forest City Realty
Trust and Skanska established a modular manufacturing facility, FC+Skanska Modular, also located at
the Brooklyn Navy Yard, to fabricate modules for the
Atlantic Yards development. This facility produced
the modules for a single-housing tower, the B2
tower, designed by SHoP Architects. In Philadelphia,
the When We Fix It Coalition of builders, architects,
engineers and environmental groups has been

lobbying the municipal government since 2004 to
support the use of Pennsylvania's concentration of
modular companies to lower the cost of affordable
and workforce housing.[13] Mid-rise, multi-unit modular housing is also becoming increasingly common
on the west coast.[14]

Modular builders across North America are
leveraging the roots of the balloon frame and the
mobile home industry, harnessing the ideology,
product and process abilities to deliver more durable housing. More recently, manufactured methods
of housing production are also being utilised for
architectural outcomes.

Conceptual Prefab

Conceptual prefab responds to aesthetic, formal, polemical, symbolic, rhetorical, or fantastical reasoning. This focus engages with prefab's aspirational and transformational promises. Conceptual prefab often follows a solutions-oriented *approach, where a solution is generated for a yet-unidentified or intangible problem. Distilling the goals of conceptual prefab is much harder than with utilitarian prefab, because its criteria are not explicit, rational, or quantifiable. To understand the logic behind conceptual prefab we must venture out through ever-widening circles that touch on the very substance of culture and meaning.*

3.3   Buckminster Fuller and his Dymaxion House concept, 1927.

Examples of conceptual prefab can be found in the striking houses reviewed in the pages of *Dwell*. Another fruitful source are the ubiquitous stock images of the newspaper articles and the 'heroic' case studies of the many historical accounts previewed in Chapter 2. A sample of well-known moments of conceptual prefab from the twentieth century includes R. Buckminster Fuller's *Dymaxion House* (1944–47) (Fig. 3.3), Jean Prouvé's *Maison Metropole* and *Maison Tropicale* (1949–52), and Matti Suuronen's *Futuro* (1968–78). This is the branch of prefab that taps into the aspirational, creative and emotional aspects of building, dwelling and living. It aims at a wider cultural, social and economic transformation, but cannot be easily reduced or instrumentalised for any clear purpose, and is thus harder to understand than utilitarian prefab.

3.4   The off-grid 'Ecocapsule', an architectural concept from Slovakia. Such proposals offer symbolic solutions for the future of building.

3.5 Thomas Edison's ill-fated single-pour concrete house. Patented in 1908, the idea relied on builders investing a large sum in the heavy and complex formwork system.

Where the 'brief' for utilitarian prefab is clear – accommodate x people for y years in location z – the brief for conceptual prefab is much less obvious. There is a long history of architects using prefab for symbolic and polemical purposes: a 'house of the future'; a prototype demonstrating mass production techniques; an open-source, customisable dwelling. In these examples, prefab stands in as a signifier of a much greater agenda. On some occasions, conceptual prefab may never be intended for more than a niche application or the exploration of key techniques or materials. But such examples still adhere to the idea that they could be extrapolated to solve the *big* problems of the day, which typically include examples such as housing supply, affordability, homelessness, or disaster relief. The purpose of conceptual prefab is often to stimulate discussion, to change expectations, to demonstrate potential

through building prototypes, and to 'talk' with (and about) building culture more generally.

The 'who' of conceptual prefab is also telling: the key protagonists are architects, engineers, industrial and product designers, inventors and entrepreneurs. This stream is more connected to the transformational power of prefab and the singular, 'heroic' author so prized in these professions. Its focus on the author, creator and inventor is, in many ways, at odds with the outward aims of many prefab ventures to provide solutions for the masses. Logically, the proliferation of such 'unique' solutions would eventually result in a mass solution, and thereby change the status of the objects themselves. Would, for example, our view of Le Corbusier's Pavillon de l'Esprit Nouveau, built in Paris in 1924, be the same if it had been rolled out en masse as Le Corbusier intended?[4] (Fig. 3.6)

These projects rehearse a well-worn balancing act – how to appear as an instance of a greater agenda to 'house' the masses, yet retain the appeal of exclusivity, the thrill of the future, or the striking touch of the genius? We will return to this problem in Chapter 6 with regard to the discussion of design value in industrialised house building.

Authorship is central to this discussion. The genius of the single author remains a hotly contested pillar of the professions of design and architecture. When absent, architectural discourses have set aside particular categories for buildings that do not come with the stamp of authorship – Gothic cathedrals and vernacular building, for example. In this context it is interesting to consider the challenge posed by the prefab house: as just one instance of a wider project. If industrialised building solutions were to achieve the success their authors wish for, this very success might erode the concept of single author. As Colin Davies points out with regard to architects dabbling in industrialised housing projects, this is precisely *not* what conceptual prefab does.[5]

Conceptual prefab has deep links with architectural culture. In the early twentieth century, architects believed that they needed to recognise and channel the underlying destination of technology. In this, prefabrication and the prefab dwelling unit

3.6 Le Corbusier's Pavillon de L'Esprit Nouveau. Temporarily erected in 1925, the building demonstrated Le Corbusier's ideas on architecture and urbanism, seeking to reject the decorative arts of the very exposition for which it was commissioned. The prototype was just one module of a larger apartment building concept.

took on very particular and iconic roles because of modernist ideas about the cultural consequences of manufacture and serial form. Architectural historian Manfredo Tafuri refers to this as the 'crisis of the object'.[6] Many architects are taught to believe they are providing utilitarian solutions when in fact they are providing conceptual solutions. Conceptual prefab is often used in this context by architects to show that they engage with the needs of the masses but can still be involved with the high-design pursuits that are highly prized within the profession. In Chapters 4 and 6 we explore the traditional structure of the disciplines and professions as a barrier to the uptake of prefab.[7]

It is this agenda of a technological breakthrough and social revolution that conceptual prefab keeps alive. If we refer back to the confusion of means and ends outlined in Chapter 1, we see that conceptual prefab positions prefabrication as the end, almost as a value to be aspired to. This – in contrast to utilitarian prefab's *problem-oriented* approach which focuses on the objectives of cost, speed and quality – is a *solutions-oriented* approach. As discussed further in Chapter 4, we believe this has been a serious impediment to the success and application of the broader venture of industrialised housing. Simply put: this approach sees designers or companies first arriving at an idea, design or system, and then setting about finding a market to sell it to – the *solutions-in-search-of-problems* phenomenon, which we identified in Chapter 1 and will discuss further in Chapters 4 and 5.

Exceptions and an Argument for a Third Way

The future of prefab and industrialised building lies in a better balance between utilitarian and conceptual prefab. Until recent decades only a few projects and companies have challenged the hegemony of these polar extremes. Now, the changing conditions of twenty-first century housing and construction are undoing this polarity. It is the 'Third Way' or the spectrum of potential position between utilitarian and conceptual prefab that is of most interest for the success of future ventures.

Qualities offered by conceptual prefab, like novelty, programmatic exploration, formal inventiveness, striking aesthetic choices, or conceptual experiments, are essential to progress thinking and practice in contemporary housing. Utilitarian prefab may have delivered on prefab's core promises, but its outcomes typically lack innovation in a spatial and material sense, have low benchmarks for sustainability, and increasingly lower the standards of quality in a way that is difficult to sustain or endorse. Our argument for a third way highlights the dramatic swings of overreach and technological over-determination on the one hand, and the often insipid, limited, and uninspired approaches to housing on the other, to show that it is this middle ground which should be our target area.

Key historical examples and a view to the future of industrialised housing ventures suggest it is more useful to think about prefab as a spectrum, rather than the polar extremes of utilitarian and conceptual. Figures 3.7 and 3.8 show a notional spectrum between these two poles of classification. The two diagrams illustrate snapshots from 1950 and 2010, to show how this distribution has changed. What was a largely unpopulated territory in the middle of this spectrum in 1950 has filled substantially in recent decades, but there remains a gap between the mid-ground and the conceptual. There are many fine examples of such mid-ground players in Europe, North America and the Asia-Pacific, some of which are discussed in this book

3.7   Mid-twentieth century polarisation of prefab companies between utilitarian and conceptual prefab.

3.8   After 60 years, prefab companies show a more even spread across the spectrum between utilitarian and conceptual prefab.

(see Case Study USA: Simplex Homes, p.66; Case Study Japan: Sekisui House, p.115; and Case Study Sweden: BoKlok, p.133).

The reason for this more even spread in the twenty-first century is found in the new conditions, expectations and technologies outlined in the introduction. Two key examples from this third way from the mid-twentieth century are especially interesting to our story: the now universally appreciated Eichler houses and the General Panel Company. Both projects arguably lie between the utilitarian and conceptual poles and play an unusual game. These companies and their products do not completely satisfy either conceptual or utilitarian camps, but demonstrate a successful compromise that is instructive for the future.

Case Study: The Eichler Houses

The so-called 'Eichler Houses' are not typically included in case studies of prefab housing. They have become universally appreciated for their marriage of aspirational and conceptual design with a mass market logic that has much in common with the core promises of utilitarian prefab. The Eichler houses demonstrate the possibility of a successful third way compromise.

Joseph Eichler was chiefly a property developer operating in California.[8] In the post-World War II decades, Eichler built his reputation and business on the introduction of modern architectural styles, materials and principles to a mass market. The Eichler houses, as they became known, demonstrate the possibility of a more moderate and polite Californian modernism adapted to a mass market. These houses responded to new design requirements and displayed novel and prudent formal and material uses. The Eichler houses are not 'prefab' in the strict sense of being manufactured off-site but they did introduce many industrialised processes. As such, they fit well into the burgeoning middle

3.10 One of Joseph Eichler's developments at Lucas Valley, California in 1962. These homes came to be emblematic of their location and time, and show a fruitful marriage between design value and commercial success.

ground between utilitarian and conceptual prefab.

These houses are of particular interest to the analysis and approach developed in the final three chapters of this book because they offered the market a balance of simplicity, good design and

3.9 Images of Eichler Homes such as this one were often used in innovative marketing brochures which attempted to stand Eichler Homes apart from their competition through a focus on design.

The Platform Approach

If the traditional construction industry operates from project to project, building to building, industrialised housing requires a more considered, longer-term approach that goes beyond the individual product, house or building. This platform approach has been used to great effect in other industrial sectors and recent decades have seen the appropriation of its techniques into industrialised housing. There are two dominant modes of thinking about platforms: the product-driven and process-driven approaches. The former is more widely known but the latter is perhaps more applicable to the particularities of housing. Over the past decade, 'Platform thinking' has also emerged as a distinct business model that relies on interconnectivity and networks to connect users and makers in new ways.

In recent times, 'Platform' has become something of a buzzword for business. Seeking innovation, efficiency and competitive advantage, companies use the term in various ways – online platform,

customer platform, process platform or product platform. Historically, manufacturing focused on product design as a singular activity, an emphasis that missed the potential for 'commonality, compatibility, standardisation or modularisation among different products and product lines'.[1] In response, the platform approach emerged to create simplified product lines sharing elements through a common family structure.

In its basic form, a product platform is a 'foundation for a range of individual product variations', which allows the creation of 'elements and interfaces that are common to a family of products'.[2] Product platforms have gained contemporary interest as companies have sought to create opportunities for successful mass customisation, diversifying their products without superfluous consumption of materials or time. In terms of an approach for product development, a company's platform can be understood as top-down (proactively designing products to create new markets), or bottom-up (responding to the market with new designs).[3] This design-focus highlights the importance of considering a company's particular platform in conjunction with its business model, market engagement and technical expertise.

A platform system has four chief parts: the components (physical parts), processes (design and production), knowledge (stored business expertise) and people/relationships (between staff internally and with the supply chain).[4]

The automotive industry has utilised a platform approach to car design and development for several decades. The traditional automotive platform was based on shared chassis and body-types, such as General Motors' Y- then H-platforms of the 1960s and 1970s. This established a consistency of product design across all countries of operation. Today, automotive platforms have developed to give greater modularity of design of general components, allowing brands to create commonality and compatibility across ranges of vehicle classes. This is demonstrated by Volkswagen's Modularer Baukasten (MB, or Modular Building Block System), which has created platform strategies based on vehicle size and engine orientation, but allows commonality across

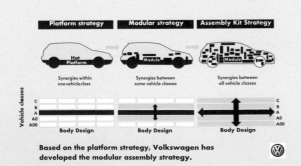

Based on the platform strategy, Volkswagen has developed the modular assembly strategy.

D.1 Evolution of the platform approach, from an automotive perspective, enabling efficiency and variety.

D.2 Summary of a platform approach for construction, showing Jansson's support methods and relationship of constructed buildings and business offerings.

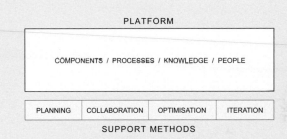

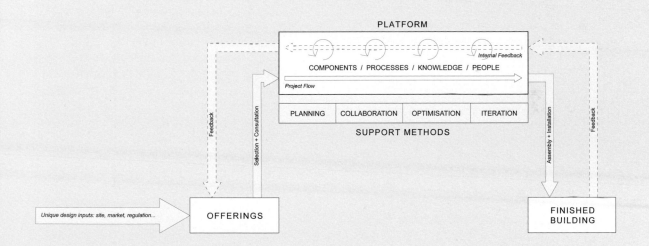

Audi, VW, Seat and Skoda brands, with branches into Porsche and Bentley (see Fig. 4.4).

There are two dominant views of how best to utilise the platform approach in construction. The first is a product-oriented view that stresses the importance of modularity and the interface design of the physical components, as applied to manufacturing platforms in the car industry, for example.[5] The second view stresses the importance of using the platform approach as a way of thinking about construction through a process focus, with emphasis on feedback and flows of knowledge.[6]

Research to define a platform approach for construction has also underscored the necessity of platform support methods in planning, collaboration, optimisation and iteration of design tasks. These tasks contain a complexity not found in traditional mass manufacturing.[7] As a result, new roles have emerged in construction such as the 'Process Owner', or 'Platform Manager', who co-ordinate feedback and continuous improvement of the overall platform. These new roles operate in addition to construction's traditional individual project manager roles.[8]

In Sweden, companies such as BoKlok (see Case Study Sweden: BoKlok box, p.133) have developed a single technical, product-focused platform to control the design, cost and configuration of their volumetric modules. This allows many permutations to be created from a standardised palette of modules, enabling the company to consistently deliver a high quality of build across the Nordic countries. Veidekke, a Norwegian company, aims to continually improve the delivery and the design of the 'kit of parts' that comprise the VeidekkeMAX platform (see Fig. A.1, p.25), which ranges from precast concrete stairs, slabs and external wall elements to steel-framed volumetric bathrooms, to internal wall elements. German house builders utilise the platform approach to increase the efficiency of their on-site operations, or to develop housing products that can act as a 'beach-head strategy' for product development in new markets.[9] In Japan, companies such as Sekisui House (see Case Study Japan: Sekisui House box, p.115) have developed a 'Standard Separation' delivery model, which comprises four catalogues that control plans, finishes, components and technology – an oblique, though distinctive, reference to the platform approach.

At a conceptual and strategic level, platforms have also been gaining traction as a method of thinking about problems in a wide range of applications. 'Platform-thinking' enables businesses to gain competitive advantage through the elimination of intermediaries or wholesalers, the creation of new forms of value, and/or enhancing connections between markets. This new value can be realised not just in the product offering through the product development platform, but across the operations of the entire company, as platform-thinking dictates new work methods.

The rise of Uber and Airbnb has demonstrated how platform-thinking can restructure the allocation of pre-existing resources and thereby disrupt traditional industries.[10] Construction too is likely to be affected by platform-thinking. The elimination of intermediaries, direct contact with end-users, new formulations of professional roles and emerging fabrication techniques and technologies hold obvious potential. Traditional procurement methods may be disrupted as building producers are put into direct contact with the end-user through communication technologies. Meanwhile designers may increasingly be able to manufacture buildings themselves through advanced digital technologies and automation (see Digital and Automated Fabrication box, p.33). These new business models, driven by connectivity and communication, are likely to create new value for the end-user by allowing more direct interactions between customer and creator.

affordability, without the excesses of formal acrobatics, technological triumphalism and experimental expressionism prevalent in many other architect-designed mass-housing concepts. It was this balance of good design, brand and pricing that prompted Steve Jobs to recall the Eichler houses that he experienced growing up, noting their formative influence on his sense of design:

> Eichler did a great thing [...] His houses were smart and cheap and good. They brought clean design and simple taste to lower-income people. [...] I love it when you can bring really great design and simple capability to something that doesn't cost much. It [the clean elegance of the Eichler house] was the original vision for Apple. That's what we tried to do with the first Mac. That's what we did with the iPod.[9]

This passage, and what it says more broadly about the Eichler houses, is significant for a few reasons. First, it demonstrates the possibility of a viable solution to Walter Gropius' early call for 'inexpensive, well-built and practical houses' that can satisfy the customer's 'individual wishes'.[10] Second, the houses demonstrate that a property developer could tread a successful balancing act between good design and commercial success (often held to be opposing forces). Finally, Jobs' statement is a rare acknowledgment that other industrial design and manufacturing sectors may have something to learn from the design and production of buildings. As will become clearer in Chapters 4 and 6, it is more commonly assumed that housing must learn from all other industrial sectors, because it is seen to lie behind the imaginary wave of technological progress.

Case Study: General Panel Company

General Panel Company is a crucial case study as one of the most important attempts to industrialise house building in the twentieth century. Through the work of Gilbert Herbert, it is also one of the best documented examples. If the venture had been successful, it might have established something close to the mid-ground

between utilitarian and conceptual prefab we support. But General Panel failed spectacularly and this holds many relevant insights today, just as it did 65 years ago.

The system and thinking behind the General Panel Company and its chief product, 'The Packaged House', emerged from a collaboration between Konrad Wachsmann and Walter Gropius, and is counted by many historians as one of the best-known and most promising examples of prefabrication from the mid-twentieth century. Both Wachsmann and Gropius had fled Nazi Germany in the 1930s, eventually settling in the USA where they spent the remainder of their illustrious careers. While Gropius was known to many at the time, both as an architect and through his foundational role in setting up the Bauhaus in Germany, Wachsmann was, and remains, the lesser-known figure.

Gilbert Herbert's sophisticated discussion and analysis of the venture and its key protagonists was published in 1984 as *The Dream of the Factory-Made House*. As indicated in Chapter 2, the book lays out the prehistory and the rise and fall of the General Panel Corporation.[11] Over half the book is devoted to illustrating how the designs and systems behind

3.11 Gropius and Wachsmann's Packaged House system was designed to be delivered 'flat-packed' by truck.

3.12   The General Panel test house, built
in Queens, New York in 1946. Showing
the controlled, modernist aesthetic
with shallow roof pitch and considered
placement of doors and windows.

Wachsmann, which went through numerous design and prototyping iterations. The panels were made in a standardised format, which could contain different options for openings, glazing, or solid walls. All parts were intended to be prefabricated in the factory and transported to site by truck for assembly.

The layouts and formal solutions for the Packaged House are an example of what good design can achieve, showing that it is more than just 'style' and aspiration. What Wachsmann and Gropius delivered was a modest suburban bungalow with efficient floor plans, shallow roof pitches, and well-proportioned, deliberately-placed windows and doors. As one would expect from two modernist architects, there was little to no trim, simple forms and planar walls. Despite this *restrained* modernism, there was still a nod to the more traditional forms of mass housing, and the houses would have been recognisable to their intended market of returning GIs and their families.

Herbert has also shown that other architects were encouraged to use the system behind the Packaged House in their own designs. Some of these designs show more adventurous and familiar mid-century modernist styles, replete with interlocking cubic volumes of varying heights, flat roofs, raised pavilions and linear or pinwheel plan-forms.

The Packaged House had a market, a highly talented team, a stream of finance, and government backing. Yet, as Herbert summarises:

> ... the bold undertaking failed completely, at least in a material sense. That failure had not only the elements of personal drama, as far as the chief protagonists were concerned, but consequences of much more general significance, whether it is with the technology of industrialized building that we are concerned, or with the processes of the housing market, or, more deeply, with an understanding of the meaning of 'dwelling'.[14]

Beyond the 'personal drama', Herbert offers an explanation for why this thinking largely failed to materialise as a sustainable (or extensive) industry in the USA.[15] The causes of failure were often internal to General Panel, but many were also 'generic to

the Packaged House were developed from a series of ventures and interests that Gropius and Wachsmann had pursued separately for decades in their native Germany before teaming up in the USA.[12]

Arriving in the USA in 1941, the destitute Wachsmann met Gropius with a roll of drawings containing details of a building system that used flexible building panels and which became the basis of the Packaged House system.[13] Gropius and Wachsmann's collaborative work on the Packaged House began during World War II but it was in the postwar period, with the Veterans Emergency Housing Program, that the full scope and application of the project and the company became apparent. The Veterans Emergency Housing Program had offered surplus factories and materials to housing companies, and the General Panel Company was expected to flourish in this environment. However, missing a number of important contracts as well as persistent financing problems led to the company's demise in 1952.

In line with Wachsmann's early sketches, the Packaged House system was modular and intended to be highly flexible in layout. It was a timber framed, panellised system, with a unique and highly intricate jointing system developed mainly by

3.13   The Packaged House System was used by other architects to develop their own 'offerings', however none were realised. Here, designs by Elsa Gidoni, Paul Bromber, Walter Gropius and Richard Neutra are shown.

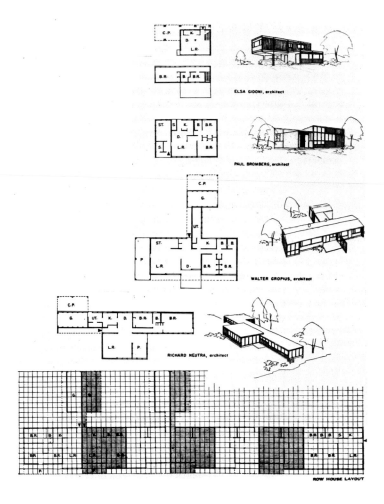

the whole movement for the industrial production of houses and combined to doom many a promising venture to failure'.[16] One issue to which Herbert returns was the Packaged House's reliance on an automotive model of manufacturing. Setting out the grounds for this analysis, Herbert covers a range of related topics that deserve longer quotation:

> ... the maker of prefabs could aim directly at the more ambitious, but hardly affluent, lower strata of the middle-class market, hoping to produce a factory-built product competitive in quality with the traditionally built houses of the tract developer, at a significantly lower price; this was the goal of General Panel, as it was of most other

prefab firms. In this formidable task, where the high costs of research, development, and tooling could only be offset by large-scale production, the advocates of the factory-built house turned again and again to the paradigm of the automobile for encouragement and for justification. But this analogy was a false one. Car prices were initially high, to cover high tooling costs and disproportionate overheads, while production slowly increased. But as a generic product, the car was unique, and its manufacturers had a complete monopoly; one either paid the high price or did not acquire a car. Eventually, of course, production rose to levels where prices could significantly be reduced, generating even larger

The Lustron Home   A New Standard for Living

First model Lustron house – 1946   America's First Truly Volume-Produced Home
Hinsdale, Illinois

3.14   The Lustron Home, another prefabricated home fuelled by the post-World War II industrial environment. An all-steel home, developed by Carl Strandlund, this was to be an affordable and low-maintenance housing option that would quickly respond to the housing shortage of the time, as well as provide support to the steel industry. Uptake was low and costs above projections. Two years after producing their first house, the Lustron company was insolvent.

demand. […] But industrialized housing did not produce unique products, the competition of the traditionally built house was an ever-present factor, and the industry was denied that sheltered growth period it needed to reach the critical level of mass production.[17]

This passage is highly significant for its analysis of the diverse conditions that bear on industrialised housing 'products' and which, if they are not taken into account, threaten to derail such ventures completely. It also shows the alluring, though misguided, power of the comparison with the auto industry, a theme to which we will return in Chapter 4.

In setting out General Panel's problems, Herbert is clear in *not* laying the blame for the failure on its 'architectural conception, nor in the technological means, nor in the translation by industry of that conception into the reality of building components'.[18] Rather, the *constellation* of conditions that contributed to failure were 'cumulative in effect', and included:

- questionable market analysis and perhaps lack of understanding of the market;
- volume/price considerations which saw the resultant houses 15 per cent more expensive than traditionally built homes;
- the approach to R&D and the requirement for its long-term amortisation;
- its reliance on a closed system, which did not allow for easy uptake or adaption by the conventional industry;
- overheads incurred by factory production and gearing up;
- the speed at which production was to rise from a standing start;
- the absence of detailed understanding of the regulatory and financial contexts for housing; and
- the uniqueness of the product vis-à-vis the parallel traditional industry and its ranges.

Herbert's account is also striking for the absence of the kinds of issues that architects, designers and some entrepreneurs have tended to obsess over, such as the design ideas and their functional and formal implications. Quite the opposite; Herbert lays a great deal of the failure of General Panel on Wachsmann and Gropius' obsession with perfecting the technical, material and construction solutions, thereby stopping the company entering the market in a timely way. By 1947–48, when the company's new facilities in California were finally up and running, the traditional housing industry had bounced back from its post-war doldrums.[19] By early 1948 only 15 Packaged Houses had been produced and sold.[20]

Herbert uses the Arthur Bernhardt diagrams we introduced in Chapter 2, developed for his book *Building Tomorrow: The Mobile/Manufactured Housing Industry*, to illustrate some of the reasons why General Panel ultimately failed (see Fig. 2.5). Herbert points to major problems in the distribution, finance, construction and land development areas, and to minor problems in the supply sector and building code regulation. The key lesson of Herbert's analysis – which echoes those of Kelly and Bernhardt before him – was that industrialised housing is much more than the technological system with which Wachsmann was concerned; it is a 'total system'.[21] Of Bernhardt's diagram, and of the mobile/manufactured housing ventures more generally, Herbert wrote:

> [the model] delineated [...] a total, complex, and integrated system, [and] was the result of the foresight and pragmatic cooperation of many individuals and firms in the various branches of the mobile house industry. It was the outcome of a slow evolutionary process rather than the single masterstroke of a brilliant mind.[22]

Had General Panel been a one-off event whose failure was easily traced to the excesses or incapacity of its developers, it would not be so important for our story. But General Panel is emblematic of a raft of attempts that came both before and after. The Lustron company, another well-known but ultimately failed business from the period, shows many parallels to General Panel.[23] Lustron started and went bust at the same time but unlike the Packaged House, technology was on immediate display in the Lustron house. Lustron – the name itself invoking a kind of futurism – was a steel-framed system, and the cladding, perhaps the most obvious point of difference, consisted of enamelled folded steel sheets. Lustron was very much a materials- and system-led enterprise and as Herbert spells out in his comparison of the two companies:

> The reasons ... for the failure of Lustron in 1950–51 are an echo of the problems bedevilling General Panel: high production costs leading to escalating prices; difficulties with organised labor; problems generated by the diversity of local building codes and a lack of sympathetic understanding in their application; the necessity of devising an adequate and properly financed distribution system; the unsuitability of bank mortgaging procedures when applied to an 'instant' product rather than an extended building process; insuperable difficulties in raising sufficient capital, which short term loans failed to alleviate; and, ultimately, the lack of a guaranteed and continuous market of adequate volume inherent in a free enterprise housing system.[24]

3.15 Components of a Lustron House laid out at Columbus, Ohio in 1949.

In several regards, this comparison of the failures of General Panel and Lustron brings the companies' location in our taxonomy into sharper focus. With the story of General Panel's rise and fall now told, where then should its chief product, the 'Packaged Home', lie along our spectrum? There are arguments for seeing the Packaged House as both utilitarian and conceptual prefab, and indeed the ambitions of the company were not without their contradictions. The Packaged House was initially intended for the mass-housing market, but it was also designed by two of the leading architects of the twentieth century and embodied many of the technical and design lessons of the early modern movement. It trod the fine line of style and market: it was not a bold or zealous modernism, rather a tempered nod to both the vernacular and speculative housing types and styles. In the Packaged House we can still see the element of style – the crispness of the detail and the overall proportions show the hand of a capable designer at work. But at the same time as it was a tightly curated stylistic exercise, it was *also* capable of being agnostic to the design style, as the alternative modern designs by other architects demonstrated.

As Herbert relays, the Packaged House was also a significant project in Gropius' oeuvre, because it marked the point where he had moved from being an 'ideologue of prefabrication' to a practitioner.[25] Despite the fact that so few houses were built, this shift in Gropius' position came with a new approach and responsibility. It demonstrated a more tempered approach to design and construction and, thus, the venture resides between our two poles of utilitarian and conceptual prefab. General Panel and the Packaged House offers valuable lessons in both how to avoid spectacular failure and how to integrate good design with novel manufacturing processes.

Why a Third Way is Important

A key observation of this book is that the success of future industrialised housing ventures will require a balance between the utilitarian and conceptual promises of prefab. But this broad observation requires a deeper mode of analysis to unlock its real potential.

Each prefab company embarks on its venture with a series of 'settings' in place, some of which may be the givens of particular circumstance, others simply arbitrary. Settings may be explicit or implicit, known or unknown, but they are ever-present. These could include the target market and location, the technique and materials to be used in fabricating the parts, the business model, the cost structure, the mode of sales and distribution, or the planning and land-use issues, to name just a few. These myriad settings provide the scaffolding within which the business is built, and can determine what the business can or cannot do. Figuratively speaking, these settings are akin to the company's genetic code, a DNA, best visualised as a series of interconnected systems that we discuss in greater detail at the end of Chapter 5.

Together, the Eichler Houses, the Packaged House and Lustron demonstrate that success and failure rely much less on luck, timing, the quality of the ideas, or the level of invention (even if these are all important). Success relies more on the successful functioning of *all parts of this total system* in a coherent way. This is why this book advocates imperfect application over conceptual purity. Such an attitude would have greatly benefited General Panel and leads us, in this book, to stress the importance of the *process* over the *product*.

To ensure the smooth running of this 'system', one needs first be aware of all the parts. We must also be aware of the various relationships and causalities between the parts; and then we must carry out the hard work of resolving the blockages and barriers to the successful functioning of both the parts and the whole and of integrating and optimising their outcomes. The results of this exercise, we hope, should be neither overzealous nor insipid, neither conceptual nor utilitarian, but appropriate, balanced and holistic.

Business Models and Industrialised Construction

A business model explains how a company operates: how it creates value, manages assets and deploys resources. Industrialised construction necessitates a different way of doing business – it requires integration, continuity and pre-engineering. This is in contrast to conventional construction business logic, which focuses on strict contracts for projects in a highly fragmented value chain. We need new ways of conceptualising and structuring the construction process and new ways of determining how companies are organised.

Industrialised construction necessitates a different way of doing business. So what is a business model and how should it be constituted and managed for industrialised house building companies?

Conventional business logic in housing construction is based on project production (deliveries) regulated by strict contractual arrangements. The value chain is fragmented because companies organise their operations around delivering discrete parts of buildings and parts of the specifications of buildings (see Construction Logistics and Supply Chain Management box, p.98). In contrast, the backbone of the business logic of industrialisation is in integration, continuity and pre-engineering allowing companies to deliver products (products are still 'sold' as different projects) that often bypass project-based contractual arrangements. This new business logic disrupts how companies are organised and how housing business and building processes are structured and coordinated. Business models are defined as a formula for value creation and asset and resource deployment. A business model concept explains the logic of companies and how they operate.[1] Today, many managers use the 'business model' as a tool to provide a structured overview of how companies operate and how investments should be exploited and protected.

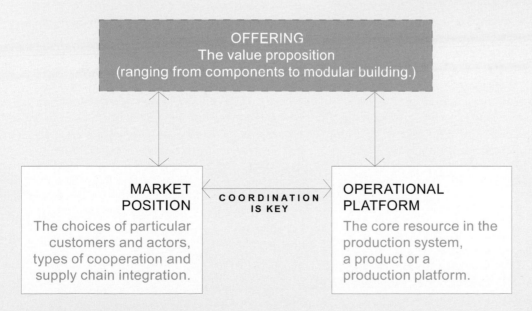

OFFERING
The value proposition
(ranging from components to modular building.)

MARKET POSITION
The choices of particular customers and actors, types of cooperation and supply chain integration.

COORDINATION IS KEY

OPERATIONAL PLATFORM
The core resource in the production system, a product or a production platform.

E.1   Key elements of the business model for industrialised house building.

The idea of the business model originated in the 1960s. Interest in them has increased since the early 2000s when forms of e-business emerged, and they now dominate the field of business strategy as a means to explain how manufacturing companies operate. Yet the building industry has yet to engage fully in such discussions. Recently, a stream of literature has emerged that adopts a business model view as an analytic tool to dissect how industrialised house building companies operate and re-organise their management.[2]

In general, a business model contains three major elements:

1. *Offering*. A 'value proposition' directed toward customers.
2. *Market position*. The company's position in the marketplace, determined through choices of customers, type of cooperation (e.g., main or sub-contractor), and the extent of supply chain integration (long-term integration or project contracts).
3. *Operational platform*. The company's resources integrated with external resources from suppliers and partners to produce and deliver the offering. The core is the production system. Some industrialised house-building companies use a product platform, some use a production/process platform.[3] The product/production platform contains the particular production resources, know-how (capabilities), partners and the (value chain) management of these assets.

The market position must be aligned with the operational platform to deliver the offering. A good internal fit between these three elements, and good external fit between the company and the market it operates in, will result in a viable business model.[4] For example, a company may attempt to produce a highly efficient and highly standardised product and to sell it to as many markets as possible; or, it may produce many highly flexible products targeted at only one market.

A company must be fully aware of the networks and resources built into its business model. If not, it risks losing its investments in platforms through the

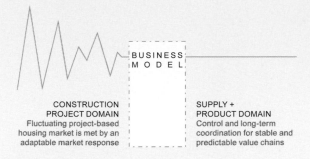

E.2   **The two domains of industrialised house building business models.**

unintended allocation of resources, which may negatively affect the company's long-term performance.[5]

A clear understanding of business models is especially important for industrialised house builders. This is because an industrialised production system, or product platform, is specialised when compared to conventional construction, which is aimed at the 'whole market' (see The Platform Approach box, p.48). One crucial aspect of this specialisation is designing a system to meet specific customer requirements (see Assembly and Construction Methods for Industrialised House Building box, p.127). For example, companies developing industrialised house building in Sweden are characterised as specialised because of two factors – first, the continuity and learning between building projects and in the use of repetitive methods and techniques; second, the defined production system aimed at specific, niche, customer segments.[6] This continuity (in the use of pre-engineered solutions, processes and partnerships) and specialisation (in terms of offerings sold in niche markets) defines how these companies operate.

Business models employed in industrialised house building follow a platform logic that can be of a product or a process type. A platform-oriented house-building company requires capabilities in two dimensions to ensure a market fit.[7] It must be capable of managing both the product and/or process domain (long-term coordination for stability and predictability) and at the same time manage the

CONSTRUCTION
PROJECT DOMAIN

SUPPLY CHAIN +
PRODUCT DOMAIN

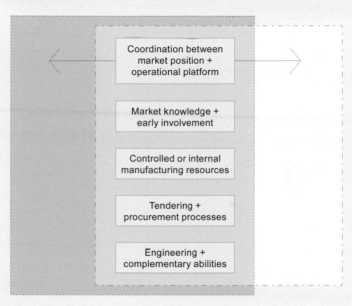

project dimension (construction project management, engineering and on-site operations).

There are five two-dimensional capabilities required by industrialised house-building companies in construction projects.[8] Together these form the company's core competencies (see Fig. E.3):

• *Coordination between market position and the operational platform*. Clients' needs (quality and delivery accuracy) must be met by the specific product offer. The ability to continuously improve to control work processes and develop products and processes is important.[9]

• *Market knowledge and early involvement*. The product logic limits the scope of the company. A clear definition of customer needs and market niche is crucial. To fully utilise the product/production platform in construction, projects must incorporate client interaction during their early stages.

• *Controlled or internal manufacturing resources*. The ability to deploy a specific product/production platform to control the supply chain in specific housing projects and at the same time create a predictable and stable supply chain to maintain the product dimension.[10]

• *Tendering and procurement capabilities*. The high monetary cost of buildings means that the client will choose a supplier from several quotations. A large amount of the total cost is subcontracted, which makes procurement capabilities of materials, resources and subcontractors necessary both to comply with project specification and product development work.

• *Engineering and complementary abilities*. Internal engineering capability is needed to configure the pre-engineered solutions exploited in specific housing projects but also for development of the product platform. Since industrialisation is based on continuity (e.g., partner alliances) complementary capabilities (dissimilar) between the partners common resource bases must be identified and attained to maintain the product dimension.

Business models are not static constructs. Changes can be triggered by macro-economic situations, increased competition, or other external circumstances. The limitation of market scope puts extra strain on industrialised housing companies to develop business models that can meet changing market demands. These capabilities are necessary to allow business models to adapt to changes.[11]

An individual capability progression management scheme should be able to change from one specific level of operational performance to another level while securing a competitive fit is proposed.[12] Five long-term management capabilities are required for companies to manage their business model over time:

- *Dynamic efficiency capability* ensures a contingent fit between the internal and external elements of the business model. This is a difficult balance to be strategically and operationally efficient over time and incorporates exploration and exploitation of the core competences.
- *Core competence extension* enlarges markets and addresses additional customers.
- *Core competence redeployment* serves new markets with the same core competence.
- *Integration mechanisms* link or separate emergent or new business models.
- *Support of the manufacturing outputs that secures the competitive fit*. The ability to initially facilitate high quality, accurate and predictable deliveries of housing. Thereafter to build capabilities offering the market increased cost efficiency in parallel with increased flexibility.

The three cornerstones of industrialisation (integration, continuity and pre-engineering) require industrialised housing companies to make substantial investments to reinforce their chosen market position and in the assets of their operational platform. They also mandate a long-term view of the expected return on invested capital. Business models will become more dynamic in the future. The key question is 'How will a business model change over time and what capabilities are needed to respond to and push these changes?' The interaction of a contingent fit between technology and market and between design and technology is needed to ensure the future of industrialised housebuilding.

4   Barriers to the Uptake and Success of Prefab Housing

This chapter outlines many of the problems that have plagued the uptake and adoption of industrialised building in the past and present. This includes the blockages, barriers, and obstructions we have discovered through our collective work with industry, overlayed with our expanded understanding of the history of prefabrication and industrialised building. Key companies and case studies are introduced to illustrate these points and to draw lessons for future practice from them.

Many of these barriers and the problems they pose are not new. Most are well documented and have not changed much since the mid-twentieth century when Burnham Kelly and others spelled them out. We offer the following as a timely warning and encourage new ventures to ensure that they learn these lessons before setting out on their own future path to industrialisation.

1   Imminent Revolution

The idea that the construction industry is on the verge of fundamental revolution is not new. The peculiar combination of outward simplicity and a deeper complexity leads to both repeated statements of imminent revolution and to many failed attempts to innovate. These failures happen because many solutions do not capture and respond to the complexity of construction generally and housing specifically.

Behind many attempts to industrialise building lies a simple motivation: surely we can do things better! The briefest tour of any conventional building site offers a window into practices that are obviously wasteful, inefficient, often chaotic, and – perhaps most importantly – very expensive (see Construction Logistics and Supply Chain Management box, p.98). It is little surprise, then, that there has been a sense of impending change, or revolution in the construction industry for some time. Take, for example, the following quotation from David Donnison's *The Government of Housing*, published 50 years ago, which discussed the problems of housing and economics in the UK:

> There has been much talk in recent years about the need for an industrial revolution in the construction industry, leading in some quarters to hopes of a spectacular "break-through" producing major cost reductions, particularly on the housing front.[1]

Despite this mood for change, Donnison goes on to point out that the actual outcomes were more sobering:

> Such hopes are likely to be disappointed, at least in their more extravagant form. Many countries have devoted years of effort and large sums of public money to this task. But in Western Europe, where conditions are most nearly comparable to our own, no country has built houses at appreciably lower cost with the aid of radically new systems.[2]

Notwithstanding the historical amnesia discussed in Chapter 2, we should pause to consider *why* so many have thought they can revolutionise construction where so many others have failed. Similarly, if the production of houses and mainstream construction methods really are as inefficient and unproductive as many suggest, why has it proved so difficult to bring about the 'breakthrough' that Donnison wrote of 50 years ago?[3]

Few people who have viewed how contemporary commercial aircraft are manufactured are likely to remark 'we can do this much better'. Aircraft are large, expensive and highly technical – the stakes are enormous if something goes wrong. Not so in construction. The motivation for change in construction, we argue, arises from the combination of several conditions fundamental to building: firstly, the outward chaos and inefficiencies of the building site and conventional construction methods (see Fig. 1.2); and secondly, the relative simplicity of the parts, materials and processes involved. Building is, for the most part (excluding highly complex one-off buildings), the assembly of low-tech, readily available parts. Complexities arise because of the scale and size of the constituent parts and owing to the complicated coordination and sequencing of building processes. Nevertheless, the actual techniques and processes of building and assembly appear simple and can be learned quickly, and the materials for building can be bought at any hardware store. Together, these conditions have engendered the misleading sense of easy fixes. A final consideration for the motivation of players seeking to revolutionise construction is found in low barriers to entry for those wishing to propose

new systems, combined with the size of the 'pie' that is the construction industry. With just a little searching on the internet, evidence of this propensity for revolution can be found in the great many building systems and inventions, developed and prototyped by individuals or backyard operations.

While not directly a barrier to the path of innovation in the construction industry, this idea of imminent revolution has been an impediment to real innovation. The history books are full of accounts of inventive systems that never made it to a building site.[4] Similarly, patent record offices contain mountains of documentation of great ideas that never reached significant commercialisation or uptake. 'Imminent revolution' provides a diversion, which, when such attempts fall flat, can bring the greater endeavour of change into question and reinforce an acceptance of the status quo.

2   The Definition of Prefab is Confusing

There is great uncertainty around the term 'prefab', its myriad synonyms and its definition, which provide a distraction from its purpose. Terms and definitions used in non-English languages can undo some confusion. The lack of consensus around 'prefab' makes it hard to communicate and to measure the impact of work in this field. Prefabrication is not an absolute description but a relative one. We do not propose new terms but focus on commonalities and intentions rather than differences.

The lack of consensus around terminology and definition has greatly impaired the ability to collect accurate data or to provide metrics on prefabrication. As such, very few countries are able to report what percentage of 'prefabricated' houses are actually in their markets. And, were countries able to collect such data, very few companies would even share the same definition for what they term 'prefabrication'. These problems are not likely to be resolved by a systematic study of usage or etymology, or by a prescriptive proposal of some majority-agreed term or terms.[5] We think it is likely that many more terms will emerge in the coming decades, particularly as new techniques and technologies change how we think about prefabrication and construction more generally.

The focus on the 'what' of prefabrication (and its various terms) has overshadowed the 'why'. Similarly, that much discussion in industry is focused on differences overshadows broad commonalities. As noted in Chapter 1 (see Fig. 1.5), in essence these terms and their associated technical approaches make largely the same 'promises', which have, in fact, changed very little over the past two centuries. Prefabrication is a fluid spectrum of options and construction methods that each project, company, or individual has at their disposal (see Assembly and Construction Methods for Industrialised House Building box, p.24). Exactly where the 'slider' is set and for what reasons is the more interesting and revealing issue. This is in accord with Burnham Kelly's observation that prefabrication is a question of degree and not an absolute, to which we might add, the reasons and intentions behind the degree of prefabrication that is pursued is ultimately more significant than the setting itself or what we call it.

This argument around terminology and definition has burned most brightly in English-language discourses. Turning to Japanese, Swedish and German-language discourses – that is, countries where prefabrication is widely adopted – takes some of the heat out of the debate.

In Japan, a range of terms have come to be associated with prefabricated house building; they are less tied to construction methodologies and more to construction materials. General terms for the industry include *kōgyō-ka jūtaku* (industrialised housing), and *purehabu jūtaku* (prefabricated housing). Material-based terms include: *mokushitsu-kei purehabu jūtaku* (prefabricated wooden housing – typically panelised); *tekkō-kei purehabu jūtaku* (steel-based prefabricated housing – built from light-gauge steel frame panels); *yunitto-kei purehabu jūtaku* ('unit-type' prefabricated housing; volumetric construction – typically built from timber or steel); and *konkurīto-kei purehabu jūtaku* (concrete prefabricated housing – precast panels).[6] Some of the Japanese terminology such as *yunitto* and *konkurīto* still hold

traces of their post-World War II origins in English as 'unit-based' or 'concrete'.

Japanese interest in industrialised construction has been driven by the cultural concept of *mottainai*, a societal interest in waste reduction and efficiency. This is not unique to building but rather to the desire not to waste time, money, food or energy. From this concept a range of well-known Japanese 'lean processes' have been derived that have found broad application across a range of industrial sectors, including prefabricated housing production (see Japan box, p.93).

Sweden, which reportedly has one of the highest uptake rates of prefabrication in the world, has, in recent years, sought to establish a definition to clearly differentiate industrialised construction from other forms of manufacturing, as well as to develop a holistic business-level view of off-site construction.[7] The *Miljonprogram* launched in the 1960s (see Sweden box, p.120) established interest in the industrialisation of construction, and two subtly different terms emerged from this period: *Industriellt byggande* is used commonly in industry to describe an approach to construction that is like manufacturing and which typically involves prefabrication, while the less common *industrialiserat byggande* reflects a repeatable form of on-site construction that is rational and mechanised. Specific Swedish terms focus on the level of prefabrication: of parts, their manufacture, and assembly on-site. Of the parts, *komponent*, *planelement* and *volymelement* refer to the prefabrication of components, 2D elements and 3D volumes. *Komponenttillverkning*, *planelementtillverkning* and *volymelementtillverkning* are subsequently used to describe the off-site manufacture of these pieces. Once on-site, the coming together of built material is described from component to volumetric installation by the terms *montage*, *monteringsbyggande* and *volymbyggande*.

As in Japan, cultural and political factors are at play in the language. This was evident in the Swedish modernists' calls for buildings to pursue a functionalist agenda and a more 'rational' form of construction, and in the Swedish government's post-World War II policy that forged a 'middle way' between capitalism and socialism. Such calls and policy permeated all aspects of life, through to construction and housing.[8]

Finally, in German language the most common equivalent of 'prefab' is *Fertighaus*, which can be directly translated as 'finished' or 'ready' house. This is a broad term that covers all building undertaken off-site and brought as finished elements or volumes to site.

3   Means and Ends

Prefabrication is a means to an end. Many companies that have attempted to make prefab housing have focused on the means while neglecting the ends. This failure to focus clearly and early on the ends, or objectives, is a substantial barrier to success.

Prefabrication is often misunderstood as being the objective in and of itself. That is, many companies have directed their ventures on the belief that once construction is moved off-site, rationalised and a smooth-running process of prefabrication achieved, all else would fall into place. One could also be forgiven for thinking that prefab itself is not merely a goal but a value, which takes on aspirational and sometimes moral connotations. We think this view to be misguided. Prefabrication does not have intrinsic *value*, nor is it some kind of *quality* to be aspired to. Rather, prefabrication and industrialisation are a means to an end.

This misconception has provided a significant barrier to the success of many prefab housing ventures, past and present. It walks hand-in-hand with the *solutions-in-search-of-problems* approach that was evident in so many historical examples. This approach can be summarised as follows:

1. An individual or company starts with a stand-out idea or concept for a prefabricated house;
2. A prototype house is run to production;
3. Although the house may have originally had a notional target market, the company looks to sell it to any group it can (because *more* market is better than less);
4. The initial high cost of production is written off to the prototyping phase, gearing up, and the like;
5. Finally, when gaps emerge between the cost of production and lack of fit to market, such costs are summarily defrayed to the need to 'scale' and extra capital required to make this jump.

This *solutions-in-search-of-problems* scenario demonstrates that the 'end' part of the means and ends equation has often received the least amount of attention. This is where, we believe, much of the trouble of failed companies lies. For example, of the General Panel venture we may well have asked Gropius and Wachsmann the simple but important questions: Is the objective of the company to provide affordable housing to the post-World War II mass market? Or, is the objective to create the most ingenious joining system and comprehensive construction kits for house building? If it is the former, it would follow that the issues of price-point, local regulations, consumer finance and market expectations would likely take precedence. Following this, it might not have been necessary to overhaul the *whole* construction system – indeed, much of the supply chain and industry structure could have remained intact or been changed gradually over time. If the answer to our hypothetical question is the latter, we have hardly to imagine any changes to the R&D-intensive mode that Gropius and Wachsmann pursued and which led to its ultimate failure.

A contemporary example of this same phenomenon is Blu Homes, a well-known company based in the United States. As the company's website states, Blu Homes make 'modern premium prefab homes'. The company was founded in 2008 and originally intended to operate across North America.[9] A few years ago, operations were reduced to significant bases on both East and West Coast USA, and more recently, operations were reduced further yet, to Northern California. The progress of Blu Homes has been closely followed in the industry, receiving a great deal of media attention, partly because it embodies the ambitious spirit of radically improving housing production and partly because of the heavy financial backing the company has received.[10]

4.1   Blu Homes 'Breezehouse', 2015.
Proprietary folding systems allowed
for larger internal spaces than other
volumetric systems.

Blu Homes developed a proprietary method for transporting shipping container-sized modules to site by truck, and assembling houses using an elaborate method of unfolding walls and a panelised roof system. This system enables the company to provide internal spaces that exceed the typical dimension possible with volumetric methods, which are limited by transportation dimensions (see Fig. C.1 in USA box, p.39). A bulky, engineered steel chassis and intricate heavy-duty hingeing were necessary to carry out this feat. Blu Homes also offers one of the most articulate customer interfaces in the industry. This interface, often referred to as a 'configurator', allows customers to interact directly with Blu Homes' ranges and to carry out customisations that become the basis for live costing and selection of models and features. With early design and systems input by architect Michelle Kaufmann and years of R&D into the backend IT system, Blu Homes has become emblematic of the ambition in prefab housing to create a fully integrated online platform for customising, ordering and specifying new houses (see Chapter 6, Section 5).

Despite the enormous investment in the company – making Blu Homes one of the most capitalised, industrialised housing ventures in North America – the commercial path of Blu has not been a resounding success. By 2015, the company was overhauling the proprietary system to make it more simple and efficient. The use of large-format heavy-gauge steel was being exchanged for standard timber sections. Proprietary hingeing and assembly

Case Study USA: Simplex Homes

Simplex Homes is emblematic of the wider modular housing industry in the United States. It has operated across the majority of conditions represented in that country and embodies the traditions, techniques and aspirations of the wider industry. These include: the early production of HUD-code, low-cost, transportable housing; permanent modular housing for conventional mass markets, both detached and attached; and, more recently, more up-market architect-designed offerings. Simplex Homes has successfully negotiated the broader construction market

and a turbulent economic period, demonstrating the success of slow and incremental growth, while diversifying and introducing business and technical innovation over a long period.

Simplex Industries Inc. (aka Simplex Homes), is representative of North American modular housing in a number of ways. First, the company is predictably located in a repurposed warehouse along the rust belt of the New Jersey–Pennsylvania border in the Northeastern United States. The company started out manufacturing coal stokers, shifted to mobile homes built to the Housing and Urban Development Code (HUD Code) in the 1970s, and then quickly transitioned to building light timber-framed permanent modular housing products for conventional residential construction (see USA box, p.39). Prior to 2010, that product was predominantly single-family housing, but in recent years the company has pursued low- to mid-rise multi-unit housing projects.[1] Modular construction business in the US is, in many cases, a family affair, and is therefore inseparable from its owners and developers. Founded in 1971, Simplex is currently led in its second generation by Patrick Fricchione, Jr.

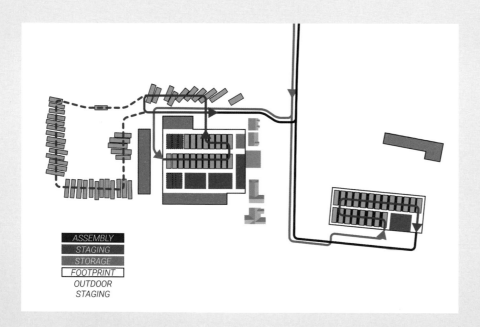

ASSEMBLY
STAGING
STORAGE
FOOTPRINT
OUTDOOR
STAGING

F.1 Input of materials and components into the Simplex facility and output of completed modules from the facility.

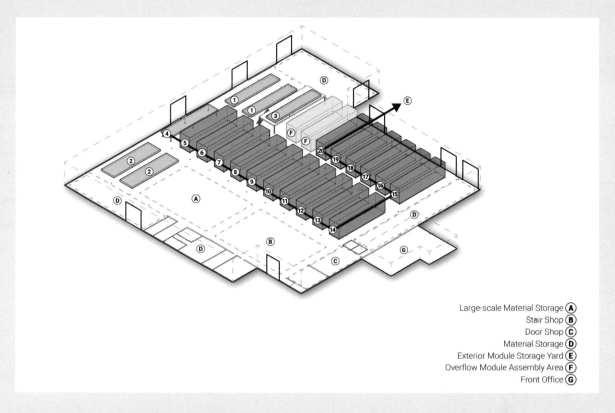

F.2   Production stages of Simplex Homes.

Not unlike most prefab manufacturers in the US, Simplex Homes makes a modular product that is 65–90 per cent factory finished using an in-line technique. Growing out of the HUD home industry fabrication process, a standard floor assembly (analogous to the HUD home chassis) is first assembled in an area adjacent to the line. That floor assembly then moves along the line on casters, with wall panels, manually built on horizontal jigs, moved into place by an overhead bridge crane to form a box structure. The boxes are finished from the inside out with pre-wiring, pre-plumbing, pre-ducting and installation of stairs, HVAC equipment, plumbing fixtures and kitchen appliances. This work is assisted through the use of Simplex's rolling steel scaffolds. Wall board is pre-installed on nearly every project, but depending on the program and client interest, floor finishes, paint and exterior cladding may be completed on-site. Modules are completed and lifted onto trailers inside the factory before being moved into the yard and shrink-wrapped for shipment. Unlike most North American modular manufacturers, Simplex Homes owns a fleet of trucks and often takes responsibility for shipping and setting of boxes on-site.

Like other Northeastern US modular manufacturers, Simplex Homes' primary products are modules for conventional houses, including single-family detached, townhouses, and low-rise, multi-unit duplexes and four-plexes. Modules are manufactured from 8' 0" to 13' 9" for standard sizes and up to super-wide 15' 9", which requires special permits and car escorts in transit. Module lengths can be manufactured up to the size of the factory facility – 53' 6". Ceiling heights are restricted to 9' 0".[2] Roof modules built from prefabricated trusses are procured from suppliers, sheathed and finished with roofing shingles and other materials. These roofs use hinges to fold portions of the roof flat to make them compact enough to meet transportation requirements.

Simplex Homes also manufacture other building applications, including light commercial buildings, dormitories, hospitality and retail structures.

Although not unique in their technical product offering, Simplex Homes has taken an innovative business approach (see Business Models and Industrialised Construction box, p.57). During a period in which other modular builders have struggled, and many have ceased to operate, Simplex has experienced steady growth. This can be attributed to the combination of relatively conservative business decisions, diversification of its product line and the development of key partnerships. Prior to the recession, Simplex planned to open a second facility in South Carolina, but these plans were cancelled when the economic climate changed. This reminds us that success in industrialised housing ventures is achieved through caution – standing costs and overheads can cripple companies in the downturns. Instead, and throughout this period of economic decline in the US and abroad, Simplex Homes launched a number of other initiatives including Simplex Solar, Cornerstone Building Solutions and Modern Architectural Modular.[3]

Business diversification is a point of difference for Simplex Homes within the broader context of North American modular companies. While the bread and butter of the business is manufacturing for conventional residences, the company's recently launched subsidiary, Simplex Solar, is developing new and alternative revenue streams. This solar installation company was set up to respond to the growing demand from homeowners for solar arrays offset by tax incentives, and also enables Simplex Homes to upsell solar in their product line. Further, Simplex has a pursued a joint venture with affiliate Cornerstone Building Solutions, a traditional homebuilder in the region. Simplex modules are manufactured for conventional construction and sold through Cornerstone, a standard homebuilding company that evokes confidence in homebuyers who may struggle with social stigmas associated with prefabrication.

Simplex Homes is also unusual in its business arrangement with Resolution: 4 Architecture, and their joint development of Modern Modular (see Fig. 1.6). This is a project design and delivery methodology developed around modular construction logics that focuses on high-quality architectural design. RES 4's initial modular work was the outcome of *Dwell Magazine*'s 2003 prefab home design competition; as one of the winners, RES 4 had their design built. RES 4 worked with Simplex Homes on this initial prototype and a partnership emerged that continues today. Together they have created a unique mass-customised system of service and living modules that can be combined in a variety of configurations to realise high-end architecturally significant homes in the Northeast. This product is targeted at the second-home market. The modules and resulting homes are scrupulously detailed and require a longer production time in the factory. This low-volume, high-margin business opportunity provides stability when the mass-housing market

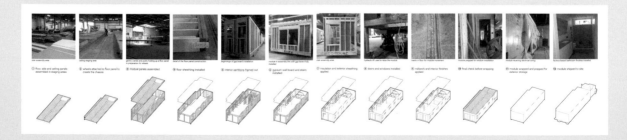

F.3   Production stages of modules for Simplex Homes.

F.4   The factory floor at Simplex Homes shows the modules under construction.

stagnates. While Simplex has worked with a number of other architects, and RES 4 with a dozen or more modular companies, both have repeatedly singled out the other as exemplary partners, with each side optimising their approach through this ongoing collaboration.

Typical of the wider trend in the United States' modular industry, Simplex Homes has begun targeting manufacturing for the multi-unit, mid-rise market including dormitories, hospitality, and multi-family housing. CEO Patrick Fricchione, Jr. states:

> Dormitories changed our business at Simplex. They showed our ability to work with architects and engineers on a large scale. They showed our ability to not just adapt to new construction techniques, but on occasion develop them. Finally, they showed our ability to handle very large scale, very expensive projects and to do excellent work under very tight time frames.[4]

Recent dormitory projects include Mansfield University of Pennsylvania, Marywood University and Pennsylvania State University. This new direction into manufacturing modules for multi-unit mid-rise construction is another diversified strategy requiring new skills from Simplex. From cost estimating and design/engineering to site logistics planning and hybrid construction integration, Simplex Homes' success demonstrates the necessity of innovation at the level of business organisation and diversification In order to maintain economic sustainability in difficult markets. Nevertheless, this jump in scale and complexity is challenging Simplex Homes to acquire new knowledge of the commercial construction sector and adds additional financial risk. Clearly, this is a risk that Simplex and many other companies are prepared to take as the broader market begins an inevitable adjustment from individual, detached housing towards denser urban housing. Manufacturing units for this market requires a high-quality repetitive module, and Simplex Homes is now exploring ways to increase its automation and production capabilities through the implementation of German and/or Swedish panellised construction equipment.

methods were being radically simplified. And, as noted above, operations had been reduced to focus on the Northern Californian market.

These changes exemplify a now-familiar path of companies that begin with radical aspirations, high design and concept-driven systems. As Blu Homes boldly state in their promotional materials: 'We looked at the history of home building and came to one clear conclusion – it was time for a radical change.'[11] Despite the well-meaning, well-reasoned arguments for change, eventually the realities of location, logistics, regulation and market reappear in a now-familiar form. That Blu Homes have spent around six years and millions in R&D but still have neither a substantial market presence nor the seamless, integrated platform that would transform housing production into an online experience, should give us pause to reconsider the lessons that General Panel offered in the mid-twentieth century. The recent changes to Blu Homes' system, along with its release of new ranges in the tiny house and auxiliary dwelling market, suggest a more end-user and market-driven focus that starts with the ends and not the means.

Unlike Blu Homes, many small to medium or start-up companies do not have the luxury of proceeding without continually increasing revenue in step with expenditure. But smaller companies are not always at a disadvantage to large, well-funded ventures – indeed they are often at a distinct advantage. Because these smaller, less well-funded players are constantly testing their product in the market, they are making the requisite mistakes and learning their lessons early. This is different to the approach taken by Blu Homes and also by General Panel. Reforming both companies would have meant moving to market with an imperfect and conceptually impure system, but this is precisely this trade-off between means and ends that is the *bête noire* of prefabrication.

As we can see, the means-and-ends confusion is as alive today as it was in the mid-twentieth century. What works in other sectors does not necessarily work in housing and many companies continue to start at the wrong end. Mesmerised by the elegance of the winning idea, grandiose plans for expansion, or the novel business plan, companies lose sight of the core markers of the value proposition and of why the business exists in the first place, and drift off the path to a sustainable and successful venture.

4   Innovation vs Invention

Many companies and individuals confuse invention with innovation. Innovation requires application and uptake, which is often evidenced by commercial success, whereas invention need only be novel. To make a difference, industrialised housing companies need to focus more on innovation and less on pure invention.

A parallel to the means-and-ends confusion is the distinction between innovation and invention. A focus on innovation over invention is particularly important in prefabricated housing because *uptake and application* in the market place, commercial success, and the product's capacity to resolve the myriad constraints that housing and building ventures need to satisfy, are the most important measures of lasting success.

A good contemporary example of this phenomenon is Wikihouse, a company founded in the UK around 2011. Wikihouse has become emblematic of the potential of digital and automated fabrication technology to transform building (see Digital and Automated Fabrication box, p.33). Wikihouse, as the name suggests, offers an open-source platform on which designers and end-users can interact. In essence, Wikihouse has developed simple-to-use software that can break down 3D forms into an automatic nesting schedule and cut-sheets for a CNC router, that ultimately cuts and spits out plywood parts. These parts are sequentially numbered and can be put together by relatively unskilled labour without the use of power tools or large-format construction equipment. Indeed, the only tool required is a simple plywood mallet (cut from the same sheet as the building parts), using pegs and wedges to make what co-founder Alistair Parvin jokingly called 'a really big Ikea kit'.[12] Significantly, this process is automated and is initiated (quite literally) with the push of a button. When the core Wikihouse

4.2   Assembly of CNC plywood carcass,
using the WikiHouse platform.

process is completed, the resulting building is an interlocking structural system – a carcass similar to an interlocking toy dinosaur – that takes the shape of a cabin, or indeed any form that the Wikihouse community have created in the platform's shared 'Library'.

The resulting structure, however, is not a *real* building. It is more akin to a life-size architectural model. Its core system contains none of the usual fixtures, cladding, fittings, or finishes. A prototype building, or indeed an actual building, is distinguished from an architectural model by the need to interact with the whole host of requirements that real buildings (such as houses) need to satisfy. This includes adherence to local/national building codes, which are likely to contain criteria pertaining to structural, fire safety, and acoustic and thermal performance. Added to these, are more prosaic issues such as waterproofing, durability, buildability, the interaction of the framing system with external and internal cladding and finishes, the fitting of windows and doors, and services integration (electricity, water, waste), site connections, and so on.

Wikihouse's publicity does not articulate the distinct discontinuity between the structural phase and the much more complex requirements of a finished building. Presumably, when the structural carcass is complete the usual power tools, trades (roofers, plumbers, electricians and carpenters), and building knowledge and expertise would need to enter the site, to make the structural carcass into a real house that people could legally occupy. In recent years, Wikihouse has taken steps to address these shortcomings and the website now includes a range of rubrics: fit out, building envelope, lighting, water, data, thermal, power, waste, air and site integration, which are likely to receive increasing input from the venture's community.

Wikihouse has developed a 'partial solution' that we might duly locate within the *conceptual prefab* category. It is also a fine example of focus on invention over innovation. Wikihouse's chief contribution has been to grow the awareness of the potential around distributed manufacturing of housing, achieved by the connection of digital and automated fabrication technologies, popularised in the first decade of the twenty-first century, with an open-source, interactive, online platform.[13] Wikihouse's efforts have achieved great success in these terms and their motivations are laudable. Yet some six years into the venture, Wikihouse has not made significant inroads into the housing problems that they so desperately wish to transform and democratise. Instead, they have developed a highly inventive platform and 'business model' that has captured the imagination of many in the industry.

It is the failure to adequately address *all* the issues that housing faces that makes Wikihouse's product conceptual prefab, and their core contribution rhetorical. Looking back over some of the well-known moments of conceptual prefab from the twentieth century, Fuller's *Dymaxion House*, Prouvé's *Maisons Metropole* and *Tropicale*, Suuronen's *Futuro*, and including the present-day Wikihouse, it is clear that such examples are rich in invention – new processes, technology, materials and visual appearance – but lack innovation.

A counter example to the inventive approach above is that of the now ubiquitous Plasterboard. Sheetrock or drywall, as it is variously known, was developed over 100 years ago to replace a labour-intensive and time-consuming manual process. Plasterboard is neither the highest quality nor most durable internal wall solution in the market, but it has become the industry standard internal wall lining around the world. This is a result of plasterboard's initial advances over traditional practices and materials, and subsequent incremental innovations. Plasterboard is not glamorous, or exciting. It is boring and infamous, but its uptake and application show us a different mode of problem solving to which we will return in Chapters 5 and 6. Plasterboard shows us that real innovation in construction need not look inventive.

5   Analogies with Other Industrial Sectors

Industrialised housing ventures often compare their activities to those of other industrial sectors. One of the most prolific and important comparisons is with the automotive industry. The auto industry holds important lessons for prefab housing but the analogy has also been problematic. A deeper understanding of the specificities of housing relative to other manufactured products is required to enable any successful translation from other industries to housing.

When some companies confuse the means and ends, or invention with innovation and drift off the path to sustainable and successful ventures, it is not necessarily because they are not paying attention or they are not capable of seeing the situation differently. There are many, very seductive diversions that can distract these companies and teams from achieving their goals.

In prefabricated housing, many such distractions have historically been provided by other industrial sectors, whose successes have served as thought-models for how the construction industry might be transformed. Astute managers, designers and strategists are taught to always be on the lookout for innovations in other sectors which, by analogy, might lead to a breakthrough in their own field. The monumental change that the telecommunications, computing, or personal electronics sectors have undergone in the last 50 years, is felt – and not unreasonably – to hold lessons for catapulting the building industry into the twenty-first century. What is the corollary of the iPhone in housing and construction? Or, as one of us was once asked in a meeting with a government agency: 'Who is the Steve Jobs of your industry?' The chief (and repeat) offender in this mode of thought has been the auto industry.

There are a number of problems in comparing prefab housing with car manufacturing. These include: sheer size, parts and compartmentalisation, site conditions, users, climate, codes and regulations, materials and construction, tolerances

4.3   A Toyota Camry being
manufactured in Toyota's Altona plant
in Melbourne.

(or factory vs site), customisation, cost relative to income, supply chain and industry set-up.[14]

The chief lesson in pointing these problems is that a better understanding of the *specificities* of housing relative to other industries – in particular the auto industry – has the potential to release industrialised house building from the trope of a perennial 'good idea' that ultimately leads to disappointing results.

Among scholars who have dealt with the house/car comparison, Herbert has done the most to explain how pervasive (and pernicious) this analogy has been. Herbert characterised the analogy in almost pathological terms as: 'The Henry Ford syndrome' and, in his analysis of the reasons for General Panel's failure discussed in Chapter 3, he notes the analogy to car manufacturing was key among these.

But the comparison between houses and cars did not end in the mid-twentieth century and it has shown itself to be both highly elastic and persistent. Beginning in the pre-World War II period, Herbert illustrated the reliance of home building companies on Fordist principles. Then, in the post-World War II period, new companies aligned their models to the rise of mass-production as advanced by General Motors. In the late-twentieth and early twenty-first centuries, Colin Davies and others point to the rise of the lean production system pioneered by Toyota. Today, new concepts like 'Industry 4.0' (see Fig. 6.8), have heralded the age of the 'smart' factory, the internet of things, big data and cloud computing, and have contributed to a model of future industrial organisation and production that again share origins in auto manufacturing.[15]

The car/house analogy is so enduring and elastic because it is powerful and we can learn much from it. It becomes a barrier to the uptake and success of industrialised housing when it is the cause of technological overreach and when it becomes doctrinaire in its application. The key lesson here is that industrialised house building ventures need to be careful in following a questionable version of progress, particularly a mode of industrial manufacturing that may already have been superseded.

Many prefabrication companies today look to Japan as the most sophisticated housing industry in the world and seek to emulate its technological advances (see Japan and Case Study Japan: Sekisui House boxes, pp.93 and 115) The Japanese industry is indeed sophisticated and a handful of Japanese companies have achieved something comparable to the auto industry in both scale and technique. Sekisui House, for example, has a factory in Japan that is almost entirely automated, where one can view a factory floor full of robots cutting, sorting, stacking and welding house components effortlessly and tirelessly (see Fig. I.2, p.94). These achievements are impressive, but they are also highly specific to Japan and its corporate traditions and structures and are not readily applicable to other countries, and particularly not entrant companies.[16]

Sweden provides a different view of how a successful industry can appear; one that does not *necessarily* rest on the widespread adoption of highly automated and digitally controlled processes (see Sweden box, p.120). This is to say, success should not be measured by the degree of technological 'advances' but by the results and the value achieved.

In Chapter 6 we return to this discussion with the concept of 'Industry Lite'. This idea suggests that one possible path in industrialised housing will involve a move away from the 'heavy' and expensive modes that are the norm in the auto industry, towards an approach that is lightweight, nimble, decentralised (much in the manner that Wikihouse has attempted). But as distinct from Wikihouse, a successful future vision is more likely to revolve around solutions and processes that can produce highly customised, flexible and cost effective solutions that respond to the full variety and specificities of housing.

Computational Design

Computational design tools are increasingly used in the construction industry. This includes parametric modelling, visualisation, automation, simulation, and optimisation, and is closely linked to both new digital and automated fabricated technologies and techniques and platforms in industrialised housing (see The Platform Approach and Digital and Automated Fabrication boxes, pp.48 and 33). While computational design can work synergistically with the methods for industrialising housing construction, these tools also create several challenges: they require familiarity with mathematical and programming concepts; and they demand a new way of working and a new organisational structure within the industry.

Computational design is most widely known through Computer Aided Drafting (CAD), a 2D and 3D drafting and visualisation tool, and Building Information Modelling (BIM), a method that enables data to be easily attached to and extracted from CAD models. Both CAD and BIM have advanced over the past two decades to become standard within the construction industry. Yet computational design is more than CAD or BIM; it delves deeply into the full potential of computational power, the expression of design intent, and its realisation.

The prefabrication of buildings requires careful consideration of the relationship between parts and wholes. In the 1920s, Rudolph Schindler's explorations of integrated spatial and component design described such a relationship as 'modular coordination of parts to wholes'. Computational design offers a powerful means of exploring these relationships through a digital process. CAD was introduced in 1963 by Ivan Sutherland with 'Sketchpad', which used a computational design user interface, via a monitor and light-pen, to create hierarchical and associated graphic elements. At the same time, Christopher Alexander was developing ideas about the assembly of parts within wholes in *Notes on the*

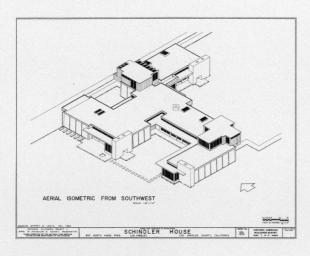

AERIAL ISOMETRIC FROM SOUTHWEST

SCHINDLER HOUSE

G.1 Kings Road House by Rudolph Schindler. Designed and built for Schindler and his wife in 1921 to be shared with another couple. The cost-effective design demonstrated a range of construction innovations for the time, such as its tilt-panel walls and modular design.

G.3 Kafka's Castle Apartment Building
by Ricardo Bofill, built near Barcelona,
Spain. An example of an analogue version
of computational design based on a 'spiral
plug-in' concept, which sees apartments
clustered around vertical circulation.

Synthesis of Form, which directly influenced software engineers and became the basis for a branch of object-oriented programming.[1]

Computational design methods may be analogue or digital. The residential project Kafka's Castle by Ricardo Bofill in 1968 is an example of the former. It utilised spatial transformations to locate modular units along spiral geometry, each module rising by 0.7m in floor level. The representation of Kafka's Castle through physical models determined assembly details on site, presaging current discussion around dispensing with traditional 2D documentation for construction and assembly purposes.

The development of CAD and its digital approach was seen by some as hampering the ambivalent nature of the creative design process. Stiny and Gips' invention of shape grammars in the 1970s demonstrated an alternative computational design tool that recognised the ambiguity of structural systems and the need to preserve the possibility of re-reading shapes.[2] This acknowledged the role perception plays in understanding shapes within shapes, a procedure that CAD is incapable of performing. With 'Instant House', Larry Sass demonstrated the possibilities of this methodology by linking shape grammars to fabrication processes.[3]

It was also thought that CAD might be a hindrance to client and end-user participation in the design and assembly of homes. This inspired Robert Aish in the 1970s and John Frazer in the 1980s to seek alternative methods. From 1985–86, and inspired by Walter Segal's modular coordinated self-built homes, John Frazer developed 'Cal Build', which incorporated intelligent building blocks intended to involve self-builders more centrally in design by providing realism of representation.[4]

Nevertheless, CAD continued development as a 2D drafting and 3D visualisation tool throughout the 1990s, with a focus on form-finding and realistic rendering techniques. This underutilisation of the power of the computer was referred to as 'computerised design' by Kostas Terzidis, as distinct from computational design.[5] Patrik Schumacher of Zaha Hadid Architects disputed this distinction and claimed the high ground of computational design theory with his notion of 'Parametricism', the style and process for which his architectural practice is known.

Computational design methods that employed computational power took inspiration from evolutionary discourse and, in particular, the algorithm's ability to search effortlessly while trading off criteria to generate optimal solutions.[6] In the context of architecture it is known as multi-criteria optimisation, a synthetic search for the best state within a model, which can be achieved by several means, including: genetic algorithms; differential evolution; and genetic programming. These algorithms were inspired by Darwinian evolution, mimicking survival of the fittest amongst a population of individuals. Optimisation is complemented by parametric modelling and together they offer flexibility in the realisation of design intent.

Modular pre-assembly in construction plays to the strengths of computational design methods as both activities consider share-ability, re-usability of parts and modules, and aspire to detect clashes and bugs in their systems.[7] However, recent attempts to improve the accessibility of computational design tools through the development of visual programming languages (VPL) – for example, Grasshopper – have made it clear that such tools lack the ability to scale up to complex design and architectural problems.[8] More sophisticated CAD tools, as used in advanced manufacturing industries, might help ease some of these problems, and there is currently great interest in the industrialised housing sector to explore their use.

The implementation of sophisticated design tools might even herald a return to an era of 'craftsmanship', as noted by Mario Carpo.[9] The potential of such tools is exemplified by a recent pioneering use of advanced CAD systems for the modular design and fabrication of a four-storey, two-family residence in Red Hook, Brooklyn, by SHoP Architects. This was the first project to use the advanced CAD capabilities of Dassault's 3DEXPERIENCE. It's also an approach that has no need for drawings, an echo of Bofill's intent with Kafka's Castle in the 1960s, and was described recently as an 'open-ended' approach to design. This cloud-based project enabled the creation, collaboration, management and the sharing of data for computer numerically controlled (CNC) machining. A further recent example completed by Tyréns AB in Sweden used computational design tools for the industrialised design and production of a multi-storey timber building system. The prefabrication strategy aligned with the parametric capabilities of the software used, and is described as 'knowledge-based engineering' (KBE) supported by automation capabilities.[10]

Computational design tools have the potential to improve industrialised housing; however, their implementation still needs to address designers' expectations more fully. For example, the methods and tools should allow designers latitude to transition with ease between ambiguous and explicit expression, to more closely reflect the way designers design. Furthermore, these design tools need to be more intelligible, flexible and adaptable to cope with change amid the dynamics of the design process, and to facilitate engagement with fabricators and constructors. Nevertheless, the past 55 years of development of computational design tools and their application to prefabricated home production confirm that a synergy exists between these methods of design, fabrication and assembly, one that can embrace the complexity of industrialised housing and design problems more generally.

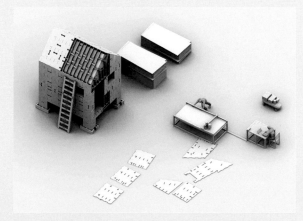

G.4 A shape grammar for timber-framed construction, developed by Larry Sass with The Center for Bits and Atoms at MIT.

6   Technology and Progress

Technology has been likened to an unstoppable force moving forward through time and inseparable from ideas of 'progress'. Such views of technology and progress are problematic, particularly in the industrialised housing field. If progress is a wave – so the thinking goes – companies must be in front of it to be right and good. This notion leads many companies to focus on 'advanced' technological solutions and less on their suitability for achieving their stated aims.

This romance of technological progress in construction having a single end or direction results in a great deal of the over-determination implied by the term prefabrication and its shriller advocates. Prefab, it is held, is more *advanced* than conventional construction. The simplistic view of technology and progress as a kind of unstoppable wave is implicit in the terms 'laggard' or 'stone-age', which are frequently heard in the description of conventional construction. This book has corroborated aspects of this view, but we also attempt to draw a finer distinction between criticisms of practices and techniques within the construction industry, on the one hand, and the technologist's call to arms on the other. Where the technologist's attention shifts unconsciously to the sparkle of the new and to loud invention over quiet innovation, we suggest that the reader be wary of such an attitude.

Again, Japan offers many lessons to help overcome this barrier. For many, admiration for Japanese industry can be traced back to its technological sophistication, and some companies aspire to emulate the level of automation evident in Japanese companies such as Sekisui House. These companies would do well to remember that the Japanese prefab industry has been operating for over 50 years and Sekisui House's company motto is 'Slow and Smart'. Sekisui House's sophisticated digital backend systems and robotic factory plants were prefigured by a highly rational paper system with extremely efficient use of human labour. As Ryan E. Smith insightfully points out with regard to the Toyota production system, the principle of automation (*jidōka*) 'is to use [it] only when the

human task has been perfected and deemed to have no handcraft value'.[17]

Many companies are held in the grip of the belief that to truly innovate they need to adopt the latest technology. They are caught in the hyperbole so common in today's culture of futurist TED Talks. A different, more appropriate, example of the successful uptake of new technology is that of SHoP Architects in New York, who designed the B2 building in Brooklyn, the tallest volumetric modular building in the world at the time of writing. SHoP have successfully made the transition to owning the design and manufacture of parts of their commissions (rather than solely providing a professional service). By taking a stake in some building projects, SHoP has the opportunity to leverage the quality of design.[18] This is a logical path that has been made possible by the emergence of, and the company's investment in, computational design and file-to-factory technology and techniques (see Computational Design and Digital and Automated Fabrication boxes, pp.75 and 33). This is forward thinking – and good business – but it requires a pragmatic view of the utility of new technologies and early investment in new types of professionals with new competencies.

It is misleading to attach moral judgments to ideas of historical and technological progress, to label a venture 'progressive' or 'retrograde' because of its level of technological sophistication. But these views abound. Some in industry scoff at housing companies that use power tools instead of automated CNC devices. It is neither 'good' nor 'bad' to have robots in a factory – rather, the question should be, is it appropriate and effective?

7   Standardisation vs Customisation

Unlike other product manufacturing sectors, and because of myriad differences between every project and its site, industrialised housing is an exercise in diversity not similarity. The ability to provide highly customised products has become one of the new promises of industrialised housing ventures, associated with the concept of 'Mass Customisation'. But to date, the degree of customisation achieved remains

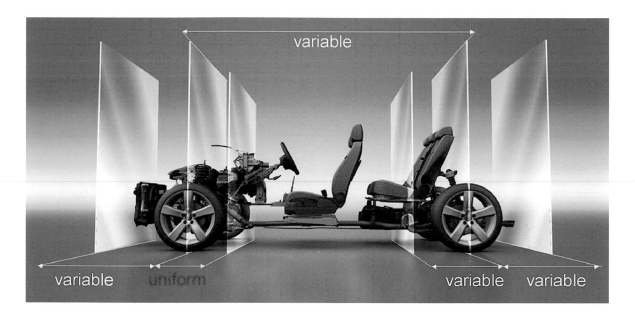

4.4   The automotive platform approach, such as Volkswagen's MB platform, allows a range of variations while keeping commonality of parts through modularisation and scalability.

very low and is more akin to the levels of superficial and highly standardised choices offered by the auto industry.

In buying a new car we have come to expect the usual types of questions: colour, engine size, transmission, stereo, climate control and wheels. The auto industry has established a successful model of combining these common 'customisations' without needing huge inventory and with short lead times. But rarely do customers ask for a new Toyota Prius with a seat on the roof (to look at the stars?), with more insulation (cold climate), or to be extra narrow (to fit into a tight garage). Once the Prius is bought, there appears to be no way to add an extra seat (for a new family member), or to change it into a commercial van (with sliding doors for easy deliveries). Such changes would seem outlandish. Yet it is precisely these changes that many think are natural choices in houses.

Many think the level of customisation achieved by auto manufacturers is industry leading but we hope to show that it is not sufficient to think about the required flexibility in housing in the same terms (see The Platform Approach box, p.48). For example, globally there are only two real differences between cars: the location of the steering wheel and the tail light colour. Even with these differences, almost any car can be driven all over the world. Most houses, in contrast, cannot be moved across a street without breaking some regulation, or making the function or design of the house unworkable (front/back, left/right, north/south). There is also the initial predicament faced by Blu Homes as they attempted to operate simultaneously in the climates and markets of San Francisco and New York, which clearly demonstrates the problems of placating both sets of conditions with one product.

It is for these reasons that conceptualising ventures in industrialised housing is an exercise in

4.5   Sekisui House's construction system changes to suit market demands. By offering timber and steel systems Sekisui House are able to respond to customer demands. This demonstrates there is no 'best practice' or 'optimal' solution within the company.

diversity, not similarity. This is another reason for being wary of the *product-driven* approach of the auto-industry or consumer electronics, and why we insist on a *process-driven* approach.

The lack of capacity to achieve real variety and diversity is one reason why many modular housing companies have remained regional players whose capacity is limited to producing highly standardised products tailored to local conditions. As Blu Homes and many other leading companies have demonstrated, achieving a 'live' and fuller range of customisations is not easy in housing, precisely because of the myriad variables that come to bear on each project. The available 'customisations' are often reduced to the choice between base ranges, and with selected curtains, tiling or stone benchtops. Customer choice that exceeds the limited range is often pushed into a more expensive price bracket for 'bespoke' or 'custom-built' solutions.

Indeed, much of what passes for mass customisation in housing and auto manufacturing is more like 'flexible-standardisation'.[19] We suggest that if industrialised housing ventures are to develop beyond being a series of regional players and to reach the mass markets to which they often aspire, the problem of conceptualising for diversity rather than similarity needs to be learned and accommodated.

8   Loose Fit and Best Practice

Unlike other product manufacturers, there is no widely agreed 'best practice' in industrialised housing. Each company has a relationship to its chosen system that is at best 'loose fit'. The method for choosing technical systems and construction methods is neither highly rational nor derived from large amounts of quantifiable data. This makes each solution difficult to transfer between places and companies. Rather, each company has a unique fusion of working solutions derived from the myriad constraints that bind each industrialised housing venture.

In reviewing the vast number of companies – both past and present – operating in the industrialised house building area, we have noted that there appears to be no dominant mode of construction, process, systems, or material. Quite the opposite: there is a vast range of approaches. Why should this be considered a problem or barrier to the uptake or success of industrialised housing? As we have seen in the history of previous attempts to prefabricate housing, many companies have approached the problem as though there were one, optimal solution. To the individuals and groups tasked with determining this 'solution', it should come as something of a liberation to find that even the most successful companies in the world do not agree which is the best system or model. The reasons for this absence of a 'best practice' are manifold.

Returning again to auto manufacturing, we note that almost all contemporary cars are put together from very similar materials. While there are most certainly differences in car construction, to the casual observer these show only minor variation. Not so for houses. Three houses that look identical might be made of timber, steel, or masonry, yet finished with the same cladding, or painted so as to appear the same colour and/or style. This holds not only for detached suburban housing but also high-rise and multi-residential buildings, which may be made of timber, reinforced concrete, or structural streel, yet appear identical to onlookers.

The chosen material and construction methodology in conventional house building is usually related to the skill set of the builder, customer preference, culture, ease of supply and cost (or potentially all of the above). This is clearly not a best practice approach, or a highly refined evaluation based on data and detailed analysis, rather one that is more related to rule-of-thumb, tradition, historical inertia or path dependency.

There is a 'loose fit' between the construction and technical systems and the houses offered by the various industrialised house building companies

we have previewed so far. One company chooses to build with steel, another with timber. Many companies build using two or three different systems. This tells us there that each company sorts through the various trade-offs inherent in every system, matching them against their own strengths and weaknesses, and customer demand, ensuring coherent relationships between *all* the parts of the system.

At the end of Chapter 3, we briefly outlined the concept of a company's 'settings', or DNA, which determines how the company can operate, what strengths it has and where it is likely to develop. The importance of this DNA and its settings cannot be overstated. Everything about the final product hinges on them, and logically, the final product is unknowable until they have been resolved. But these settings are not universal, nor are they immediately transferable. This is why no 'best practice' exists in modular housing as it exists in car manufacture – the constellation of settings for housing is so different every time, precluding a definitive answer or optimal solution across the board.

9   Partial Solutions

Innovation in industrialised housing favours comprehensive or end-to-end solutions. Partial solutions emerge when new approaches, technology and ideas are not integrated (or able to be integrated) into the larger whole. In some fields, this problem-solving methodology is appropriate; in housing it can lead to the collapse of the whole venture.

A partial solution does not incorporate a comprehensive view across the whole of business, identifying strengths and weaknesses and how to build on these; rather, it focuses effort on one or two problems in the belief these will pay off. The Packaged House, for example, was based on a highly sophisticated panelised construction system (see Fig. 3.11) that had undergone several major overhauls by

Wachsmann before finally being released to the market. As Herbert's analysis has shown, the company's ultimate failure can be traced to the poor integration of this ingenious system with the whole spectrum of systems spelled out by Kelly, Bernhardt and later Herbert himself. Similarly, Wikihouse's elegant automated cut-sheet algorithm (see Fig. B.2, p.34) is a partial solution because it fails to deliver the whole, settling too soon on solving only part of the problem (the building carcass).

A partial solution does not integrate, which is where true value can be created in industrialised house building. Other industrial sectors can more readily develop what we have termed partial solutions. Industries such as consumer electronics or auto manufacturing use such solutions as a viable means for delivering innovation because their products may: 1) make their own markets (e.g. a new toy or game), or 2) not need to be integrated into a tightly woven regulatory framework that has taken centuries to develop.

A partial solution is much easier to recognise in the past than it is in the present or future. Determining what is a partial solution and what is a comprehensive solution requires trial and error, iteration and troubleshooting. This is a question of analysis and choosing the appropriate means of problem solving, which we discuss in depth in Chapter 5. Nevertheless, we can ascertain that an approach that relies on the proverbial 'silver bullet' is likely to bring with it a high degree of risk for its inability to be part of a wider constellation of solutions.

10   Change Management and the Construction Industry

The traditions and structures of the construction industry have been a barrier to change. Buildings are part of social, economic and cultural life, and cannot be separated from the responsibilities, risks and environments with which they are intrinsically linked. The organisation and structure of the traditional industry are particularly stifling obstacles to change. New business models and modes of organisation in industrialised house building have the potential to remove such obstacles.

It is something of a commonplace to say that the construction industry is deeply resistant to change, or that it fails to embrace the spirit of innovation that is the daily bread of other industrial sectors. Yet, this does not do justice to the appetite for change or the mood of the industry. As we explained in Chapter 1 and in our discussion of 'Imminent Revolution' above, it is paradoxical that so many players in construction firmly believe that practices of the future will be very different to practices of today, yet so few can agree what this future will look like. Some think that all houses will be 3D printed in 10 to 20 years, others think new materials will fundamentally change construction.

A large part of the resistance to change in construction can be traced to financial and safety risks. Buildings are tremendously expensive, take a long time to build, and their construction requires complex coordination to ensure the work is done on time, in the right order, and safely. Delays in construction can quickly lead to very expensive penalties, or additional costs incurred by problems with scheduling. Construction companies are also required to provide a guarantee of the quality of their work and a warranty on the finished product. This is much easier to do if there is a clear track record and empirical evidence for how a particular construction method or material has performed, not just during the construction phase but in the years and decades to follow.

Some examples of these risks are illustrative. A common problem in adopting prefabricated systems or new materials are concerns around durability and performance. Volumetric prefabrication, for example, can often experience issues with watertightness. When modules are stacked together on site traditional approaches to layering and tolerances may not work. In a context where a contractor may need to come back to site months or years after completion to fix problems that have occurred during the placing and mating of modules, the compensatory rewards for trialling new systems and methods must be substantial. Such risks can only really be reduced

SIMPLIFIED DIAGRAM OF THE CONSTRUCTION INDUSTRY

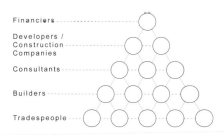

Financiers

Developers /
Construction
Companies

Consultants

Builders

Tradespeople

4.6   The structure of the construction industry, a barrier to change in itself.

by building large prototypes or by rolling out incremental change over a long period of time.

Safety risks are equally important and often compounded. This includes both public safety (what happens if the building fails) and workplace safety. Failure in both areas also leads to financial risk, which is difficult – from an actuarial point of view – to define because, by definition, new practices are new. Together, these risks provide added costs to new building methods and act as a counterweight to the argument for change. This is often referred to as the business-as-usual approach of the construction industry, but it is perhaps more accurate to think about it as historical inertia.

The culture and traditions of the construction industry are also an important part of this story. The system of apprenticeships, the nature of the labour that is located on a building site, and the way that the human group is at the centre of most construction projects are important foundations of construction culture. Most commentators allude to the problems arising from historical ventures that have required the negotiation of unionised labour and industrialised housing ventures. Today, this relationship appears more urgent as technologists and futurists in the industry are convinced that most manual labour will be automated, and where moving labour off-site (even in its current form) has become synonymous with such problems.[20]

Another significant barrier to change in the construction industry comes in the form of its conventional project management systems. Because each building and each site is different, construction companies manage them episodically on a *project-to-project* basis. As the project develops, a team will be formed to execute the building construction. This team will grow and disband as each part of the team is needed or becomes redundant (see Integrated Building Performance box, p.84). Prefabrication requires a *process-based* approach that goes beyond the life of any one building or project. This process must be implemented before any building begins construction. Such a process can take many months or sometimes years to fully develop, during which time buildings are not being built and money is not flowing. The project-to-project approach is problematic because it does not provide the kind of continuity of experience and knowledge needed for the process-intensive approach, which relies on integration with the entire team and on receiving feedback from each built project (see The Platform Approach box, p.48). Such a change to the fundamental operating structure in building construction is expensive and time-consuming and, above all, requires a strong commitment by management to change.

A final barrier to change in the construction industry is provided by the very structure of the industry itself. In most Western countries, the construction industry is based on a subcontracting model, a diagram of which is shown in Fig. 4.6. Each layer in the industry adds a margin, and each layer is required to encapsulate the risk it takes. This results in a kind of 'risk firewall' running between each stratum. At the bottom of this structure are the individual tradespeople and contractors who carry out the work on site. At the top are the financiers and developers. Apart from the obvious inefficiencies in the cost structure (whereby any unit added at the bottom must be subjected to several margins before even reaching market), this diagram also demonstrates the lack of incentive for change in the sector. In conventional projects, all players take a margin proportional to the total cost and their relative position. If the total cost is reduced, so too is the final profit.[21]

Integrated Building Performance

A more industrialised approach to construction has the potential to improve built outcomes, to unlock new ways to conceive the design and manufacture of buildings, and to enable new ways for professionals to contribute expertise. Conventional construction approaches are fragmented and stratified, revealing fundamental paradoxes that lead to suboptimal solutions. An integrated approach to building performance has the potential to unify and consolidate problem solving, allowing new and better solutions to emerge, in a more flexible and timely way within the planning and design phases.

Traditionally, a building project starts with the architect understanding the site, user requirements and budget, and then delivering a conceptual design. This is then developed by architects and structural engineers to establish viability and a basic structural solution. Other specialists enter the process sequentially, introducing their particular requirements (acoustics, services, thermal, fire safety, for example). These interactions lead to multiple iterations that may redefine the design at all levels. However, the later in the sequence a professional discipline enters the iteration, the smaller its overall impact on the design (see Fig. Q.2 in the Life Cycle Analysis box, p.144). Exceptions include fire safety, where the responsibility of protecting occupants and emergency responders requires an approvals process that can dramatically affect the design at every stage. As a result, architects will often embed basic considerations from the outset of the design process to avoid major changes downstream and minimise risk in the approvals phase. Eventually, the design is completed and implementation follows. Each building is a bespoke solution that responds to the unique combination of site, stakeholders and functionality; understanding its specific performance offers few lessons for future designs.

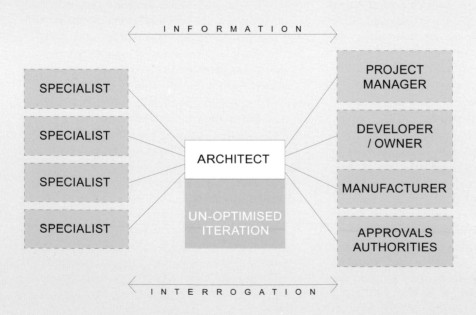

H.1   Traditional construction information flows, resulting in a lack of integration.

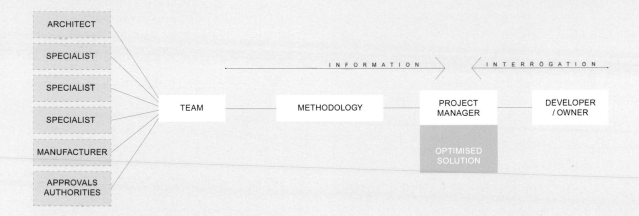

**H.2 Greater project team integration
in the early conceptual and design stages
leads to greater optimisation of the final
product.**

This traditional process is characterised by the dominance of a design leader (usually the architect), a bespoke outcome, and the design atomisation of performance metrics. The architect sees the big picture and has some level of knowledge of all the different components, and therefore puts all the parts together. Each component of the building falls under the remit of a specialist consultant, although standardised metrics (for example, 'U-values', fire ratings, maximum allowable deflections) often enable the architect to choose pre-assessed solutions. In other cases, the specialist will provide an answer to a need expressed by an architect. Once all specialties are incorporated a solution emerges. This solution has the following characteristics:

a. It is limited by the understanding of the architect, as they ask the questions and set the parameters of the possible solutions;

b. The outcome is a compilation of independently derived solutions that can only deliver performance trade-offs in a very limited manner;

c. System performance is never established. Specialties will define component performance, but as each solution is unique the integrated performance is not perceived to have value.

Ove Arup was the first to recognise the potential of integrated performance, which he describes as 'Total Architecture', in a 1970 speech:

The term 'Total Architecture' implies that all relevant design decisions have been considered together and have been integrated into a whole by a well organised team empowered to fix priorities. This is an ideal which can never – or only very rarely – be fully realised in practice, but which is well worth striving for, for artistic wholeness or excellence depends on it, and for our own sake we need the stimulation produced by excellence.[1]

This statement embodies a number of key points for integrated building performance. First, Arup emphasises the pre-eminent role of the architect as the orchestrator. Second, by recognising that this architect is actually 'a well-organised team' he suggests that, due to the multi-disciplinary nature of the process, a single professional cannot be the holder of all necessary knowledge. Third, the main objective of this team is the 'empowerment to fix priorities'. Finally, while excellence 'depends' on achieving 'Total Architecture', Arup concedes that it is an ideal that can never 'be fully realised in

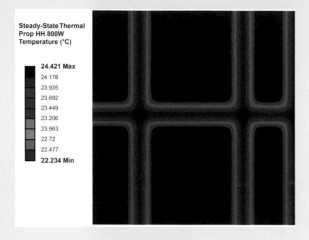

Steady-State Thermal
Prop HH 800W
Temperature (°C)

24.421 Max
24.178
23.935
23.692
23.449
23.206
23.963
22.72
22.477
22.234 Min

H.3   Thermal measurement and analysis
of the built form, commonly understood
from the specialist's perspective, who
sets quantitative parameters that the
designer must respond to.

practice'. The consolation prize is to strive for this
ideal.

The two-way relationship between architect and
specialists predicted by Arup has rarely materialised,
despite many variants being proposed. A hint of this
ideal is perhaps found in the symbiosis between
structural engineers and architects in projects like
bridges or towers, where close collaboration is
mandatory. But we have yet to see a truly optimised
construction process.

A fine example of this phenomenon is found in
the push to reduce energy consumption. This has
led to the widespread use of low-density plastic
insulation, which has resulted in the need for encap-
sulation by means of non-combustible materials,
thereby reducing ease of construction and robust-
ness and increasing the level of labour skill required.
Similarly, new building aesthetics have created
facade systems that pose fundamental problems
in compatibility between structure and building
envelope, resulting in multiple large-scale fires.
Sustainability encourages the use of materials, such
as timber, in a manner that introduces complex challenges when dealing with acoustic requirements.

Furthermore, the numerous drivers, the accelerated
entry rate of technologies, and the increasing complexity of construction logistics are hampering the
ability of the traditional architect to take the role of
the 'well-organised team' described by Arup.

Bespoke building design also provides no incentive to assess building performance holistically – the
time and resources invested cannot be recovered
because the combination of variables is unlikely to
be repeated. Prefabrication changes this paradigm.
Repetition and predictability are key characteristics of prefabrication – the more a solution can
demonstrate and deliver excellence in a holistic
manner, the more value it acquires. While value
will always be a complex property, the incentive for
holistic assessment clearly grows as construction
moves from the site to the factory. At the crux of the
problem is the capacity to deliver the performance
of the ensemble as a well-characterised extrapola-
tion of component performance. A methodology
that enables building professionals to predict
overall performance of a building as a function of
the performance of its components will assist those
involved to realise Arup's 'Total Architecture', where
the designer is now aided by a method that 'fixes priorities' to achieve an optimised solution.

This methodology is very different to traditional
approaches and cannot be framed around compliance, pre-defined solutions, or specialised answers
to specific questions. It needs to be framed as a
function of goals. Some of these goals will be subjective and others will be quantitative. Nevertheless,
they all need to be defined from first principles.
A subjective goal might be aesthetics, while a
quantitative goal could be minimisation of energy
consumption. Goals such as aesthetics are likely to
fall within the traditional role of the architect, but
the architect alone will not be driving the design at
this stage. Rather they will provide the basic principles by which desirable aesthetic outcomes can be
achieved. Similarly, thermal performance might fall
within the role of the specialist, but the specialist
sets the quantitative parameters that define thermal
performance. The compilation of these parameters
will result in a matrix for different performance
criteria. The multi-disciplinary team works at the

nexus of these explicit parameters to establish an integrated optimisation methodology, which can be applied to specific projects guaranteeing an optimal combination of components and delivering quality in a holistic manner.

An integrated building performance approach has an added advantage in that it matches delivery times for engineers, architects, project managers, developers or clients. In a traditional design, the time scales of the stakeholders are very different. Engineers require long periods of time to innovate, particularly if novel solutions require regulatory approval. In contrast, architects can iterate solutions more rapidly and waiting for engineers to solve problems may simply result in a loss of time. The inevitable outcome is that architects will iterate within the bounds of existing solutions, leaving engineers only limited scope for innovation. As a result, engineering innovation tends to happen at the component level, outside the cycle of design and construction, and as an optimisation process independent of other variables particular to a project. Similarly, timescales for developers or clients are governed by financial constraints. These impose complex schedules on project managers who have to balance the long time frames associated with procurement and approvals with the design process, which defines when these processes can start. For example, the thickness of the outer lamella of a cross-laminated timber product is defined by the need to protect the glue that bonds the different lamellas from fire. The nature of the fire depends on the design choices. Thus, design choices will determine the thickness of the outer lamella, and this information is necessary to ascertain cost and other information that must be defined before procurement starts. A common outcome is for design time to be minimised, with the quality of design inevitably suffering under such time pressures.

Prefabrication allows all these processes and time frames to be embedded into a methodology. As a result, quality and optimisation are achieved outside the typical construction cycle. That is, prefabrication is typically 'front-loaded', with detailed planning and optimisation happening before any building, or indeed any approvals or procurement process, has begun. The subsequent application of the methodology is delivered in a manner that guarantees all timescales are compatible within the construction cycle. This is the last optimisation variable and potentially the one that will result in the greatest gain.

It may be through prefabrication that 'Total Architecture' can be achieved.

H.4   Fire testing conducted on Cross Laminated Timber. Building performance during fire is vital for the protection of occupants and emergency response teams and can have a significant impact on design decisions. Early identification of such parameters can have enormous benefits downstream.

Any change to the status quo of this industry structure can appear as an increased risk of lower profits. To reverse this situation and transform it from a vicious to a virtuous cycle, in Chapter 6 we propose that industrialised housing needs to incorporate a process of vertical integration.

11 Reputation

Prefab housing has been plagued by a poor reputation for quality and design because, historically, it was widely associated with utilitarian prefab. This situation has changed dramatically in recent decades.

The market reputation of prefab is inescapably linked to the public's experience of schools, hospitals, temporary site sheds, military camps and facilities, mining accommodation, prisons, or refugee and emergency housing (see Fig. 3.2). These buildings often come with a range of unfavourable terms used to describe them: dongas, site sheds, demountables and double-wides. In the UK, the post-war 'prefab' housing estates have ultimately been mired in the low-quality, poor-design reputation. In Sweden, the legacy of the Million Homes program has also led to industrialised housing companies making a distinct break with its large-scale and often repetitive formal and material choices. A similar experience can be seen in European Eastern Bloc countries and their post-war mass-housing schemes that used precast concrete building systems. Together, such a reputation has tended to damage, rather than enhance, the image of prefabrication and system building.

Much of this poor reputation can be traced to utilitarian prefab delivering the bare minimum in response to core criteria. It remains a legacy issue but this reputation – as evidenced within popular-literature accounts in Chapter 2 –is being spun towards quality, customisation, design credentials and futuristic appeal. As more and more companies are able to demonstrate greater uptake and acceptance, we expect this trend to continue to gain greater public prominence.

12 Regulation and Planning, Site and Location

Traditional construction is developed project-to-project, site-to-site. This provides inbuilt flexibility to accommodate changing circumstances. All industrialised housing ventures must determine their 'settings' which constrain how much can be known in advance about a project and what can be adapted. By its very nature, this setting will provide a barrier to entering new markets, planning jurisdictions and sites.

Building and planning regulations are also frequently listed as a barrier to the uptake of prefab. This has prompted some countries to implement building codes and norms specifically designed to encompass prefab. In the USA and Europe, houses that are built off-site must typically comply with site-built regulations. The USA has a dispensation for the mobile, or manufactured, home industry, which is not required to comply with as many regulations (see USA box, p.39). Europe has used building regulations to drive quality improvements and harmonise standards across the Union to reduce trade barriers. Not specifically targeting prefab buildings, this approach has incentivised off-site production as it is able to meet these standards more effectively.[22] Australian industry groups recently launched a draft Modular Construction Code, which seeks to separate approvals for off-site construction from traditional approaches.

Housing, construction and planning codes are notoriously idiosyncratic and can change radically, not only from state to state but from street to street. Different sites often have different planning overlays, which might include fire, flooding, character and heritage criteria, and many greenfield housing estates have very specific design covenants that govern material choices and in what configuration they may be used. Similarly, certain trades have asserted regulatory influence such that particular tasks in electrical, plumbing or roofing, for example, are subject to highly specific local laws, often requiring on-site certification and approval, thereby ruling out full factory finishing.

Together, these factors have an enormous impact on prefab housing companies, principally because the front-loaded design and engineering systems need to incorporate any *possible* local variations, as retroactively modifying a standardised product made in the factory can be very costly. This means that companies need to be more restrictive in terms of their chosen markets and locations upfront, or they need to devise processes or solutions that enable them to adapt to unforeseen circumstances.

The final consideration here pertains to the wide variety of sites with which all housing must interact. This variety includes differences in: orientation; pre-existing physical features such as neighbouring buildings; connections to utilities and infrastructure (water, storm water, sewerage lines, electricity, gas, data/phone); vegetation; landform; or historical, cultural and social features. Geotechnical conditions alone cause some of the largest surprises on building endeavours – where one site requires little or no ground preparation, a neighbouring site may require extensive underpinning, incurring enormous cost differences through design, material and construction changes. Conventional housing construction, where buildings are developed on a project-to-project basis, can modify their practices from place to place to accommodate many such eventualities. Prefab, for the reasons outlined above, has a predetermined set of responses.

13   Finance

Many construction projects, large and small, rely on complicated financing and loan structures that are ultimately configured around accepted norms for building delivery. Industrialised building challenges these norms because of the location and timing of building activities which has proved a barrier to uptake.

Many companies and end users have reported problems in securing financing for prefabricated housing projects. While we expect these problems to diminish as prefab and industrialised house building become more widely adopted, finance remains a sticking point for some ventures. Typically, these problems stem from uncertainty among lenders who, much like the construction companies, are wary of change, and may not be familiar with new processes. This leads to a higher risk assessment and, therefore, more expensive or restrictive lending.

Paradoxically, another financial barrier arises from one of the key benefits of prefabrication: an accelerated construction program. If a conventional apartment building takes 18 months to complete and a prefabricated building takes 12 months or less, holding costs will be down for the developer, which counts as an intended benefit for the end user and as a key argument for using prefab. But the corollary of this 'benefit' is that lenders will receive proportionally less money. This provides yet another reason for conventional building's first-comer advantage, and why inefficient practice may not be a disadvantage to all parts of the industry.

The final problem in finance and prefab arises from the traditional flow of money during and immediately after construction. Typically, banks and lenders will release progress payments on agreed milestones and when certain phases of construction are complete. This process limits the risks involved with lending, ensuring that if the construction companies or developers go bust during construction, the bank will be able to take possession of the partially completed building and site and still have funds to complete the project for sale. With prefabrication, large building components (indeed whole sections of building) are made and stored off-site and delivered to site for final assembly. This is problematic both for companies and lenders, particularly in the eventuality of default, catastrophe, or any other unforeseen event, because a bank may have provided 80 per cent of total project funding but have little more than foundations on site to show for this.

14   Cost

Cost benefits are held to be one of the core promises of prefab, but in many cases prefab housing solutions are not the cheapest solution in the marketplace. There are several factors that make a more industrialised approach to house building costly, but there are also problems in the way that cost is compared with the wider industry that suppress the advantages of prefab.

Cost can be counted as one of the greatest misunderstandings surrounding prefab, because it is often not the cheapest form of building in the marketplace (see Affordability and Industrialised House Building box, p.127). Contributing to this misunderstanding is the fact that cost and price-point in housing construction are much more complex than first meets the eye. Many customers are groomed by the industry to ask for area-price rates, such as square metre or square foot prices, as a benchmark for value. But this method is problematic (and even cynical) not only for its numerous and curious 'exclusions', but because it applies an average price across a whole building. Highly serviced parts of buildings (kitchens and bathrooms, for example) and more simple enclosures (dining rooms or bedrooms) are lumped together. This model rewards bloated designs with low-value rooms that may incur high operational cost, while punishing quality and efficient designs. While the problems inherent in square metre comparison may be said to apply across the whole industry, its downsides are particularly disadvantageous for prefab, which tends to focus on quality both of the building fabric and of design.

This brings us to the wider problems of cost and price-point. As anyone who has ever tried to buy or build a house knows, housing purchases are fraught with exclusions (fixtures, fittings, even planning permission!), taxes and fees. Build cost is separate to land cost but one may provide subventions to the other. Depending on the quality of design, construction and the materials, operational costs can vary wildly, leaving some end users with a virtual time-bomb of utility expenses. Similarly, the time and convenience benefits offered by industrialised housing methods are difficult to quantify, particularly in markets where end users are not involved in the development and construction processes but are conventional buyers with a turn-key arrangement.

For these reasons, and in combination with the argument for a higher quality product, we suggest that prefab companies – and indeed their customers

– use a whole-of-business approach to quantifying the benefits of their products and take time to educate their target markets to be more critical and demand better products.

15 Open vs Closed Systems and 'IP'

In line with other industrial sectors, such as the auto industry or personal electronics, many prefab housing companies have seen the development of a series of protectable innovations as the key to developing a successful venture. However, developing highly idiosyncratic and 'closed' technological solutions is not a necessity but a choice, and one that has advantages and disadvantages.

Many prefab companies have placed a high value on the 'means', seeing the objective of their efforts as the development of a unique or patentable system. This, as we have discussed above in terms of innovation (Section 4) and technology (Section 6), is problematic. It is important for companies – who are in the process of designing and engineering the various systems needed to produce housing – that they are aware that whether to adopt an open or closed system is a choice, which will have implications for Intellectual Property (IP).

On the one hand, a company may create a construction system or processes that are highly particular to its objectives and the problems they have identified. This might be in the form of a proprietary building system that is intended to dramatically reduce material use, or an IT tool that will streamline the manufacturing process but require heavy investment to build from the ground up. On the other hand, a company might look at what is already available in the market and choose, adapt, patch and develop only those parts that are missing or defective. These are business choices but they are also choices between closed and open systems and can provide barriers to the success of the company if incorrectly conceived.

Some companies think that the development of proprietary systems and the much-bandied-about 'IP' is what investors look for in a successful venture. Furthermore, trade secrets, patents and copyrights are seen as protection from other companies, throwing up a barrier to entry against them. Both closed and open systems offer advantages and disadvantages; the key issue is the *appropriateness* of the technological solution. For example, if the business model outlines the development of a building system that requires local labour to build it, the fact that this labour will not be skilled in the particular mode of construction needs to be considered. This might suggest an open solution, and a strategy whereby local skills, materials and equipment can be readily integrated. Failing to do this results in the problems associated with high defect rates and time delays that are difficult to predict because the labour component is out of the control of the core business.

The most important lesson in choosing an open or closed system is in making sure that choice is in accord with the wider business model and the operational and technical platforms behind the business (see Business Models and Industrialised Construction box, p.57).

16 Fluctuations in the Housing Market and Scaling

Many companies assume scaling up their operations to produce greater unit volumes will solve financial and market problems in their businesses, including the inevitable peaks and troughs of the housing market. Previous attempts show that rapid scaling brings many problems and is not a panacea, and that companies need to develop business models that can adapt to the now predictiable fluctuations in the construction sector.

Many of the most successful industrialised housing companies in the world have grown over many years, indeed decades. In this book we include three examples: Sekisui House, Simplex and BoKlok. These companies all exhibit a slow process of incremental and patient growth, exemplified by Sekisui House's 'Slow and Smart' company motto. In contrast, the history books are filled with accounts of grand plans for large-scale deployment and rapid development that have ultimately failed. Many prefab companies are convinced that they need to scale up to achieve constant and steady growth and to enable them to weather the ups and downs of the housing market.

Scaling rapidly has many problems and disadvantages in prefabrication, problems to which the conventional industry is relatively unsusceptible. Prefab housing businesses typically have large overheads including: factories, tooling and equipment, a workforce and an R&D process undertaken at the beginning of the venture that is amortised over many years. A conventional large construction company may have none of these items, or maintain only a standing inner core of construction managers, for example. Yet they compete on price-point with prefab companies in the same market. Such overheads are a barrier to adjusting flexibly to market peaks and troughs where demand is fickle. This is not to say that rapid growth will necessarily fail, but that if entrant prefab companies are not aware of the pitfalls of this approach they may be dooming their venture with the first purchase of equipment.

Housing markets are famously volatile. Indeed, development and construction on a large scale generally happens when the market is on a high. This has a twofold effect on prefab. In the troughs and downturns, many prefab companies go out of business because, unlike the rest of the industry, they have standing operational costs that must be maintained. This leads to a boom–bust logic where each successive cycle sees the knowledge and experience it has developed being lost, leading to massive discontinuity in an industry that can take decades to re-establish. The other reason is that during the boom, when money is flowing, the emphasis is on low-risk, quick returns. At these times, there may be less interest in taking more risk for the marginal return typically offered by prefab, which is often best developed incrementally over time. As one leading company relayed: when the market is strong we do ok, when the market is weak we do better.

17   Professions and Disciplines

Professional and disciplinary boundaries affect the ways that problem identification and solving occurs in the construction industry. Each profession has cultural baggage that can weigh down the agility of the venture and the potential to bring about change. Architects, for example, have used prefab housing as a way to achieve difficult and deep-seated professional objectives, which may not be in accord with the broader 'ends' of industrialised housing.

As our discussion of the poles of conceptual and utilitarian prefab showed, the mindset – and indeed failures – of prefab walk hand-in-hand with the mindsets of the various professions and disciplines involved in the process. This relates to the culture of those professions and disciplines. For example, if manufactured housing was only about price and supply, architects and industrial designers would not be so interested. What interests these disciplines is a mixture of the following ideas:

- a generic building that can be fitted artfully to a variety of sites while maintaining its sense of standardisation and design value;
- overcoming the aggrandising effects of bespoke design with an authentic judgment of use value and forming a collective rational taste in building;
- that architecture and design would not only be seen as unique exercises in conspicuous expenditure, but as being capable of addressing social and economic realities that lay at the supposed heart of the modernist project; and
- the idea that each prefab house would hold, and be seen to hold, the DNA for assembly into larger buildings.

The entrepreneur operates from a different culture but brings similar baggage that may not accord well with a successful industrialised housing venture. Herbert's 'Henry Ford Syndrome' attracts the entrepreneur to the auto industry as the moth to the flame. In the auto industry, the entrepreneur sees the ever-increasing offering of features, performance and technological change against reliably dropping

price points, and wishes (naturally) to extrapolate this trend to housing. To achieve this, rapid growth and scaling is required (discussed at Section 16 in this chapter). Such a view is further based on the false assumptions that housing can be a highly standardised product (see Section 7 in this chapter), much like a car.

A final problem in the uptake and success of industrialised housing can be found in the ways that professions and disciplines regard problem solving. This, as we discussed above in regard to partial solutions (see Section 9 in this chapter), leads each group to see different problems. Each profession risks solving a particular part of the problem (with which they are uniquely concerned) at the expense of the whole. The key point here is to see the problem not through the lens of the professions but upon the merits of the problem and the wider objectives of the venture itself. In Chapter 6 we discuss a way to offset this problem through the redefinition of the roles of professions and discipline with particular regard to the industrialised housing field.

What These Problems and Their Examples Tell Us for the Future

The 17 barriers to the uptake and success of prefab housing listed above do not attempt to be comprehensive or exhaustive. Rather, they aim to bring particular issues to the fore and illustrate that a successful future approach can only be founded on a better understanding of the past and present barriers. Building on the issues and ideas laid out in this discussion, Chapter 5 outlines what an appropriate problem-solving approach might look like, that could help resolve these barriers. Chapter 6 revisits the problems we have identified above to formulate a series of recommendations aimed at overcoming them, thereby describing a viable and future-oriented path to prefabrication.

Japan

I.1 Daiwa House's 'Midget House', a prototype prefabricated house, released to the market in 1959. Housing concepts like this were developed after the successful launch of the company's first prefabricated construction called 'Pipe House' in 1955 and set the foundations for the Japanese prefabricated housing industry of today.

Japan's prefabricated housing industry is one of the largest and most successful in the world. With a market share around 15.7 per cent (or 140,000 detached houses per annum) and including companies such as Sekisui House (48,245 detached houses per annum) (see Case Study Japan: Sekisui House box, p.115), Japan offers valuable lessons. Beginning in the decades immediately following World War II, and growing consistently since then, the rise of prefabricated housing companies was aided by the emergence of other Japanese manufacturing industries, such as automotive and consumer electronics. These industries have provided many useful technologies and techniques, such as lean manufacturing, which have contributed to making Japanese prefabricated housing one of the most organisationally and technologically advanced industries in the world. The Japanese industry is now regarded as a premium producer, with heavy emphasis on quality, customisation and customer service.

One of the major achievements of the Japanese prefabricated housing industry has been the transformation of its reputation – from being seen as providing low-quality houses to supplying a premium product. In the early stages of industrialised housing, manufacturers encountered many difficulties, including problems with strict building codes, building officials, local unions, banks and poor consumer impressions. The resulting monotonous, boxy units were not popular or well regarded.

Housing manufacturers overcame these difficulties by developing a quality-oriented approach that married efficient production methods with specially developed marketing and communication techniques. These solutions skilfully satisfied local housing needs and demands and overcame the image of inferior quality. The focus of this approach was on responding to consumers' requirements, desires and expectations of housing *quality*; housing *affordability* became less of a consideration.[1]

The Japanese prefabricated housing industry started in 1955, when the Daiwa House Industry Co. Ltd pioneered the Pipe House, Japan's first prefabricated housing. In 1959 the Japanese Lightweight Iron Construction Association certified Daiwa, paving the way for the mass production of a practical prefabricated housing unit called the Midget House.

The successful commercialisation of the Midget House spurred both the government and private enterprise to focus on the productivity benefits of prefabrication. By 1963 the Ministry of Construction

I.2   Japanese manufacturing is commonly known to have embraced high technology, the house-building sector is no different. Here Sekisui House has implemented wide-scale automation and robotic processes, drawing on experiences from other manufacturing sectors.

and the Ministry of International Trade and Industry established the Japanese Prefabricated Construction Suppliers and Manufacturers Association (JPA) in an attempt to improve the public image of prefabricated homes. In 1976, the government ran the House 55 competition to encourage housing manufacturers to improve the quality of their products and to demonstrate to the public that industrialised housing need not be low quality.[2] Since then, Japanese housing manufacturers have continuously improved the design and performance of their products, while adhering to higher standards than those prescribed in building regulations for the wider construction sector.

The eight largest housing manufacturers are Sekisui House, Daiwa House, PanaHome, Misawa Homes, Sekisui Heim (aka Sekisui Chemical), Asahi Kasei Homes, Mitsui Home and Sumitomo Forestry. In 2014, a total of 892,261 houses were built in Japan. Of these, 140,501 homes (15.7 per cent) are estimated to be prefabricated, using post and beam, panelised, or volumetric modular systems.[3] In Japan, a modular volumetric system is called a 'unit system', and a modular house consists of a number of three-dimensional modules, or units, fabricated in a factory and assembled on site.[4] These factory-built units include structural frames, interior and exterior finishing materials and service facilities.

Early prefabrication was rooted in the standardisation of parts, components or entire units; in this system, end-user products are mass-produced and material and labour costs are reduced through economies of scale. In recent decades, Japanese housing manufacturers have pursued a 'mass customisation' strategy and are now at the forefront of this approach.[5] An important part of mass customisation is that the user directly determines the housing configurations through choices made during the design stage. This is difficult to achieve without standardising housing components for the structural, exterior and interior arrangements. The concept of component standardisation is best illustrated through the analogy of Lego building blocks: a number of simple, modularised blocks can be connected in a variety of ways, because of their interlocking tabs and holes. Likewise, Japanese manufacturers offer a variety of housing components and then encourage their clients to participate in combining the components to design their new home.

Japanese housing manufacturers are now synonymous with premium housing products and offer extensive customer services. Prefabricated

I.3   Reasons for choosing
a prefab house. Results of
a 2014 survey of Japanese
customers.

BUYER REASONS FOR SELECTING THEIR PREFAB COMPANY IN JAPAN

RELIABILITY OF THE COMPANY
SUPERIOR PRODUCT QUALITY AND PERFORMANCE
CONVINCED BY THE SALES PERSON'S EXPLANATION
GOOD PROPOSAL THAT REFLECTS EXPECTATIONS
GOOD POST PURCHASE SERVICES
GOOD EXTERNAL APPEARANCE AND DESIGN
RECOMMENDATION FROM ACQUAINTANCE
ENABLED TO CONFIRM THE ACTUAL PRODUCTS

0 10 20 30 40 50 60 70

YEAR 2014 (%)

houses come with extensive warranty and service arrangements, often for 25 years. This extends the relationship between company and customer (reinforcing the need for high quality products) and facilitates a feedback loop from customer to company. Despite the increased cost associated with pursuit of quality-oriented production, the manufacturers have retained a positive reputation for their innovations through effective marketing and communication. In 2014, the JPA carried out a survey to identify what buyers consider when selecting prefabricated housing manufacturers.[6] The results, shown in Figure I.3, indicate that the reliability of the company was the foremost factor affecting buyer preference (64 per

cent of respondents). The second most significant factor was the product quality and performance, followed by trust in the expertise of the salesforce. These results suggest that homebuyers in Japan consider housing quality as the top priority and that consumers are willing to purchase an expensive prefabricated house if they are convinced of the superiority of the product and the company.

Although many companies advertise their price ranges as comparable to those of conventional housing, this is rarely the case. For example, a site-built timber house in Japan costs, on average, $1,384 USD per square metre, while a prefabricated house costs an estimated $1,499 USD per square metre.

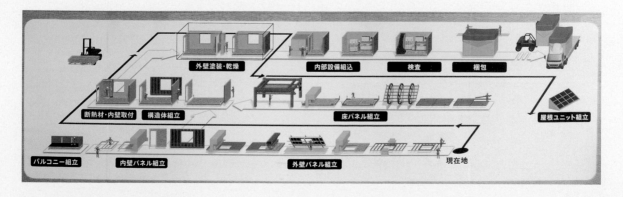

I.4   A controlled flow of materials in
the Sekisui Heim factory results in the
completion of their volumetric offering.
This factory produces both timber and
steel-framed systems, but with different
production lines.

I.5 The evolution of Misawa House's
offerings on display in the company's
customer showroom at Nagoya.
The history and story of Japanese
prefabricated builders is an important
aspect of their marketing process.

That is, a prefabricated house in Japan is, on average, approximately eight per cent more expensive.

The market appetite for high-quality and high-cost products, highlighted in the survey, has resulted in a 'cost-performance' marketing and sales strategy.[7] This strategy, familiar from other consumer-oriented products such as cars, dictates that, despite consistent rises in productivity, cost can be kept stable if the performance of the product is consistently improved. Cars, for example, are still generally regarded as expensive. However, the list of items offered in new cars is ever increasing and many features once offered as expensive options are now standard across all ranges. The same is true for the Japanese housing industry. Quality-oriented production contributes towards a high cost–performance home in which high-tech modern conveniences, previously installed as options, have become

standard equipment. Despite drastically reduced production costs, today's tendency among Japanese housing manufacturers is to compete to improve the quality of their products rather than to reduce the selling price.

This marketing strategy has led to the introduction of a number of green building features, such as solar photovoltaic power generation systems, domestic batteries and home energy management systems (see Environmental Systems box, p.139). These systems are installed in prefabricated homes partly because of the cost–performance strategy, but also in response to market demand for low-to-zero energy sustainable housing. This demand is fuelled in large part by ambitious regulations – Japan is currently preparing for the implementation of a housing policy that will require all newly built homes to be zero net energy by 2020.

5 A Problem-solving Approach for Industrialised House Building

True innovation in the area of industrialised house building comes not through the 'product fixation' typical of conceptual prefab, but through an approach that prioritises a close attention to process. It comes through a revised conception of innovation over invention and a rebalancing of an interest in both the ends and means, conceptual and utilitarian prefab.

In the previous chapter we introduced the significant past and present barriers to the uptake and success of industrialised housing. This chapter first takes a step back from the day-to-day operations and the struggles of the industry to examine the wider framework, method and approach to research in this area. With this overview in hand, we return to the realities of industrialised housing ventures with a new approach, and a new way of visualising and analysing the *total system* or pattern of such ventures.

As outlined in Chapter 1, the observations made in this book are less about the production of *new* knowledge than the combination of *existing* knowledge in new and perhaps more productive ways – it is a joining of the dots.

Knowledge

Knowledge generation and dissemination is faster now than ever before. The production of knowledge outstrips our ability to properly understand it and to apply its lessons. With the expansion of knowledge come ever more, and narrower, divisions of fields and sub-fields. The study of industrialised housing needs to be broad and comprehensive to be effective. Knowledge in the construction industry is currently spread across scores of sub-professions, making it difficult to achieve the kinds of innovation proposed in this book.

Since the Industrial Revolution, two broad trends can be observed in regards to 'knowledge': 1) a constantly expanding field of knowledge; and 2) an ever-increasing number of subdivisions within it. The German language has a term that describes the human casualty of the splintering of knowledge; a *Fachidiot* is an expert and specialist in his or her area but, with no knowledge outside of this area, can also be regarded as an idiot.

Today, it is customary to divide knowledge into broad fields, such as the sciences, social sciences, humanities and arts. Each of these broad fields brings a different approach to knowledge production, and comprises an enormous array of sub-specialisations, which have rapidly increased over the past two centuries and continue to grow.[1] Logically, it is hard to see where this growth and subdivision will end. But with the growth of knowledge come different problems.

The latter part of the twentieth century saw something of a correction to the acceleration of specialisation in the move towards cross-disciplinary knowledge and research as certain problems had begun – as it were – to fall between the gaps. This inter-disciplinary, trans-disciplinary, or multi-disciplinary research, as it is variously known, has itself become subject of study. The now ubiquitous 'wicked problem' found one of its chief causes in such narrowly defined disciplines. The term was launched in an influential paper entitled 'Dilemmas in a General Theory of Planning' by Horst Rittel and Melvin Webber in 1973, and has gone on to be widely invoked for every seemingly intractable problem that conventional disciplinary or professional wisdom cannot solve.[2] This leads to a paradigm where the 'optimal solution' no longer exists, where there is no binary possibility of distinguishing good/bad or true/false, and where it is no longer possible to definitively formulate what a wicked problem is precisely, because it is dynamic, contingent, interdependent and constantly changing.

It is now a commonplace to see housing affordability, for example, referred to as a wicked problem.[3] Extending Rittel and Webber's terms of reference, it is perfectly reasonable to think that the barriers to the uptake and application of prefab raised in Chapter 4 are also symptomatic of a certain wickedness.

Housing construction invokes most of the broad fields of knowledge. From the master builders of the twelfth-century Gothic period to the daylighting analyst of a contemporary high-rise office building, the design and construction of buildings has splintered into hundreds of specialties, and this proliferation shows few signs of abating. How then to accommodate this rapid expansion of knowledge on the one hand, with the realisation that traditional disciplinary and professional frameworks are inadequate to solve many contemporary problems on the other?

Construction Logistics and Supply Chain Management

Logistics and supply chain management (SCM) are key to all types of production systems; construction is no exception. Industrialised house building must consider a number of logistics systems: the inbound logistics to the manufacturing facility, the outbound logistics between the manufacturing facility and the construction site, and the logistics at the construction site itself. There are many opportunities to improve logistics, and SCM in particular, including a focus on the 'upstream' of the off-site facility to include a fully integrated supply chain. In this endeavour, construction can learn from other sectors that have developed sophisticated platforms capable of handling low-cost standardised products to high-cost customised products.

Supply chain management (SCM) has been around since the early 1980s and is often defined as the integration of business processes throughout the supply chain, from suppliers through to end users.[1] That is, SCM is the management of existing networks comprising multiple businesses and relationships.[2] Logistics management is at the core of SCM in construction and is defined as 'that part of the supply chain process that plans, implements and controls the efficient, effective forward and reverse flow and storage of goods, services, and related information from the point of origin to the point of consumption in order to meet customers' requirements'.[3] In construction this includes flows of materials and resources such as labour and machinery.

ROLE 1
CLARIFY 'THE INTERFACE'

ROLE 2
IMPROVE THE SUPPLY CHAIN

ROLE 3
IMPROVE SITE LOGISTICS

ROLE 4
TRANSFER VALUE ADDING ACTIVITIES FROM THE CONSTRUCTION SITE TO THE
SUPPLY CHAIN

ROLE 5
INTEGRATE THE SUPPLY CHAIN WITH THE CONSTRUCTION SITE
'SUPPLY CHAIN MANAGEMENT' (SCM)

J.1 An increased focus on Logistics and
Supply Chain Management can play five
key roles in process improvement.

Managing logistics is at the core of SCM for the
construction industry and is identified as having five
potential roles:[4]

1) Clarifying the interface between the supply
chain and site activities;
2) Improving the supply chain;
3) Improving logistics at the construction site;
4) Transferring activities from the site to the
supply chain; and
5) Managing the site and the supply chain as an
integrated domain.

The first four concern logistics management, while the fifth covers all aspects of SCM.
Construction companies that successfully implement SCM typically start with role 1, 2 or 3, and then
purposefully add more roles over time. (Trying to
address role 5 without first mastering the other four,
especially roles 1, 2, and 3, often leads to failure.)

In contrast, construction companies that ignore
these roles perform poorly in terms of logistics – for
example, poor delivery performance with only 38 per
cent perfect order fulfilment – and are likely to incur
a general cost mark-up of 20–30 per cent (which also
affects clients and developers).[5] There are no quick
fixes and companies must work strategically and
systematically to realise the benefits of SCM and the
integrated supply chain.

The industrialised house builder must also take
account of the structure of the supply chain when
considering SCM. Entities in these supply chains
include all activities upstream from the client – the
construction on-site, suppliers, sub-contractors and
all transportation activities in the supply chain – and
typically at least one off-site (or prefab) factory. As
Figure J.2 shows, the value-adding activities carried
out off-site may vary widely.

To ensure effective logistics, production and
construction activities, logistics and SCM activities
must be adjusted in response to the balance between
on-site and off-site activities. Jonsson and Rudberg
have developed a matrix for classifying production
systems for residential building to facilitate this
(see Fig. J.3).[6] The matrix classifies production

systems along two dimensions: the degree of product standardisation and the degree of off-site assembly.

The horizontal dimension in the matrix represents the degree of product standardisation, ranging from pure customisation to pure standardisation.[7] The vertical dimension embodies the degree of off-site assembly represented by four typical production systems.[8] The Component Manufacture and Sub-assembly (CM&SA) production system is the traditional approach for on-site production of residential buildings, with most value-adding activities carried out on-site. Prefabrication and Sub-assembly (PF&SA) represents a situation with a high degree of prefabrication off-site and bought-in sub-assemblies, but with the majority of assembly activities performed on-site. Prefabrication and Pre-assembly (PF&PA) includes a high degree of prefabrication and some degree of pre-assembly off-site. Finally, Modular Building (MB) entails a high degree of off-site production and assembly, with volumetric modules fabricated to a high level of completion off-site. In MB the only work performed on-site is the assembly of the modules and finishing operations (see Fig. A.5, p.27).

There is usually an ideal match between the degree of product standardisation and the degree of off-site assembly along the diagonal indicated in Figure J.3. Positions too far off the diagonal match

can be effective, but risk being outperformed by better-positioned companies.[9] Two Swedish industrialised house builders, Peab PGS and BoKlok (see Case Study Sweden: BoKlok box, p.133) provide apt examples. BoKlok's Classic concept produces a highly standardised modular building in a factory with dedicated manufacturing and assembly lines. Most value adding is done in the factory, with only final assembly of the modules performed on site. The company is positioned well on the diagonal, matching the standardised product with a very efficient production system off-site. Peab PGS is also well positioned on the diagonal, but with a very different production system offering a more varied product that can be adapted to customers' needs. Both companies are competitive, since they serve different markets with different competitive priorities. BoKlok Classic targets low-cost markets for customers who cannot afford high demands in customising the product. Peab PGS offers more variety to customers who are willing to pay a premium for this. Interestingly, BoKlok has recently introduced a new product concept that offers more variety and more choices for the customer. In doing so they have made a shift along the horizontal axis in Fig. J.3, which will put new and different demands on the production function in the factory.

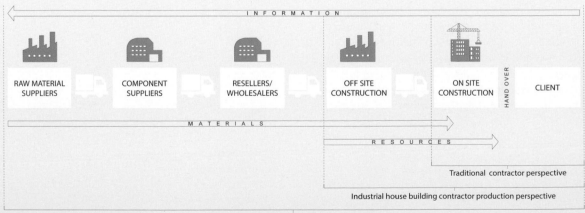

Industrial house building supply chain perspective

J.2   The Industrialised House Building supply chain, charting the flow of materials, other resources and the reciprocal flow of information.

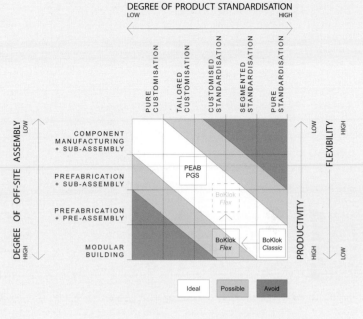

J.3 Classifying the production systems of Swedish Industrialised House Builders, to describe the construction method and its resulting flexibility in terms of customisation and standardisation. This diagram shows how a particular company can make strategic decisions.

DEGREE OF PRODUCT STANDARDISATION
LOW — HIGH

PURE CUSTOMISATION
TAILORED CUSTOMISATION
CUSTOMISED STANDARDISATION
SEGMENTED STANDARDISATION
PURE STANDARDISATION

DEGREE OF OFF-SITE ASSEMBLY
LOW — HIGH

FLEXIBILITY LOW — HIGH
PRODUCTIVITY HIGH — LOW

COMPONENT MANUFACTURING + SUB-ASSEMBLY

PREFABRICATION + SUB-ASSEMBLY — PEAB PGS

PREFABRICATION + PRE-ASSEMBLY — BoKlok Flex

MODULAR BUILDING — BoKlok Flex — BoKlok Classic

Ideal — Possible — Avoid

Every company must adjust their logistics and SCM activities relative to the structure of their particular supply chain, including the type of production system employed in the off-site facility, and the nature of the activities performed on-site. This balance affects all five SCM and logistics roles. Interfaces between site, manufacturing facility and supply chain are different for different types of industrialised production systems, and the supply chain and transportation activities need to be designed and managed accordingly. For example, delivering pre-fabricated 'flat' packs is very different to delivering volumetric modules. Site activities also vary between the different production systems. Transferring activities from the site to the supply chain (role 4) brings into play the strategic position identified using Fig. J.3 and the resulting balance between on- and off-site activities.

In summary; to be effective and efficient, different supply chain and logistics platforms need to be developed depending on the types of industrial production systems used.[10] By addressing all five roles,

the logistics and supply chain system can be aligned with the production system to facilitate efficient operations. Swedish construction company Peab provides an excellent example. The company has explored different logistics platforms in a number of pilot projects. In one project (including some 350 apartments) the company managed to reduce total production time by 17 per cent (as compared to a baseline reference project) by fully adapting the five roles to the production system.

Many industrial house builders are realising the competitive advantage offered by logistics and SCM. These focus on the off-site facility and the site, but also on the relationship between them, including logistics. The most proactive industrialised house-builders also include the supply chain upstream of the off-site facility, providing coverage for a fully integrated supply chain.

Knowledge Production

As knowledge and its fields and sub-fields have grown, the demands placed on research have changed. New modes of knowledge production have emerged that promise a closer fit between research and its intended technical, economic, social, and cultural outcomes.

There is no simple solution to the complicated tensions between specialist and generalist knowledge; both are required to realise the kind of problem-solving approach we describe in this chapter.

Housing demands a *holistic* approach, where solutions are not arrived at through a process of exclusion but through the *inclusion* of the myriad problems, constraints and particularities that bear on housing. This approach, as Rittel and Webber have noted, is very different from the scientific method, which must often eliminate many variables in order to solve a problem in a conclusive and repeatable manner. In line with Rittel and Webber's observation that the 'optimal' solution no longer exists and with our earlier discussion of 'Loose Fit and Best Practice' (see Section 8 in Chapter 4), most leading industrialised housing companies' systems are neither conclusive nor repeatable.[4] As described in the Integrated Building Performance box, p.84, new roles and working methods are needed to advance building.

The demand for a holistic approach to industrialised housing is not new. Burnham Kelly noted this almost 70 years ago in his landmark book:

> We have emphasized throughout the book the importance of treating the prefabrication of houses as a complete pattern of operations of which management, design, procurement, production, and marketing are the major subdivisions.[5]

Arthur Bernhardt and Gilbert Herbert agree with Kelly, pointing to the necessity of the 'complete pattern', and the 'total system' that is based on a full integration and synthesis of the parts. But what tools do we have to carry out such complex, dynamic and interconnected work?

It is this broader societal undercurrent that is the subject of *The Production of New Knowledge: The Dynamics of Science and Research in Contemporary Societies*.[6] First published in 1994, the book was the product of a large collaborative effort by six international researchers led by Michael Gibbons. The book's core contribution was the identification and definition of a new mode of knowledge production that could explain and respond to emerging demands. Where the traditional mode of academic and 'scientific' knowledge production was termed 'Mode 1', this emergent mode of knowledge production was termed 'Mode 2'. As the authors describe:

> Our view is that while Mode 2 may not be replacing Mode 1, Mode 2 is different from Mode 1 in nearly every respect. The new mode operates within a context of application in that problems are not set within a disciplinary framework. It is transdisciplinary rather than mono- or multidisciplinary. It is carried out in non-hierarchical, heterogeneously organised forms which are essentially transient. It is not being institutionalised primarily within university structures. Mode 2 involves the close interaction of many actors throughout the process of knowledge production and this means that knowledge production is becoming more socially accountable.[7]

In many ways, this text describes a mode of working familiar to those engaged in R&D projects between the university and industry:

- the problems it addresses are those derived from real-world application;
- they operate outside traditional disciplinary frameworks and have little regard for traditional institutional roles;
- its social structure is not hierarchical but distributed, relying on teamwork and laterally fluid networks which are transient; and,
- as distinct from traditional forms of 'expertise', Mode 2 knowledge production must operate in close interaction with the entire process and its attendant personnel, and is not reducible to any individual or small group.

The full implications of the analysis of Mode 2 by Gibbons et al. go beyond the scope of our enquiry. What is important to note is that a deeper understanding of this societal change and an appreciation of the need to rethink the modes of knowledge production are the first steps to developing tools for the complex, dynamic and interconnected work required for the success of industrialised house building.

Design Research and Design Thinking

Design thinking, design research, axiomatic design and fuzzy logic are all examples of new modes of knowledge production that are relevant to our field, as they imply a revision of the meaning and utility of knowledge, and because they offer novel tools and methods that are more appropriate to the tasks at hand.

Among the many advances made in research methods in recent decades has been the emergence of 'Design Research'.[8] A key reason design research is of value in attempting to solve complex problems in industrialised housing is found in its capacity for the kinds of holistic and integrative approaches we flagged above. Design research has the capacity to synthesise a range of incongruous or even conflicting inputs and still generate a solution. Design research methods can be creative, generative and speculative. This approach draws on techniques and methods from traditional artistic practice, and its outcomes are sometimes highly subjective, precluding the kinds of objectivity and repeatability so cherished within the sciences. We refer precisely to the value of design research when we say, 'It is more art than science', by which is usually meant that we can reach a conclusion, but that this conclusion involves intuition, rules-of-thumb, emotions and feelings, and a kind of speculation that would be anathema to conventional scientific sensibilities.

Design research employs a series of techniques with which many designers and inventors are familiar. Many non-designers are surprised by how fluid and seemingly random such techniques appear, especially during the process, as they are perhaps more familiar with the polished outcomes of such processes. For example, rather than applying a linear approach to problem solving, design research uses a circular or iterative approach. Each successive pass adds a new layer of meaning or resolution. Such an approach prohibits jumping ahead to the final or optimal solution; rather, with each iteration, the variables of the problem are brought into a more harmonious and *intentional* alignment. This process is augmented by prototyping, which might include drawings, illustrations, models, mock-ups, or indeed a full-scale building. Prototyping allows the designer to 'test' a solution, concept, or idea before carrying out a further iteration. Similarly, a designer may use speculative approaches to problem solving through the invention of scenarios, again to test a premise for its advantages or disadvantages in an agile and lightweight manner.

It is important to note that design research methods are not restricted to designers or inventors but can be learned by other professions. It is this potential that has captured the interest of a wide range of professions

Design research is still counted as a new mode of research in academia but design thinking is newer still. Tim Brown's well-known book, *Change by Design: How Design Thinking Transforms Organizations and Inspires Innovation* (2009), is a key source in this area.[9] Before Brown, Roger L. Martin's *The Opposable Mind: Winning Through Integrative Thinking*, first published in 2007, carried many similar recommendations but with less focus on traditional creative process from design and the arts.[10] These books, and a slew of others to emerge in the wake of these studies, have been applied to a wide range of problems, from business, leadership, marketing, communication, to health care, for their capacity to identify different problems using new analytical tools.

The emergence of design research, and the more popular design thinking, are not random events. Standing behind these developments is a longer, deeper, and more complex change in the way contemporary society and its institutions view and value research and knowledge. Design research presents tools that researchers have at their disposal for diagnosis and analysis, and for developing appropriate solutions.

Problem Solving

A deeper view of the history of knowledge and the modes and methods of knowledge production can help to clarify and generate a new, more appropriate approach to problem solving for industrialised house building. This approach needs to be inclusive, holistic and iterative, rather than exclusory and linear. This approach does not result in 'perfect' or 'optimal' solutions but rather a series of 'trade-offs' which depend on the tactical shifting of criteria in line with a greater strategy.

At the close of Chapter 3, we briefly outlined a problem-solving approach useful in industrialised house-building ventures. It can be summarised as follows:

1. First we must acknowledge all the parts of the system that come to bear on housing;
2. We must then determine the various 'settings', objectives, or 'ends' of the product or business;
2. Finally we can develop solutions for the several parts of the system.

These solutions and the various settings are the *means* used to achieve the stated ends. The goal is a coherent, smooth-running total system, which we refer to in this book as *the process*. It is important to recognise that this problem-solving approach might appear to run in reverse to the more traditional R&D approaches, which often begin with an idea for a winning product, a new technology, or a stand-out business model, and set about trying to make commercial and operational success after that.

The approach to problem solving we advocate in this book is not derived through the 'pure' application of a single method, but through a hybrid, iterative process of trial and error, testing and analysis, and troubleshooting. The criteria for evaluating a solution is its *appropriateness* and not the application of rigid theory or doctrinaire research methods. The design research method is particularly relevant because it rarely exists in a pure form.

Unlike experimental scientific methods, for example, design research draws on a variety of traditions and methods from other fields, and can therefore be seen as a truly hybrid method, one that can accommodate variation and dynamic inputs.

With the advantages of this approach come different types of outcomes. For example, design research can draw on deeply subjective views and involve large amounts of discretion. It therefore (and often) lacks the customary legitimacy offered by scientific 'objectivity' and 'repeatability'. For these reasons, design research is not only hard to define, it is also hard to measure. Nevertheless, we argue that this should not undermine the value it can bring to the process.

Eric Ries' influential book, *The Lean Startup: How Constant Innovation Creates Radically Successful Businesses* (2011), shows how such a method can be applied to the development of startup businesses. Ries' book introduced many novel concepts to explain this approach, perhaps the best known of which is the 'Minimum Viable Product', or MVP. An MVP is what Brown would term a 'prototype', and it recommends that startups take their products and ideas to market as soon as possible in order to get critical early-stage feedback and to begin measuring outcomes. Like a prototype, an MVP is a kind of mock-up, or placeholder, intended only to be plausible enough to be measured. To carry out this measurement, Ries developed the concept of 'Innovation Accounting', which he contrasts with the kind of 'vanity metrics' at play in almost all new business ventures. These concepts are significant because they tell us not only how to make better R&D by applying a framework that can know whether the process has been successful, but also how to evade the kinds of wilful and highly subjective outcomes with which some designers (indeed new businesses) benchmark themselves (vanity metrics).

This process, it should be pointed out, is not a process of simplification or reduction but allows the complexities of the problem to emerge, coalesce and be measured in a realistic way in direct relation to the MVP. This might be testing how a new community interacts with a web platform, or measuring consumer reactions to a new running shoe design.

PROBLEM A
STRUCTURAL WALL SYSTEM
Develop a structural wall system that has the highest strength using the least material.

PROBLEM B
WALL SYSTEM FOR MARKET APPLICATION
Develop a building wall system that can be used in the market for prefabricated housing.

Problem A Criteria:	Problem B Criteria:
- Span (metres)	- Building Code
- Weight (kg)	Compliance
	- Structural Compliance
	- Acoustics
	- Fire
	- Waterproof
	- Design Flexibility
	- Variety of Expression
	- Cost
	- Buildability
	- Sustainability
	- Logistics
	- Market Acceptance
	- Perceived Quality

5.1   Reductive (Problem A) and holistic (Problem B) approaches to problem solving. The holistic approach to Problem B results in trade-offs. The reductive approach to Problem A results in optimised solutions.

The MVP and innovation accounting techniques allow new questions and answers to emerge, and outcomes that could not have been forecast or envisioned. The application of this method in industrialised housing ventures is likely to be different because houses are large, expensive objects, and many companies do not make the kinds of mock-ups the MVP process demands. Instead, test sections are built to see if a wall build-up will work, or if finishes are appropriate. These tend to be technical, mechanical tests, and are very much focused on the 'hardware'. Some companies make prototype houses, usually for marketing purposes but they are rarely used to undertake the requisite innovation accounting. In industrialised housing, this might include the 'software' of the houses. Such accounting might involve: analysing the way families use a new house range; testing the 'look' on the target market; identifying key gaps and glitches in the process; and, generally gathering data that would help them to identify future improvements across the whole process beyond the physical structure.

These iterative, reflexive and tactical problem-solving techniques are central to design research and design thinking. The methods outlined under design research above are of value in exploring solutions to tricky, dynamic problems because they have the capacity to synthesise a range of complex inputs and generate coherent solutions. Together, such techniques do not offer a conclusive argument for efficiency, perfection or optimisation, but rather a series of what we might call qualitative and quantitative *trade-offs*. In the case of industrialised housing ventures, these trade-offs are broadly the same as the 'settings': essentially a dynamic weighting across a broad range of criteria.

The difference between the application of this method and that of an inventive, blue-sky, curiosity, or concept-driven approach, can be seen clearly in the following two problem statements (Fig. 5.1).

Problem A demands a structural wall system that has the highest strength using the least material. Problem B demands a building wall system that can be used in the market for prefabricated housing. Problem A is reductive and Problem B is holistic. Where Problem A relies on two main criteria, strength and weight, Problem B must satisfy, in some way, every criterion listed if it is to be a valid, market-ready solution. No matter how high the performance of a particular solution to Problem B may be in terms of structure, cost, buildability, or acoustics, for example, it is *not* an acceptable solution if it poses a fire hazard, or is not watertight, or its materials are not readily sourced. Clearly, the solution to Problem B must result in many trade-offs, because not every criterion can have an optimal outcome.

This concept of a trade-off is very simple but not easily digested by fields who are not fluent in the above-mentioned strategies and techniques. It is similar to the 'Theory of Constraints' developed as a management strategy but applied at the product and process levels.[11] A trade-off is fundamentally different to an optimal solution, because it is the best possible solution when triangulated within a set of potentially competing criteria.

Finally, the concept of the trade-off is also highly relevant to our problem-solving methodology, not just because it is key in generating solutions to complex problems, but because it also explains why *precedents* are so important in complex problem solving. Precedents, like prototypes and MVPs, have the power to demonstrate the successful resolution of multiple criteria and trade-offs in a tangible way. These are *proxy* resolutions that are transportable and graspable. Where the satisfaction of the 13 criteria outlined in Problem B may seem hard to achieve from the outset, knowledge of a competing wall system that has already made a series of trade-offs can accelerate the process of development immeasurably.

Innovation and Problem Solving

Innovation is different to invention because it demands application and uptake. Historically, many prefab housing companies have pursued inventive solutions, often at the expense of real innovation (see Section 4 in Chapter 4). The term disruptive innovation is now widely used to explain any business or technology that disrupts an existing field or sector, yet its original meaning referred to a particular approach to innovation that is often low-quality, low-cost and market changing. Mobile homes and plasterboard are examples closer to the original meaning of disruptive innovation, which raises the question of how companies can pursue such innovation in the present.

Problems A and B above also pose a different question: within the context of industrialised housing, what is the appropriate mode of innovation? An elegant, lightweight structural wall system as an outcome of Problem A shows a great capacity for invention. Here we might think of similar systems by legendary inventors such as Buckminster Fuller in the 1920s and 1930s, or Jean Prouvé in the 1940s

Design for Disassembly

'Design for Disassembly' is becoming a familiar part of discourses on environmental strategies for construction and sustainable design. The concept originates in industrial design and pertains to a wide range of strategies for reuse and recycling, all of which highlight a whole-of-life approach to materials and buildings. Design for Disassembly is particularly relevant to prefabricated and industrialised construction, as such methodologies already contain within them the possibility for easy dismantling, whether for maintenance, refurbishment or reuse.

'Design for Disassembly' refers to strategies that enable products, structures or edifices to be dismantled (in part or as a whole) to enable changing or removing pieces. The idea started in industrial design and is related to the logics of mechanical engineering – particularly the design processes of engines and machinery – by which parts are either fixed or replaced. Here cars or consumer products serve as pertinent examples (see Fig. K.1).

Awareness of the negative environmental consequences of consumerism and the scarcity of natural resources at a global level has provided the impetus for developing design for disassembly strategies.[1] Most countries and companies now have sustainable resource agendas in place, or are being pushed to develop them. In 2005 the European Commission proposed a 'Strategy on the Sustainable Use of Natural Resources used in Europe', with the objective of reducing the environmental impacts associated with the use of resources in growing

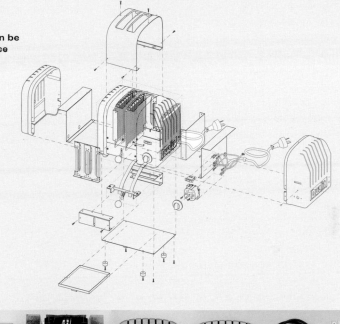

K.1 A dismantled Dualit toaster, demonstrating that with care and consideration during design, even a complex device such as a toaster can be disassembled for repair, maintenance or end-of-life processing.

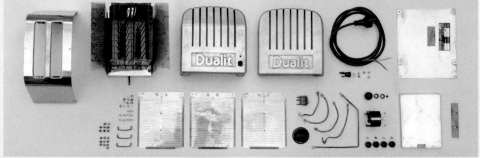

economies. This strategy was followed by the Circular Economy Package in 2016, which includes measures covering the whole life cycle: from production and consumption, to waste management and markets for used raw materials.[2]

Design for Disassembly helps to manage the cyclic phases of the resources, to minimise harmful substances in the environment and the consumption of new raw materials, and to harvest the embodied energy (see Fig. K.2). It may include the full lifecycle of material resources, products or buildings and their fabrication processes. It is based on the actions summarised below:

Minimise
• Quantities of resources and materials in general;
• Number of different kinds of materials;
• Number of parts and variation of joints; and
• Use of environmentally problematic materials.

Categorise
• Use pure (natural) and unpolluted recycled materials over polluted materials;
• Lifespan of different materials (deterioration, weathering, wear and tear); and
• Lifespan of the building elements (accessibility, versatility).

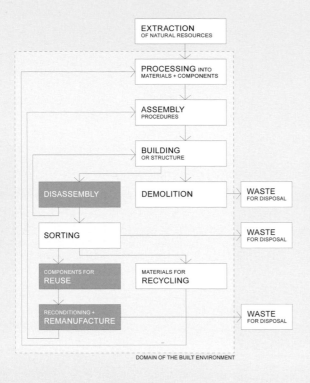

K.2   Flow of materials within the domain of the built environment.

Standardise
 • Use modular design and 'generic components' – compatible with other systems;
 • Construction principles and information in order to share knowledge more easily; and
 • Permanent identification of components – similar to material ID.

The ability to take buildings apart is not a new idea. Structures built to permit reuse of the materials, or to benefit from highly developed assembly systems, have existed as long as humankind itself. They appear among nomadic cultures as lightweight tent structures of 'sticks and skins' and among settled cultures as human-scaled building systems of various robust materials – bricks, stones or full timber – that were intended to have a longer lifespan. For example, Figure K.3 shows timber joints of Swedish mediaeval churches.[3]

These building systems share a number of features. First, they use very efficient modes of construction, are portable, and are fast and easy to assemble. Second, they are made of individual parts that can be renewed in case of damage or weathering. Third, the materials or crafted building components were considered valuable resources that had to last and could be kept for possible future use. The ability to share knowledge through clear structural principles and well-organised construction procedures was handed down through generations, and this knowledge provided the basis for a great variety of building techniques and systems influenced by specific cultures and contexts.

Contemporary building practices can learn significant lessons from historical building techniques developed for these purposes. They can be roughly grouped into ideas about material properties, structural systems, accessibility, joining typologies, sum of components and appropriate technologies.[4] These building techniques were originally driven by similar motivations – a need to conserve materials and save energy. They were primarily formed by local conditions, whereas current building techniques are ruled by policies and environmental challenges at a global level. Today, buildings designed for disassembly enable flexibility, adaptability, convertibility,

Systemise
 • Design an open-building system, where parts are freely interchangeable and less unique to one application;
 • Specify performance criteria and guidelines for assembly/disassembly procedures;
 • Identify points of disassembly that are clearly identifiable and will not be confused with other design features; and
 • Order the parts while allowing for an infinite variety of the building as a whole – (this will allow minor alterations to the building without major building works).

additions and subtraction of whole buildings. These practices may help to avoid the demolition of a building and serve as the most energy-saving approach. The diagram by Philip Crowther (see Fig. K.4) tracks the value chains and loops.[5]

Design strategies for reuse and recycling are not interchangeable. Design for reuse is generally preferable to design for recycling due to the overall environmental impact. Reuse prescribes that materials and components can be removed intact and maintain service and aesthetic qualities with minimal alterations. Reuse preserves the invested embodied energy of materials, thus reducing inputs of new embodied energy during the material's reprocessing or remanufacturing.[6] Examples include the joint of a concrete column and the Stavna timber block system, which are both designed for disassembly.

Design for recycling, on the other hand, can involve destructive disassembly processes that degrade the materials. This may result in unacceptable levels of pollution and mixing that prevent economic further processing.[7]

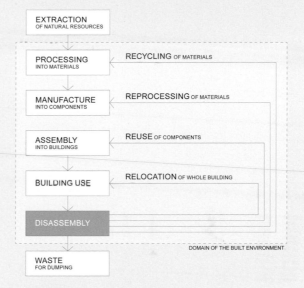

EXTRACTION OF NATURAL RESOURCES

PROCESSING INTO MATERIALS — RECYCLING OF MATERIALS

MANUFACTURE INTO COMPONENTS — REPROCESSING OF MATERIALS

ASSEMBLY INTO BUILDINGS — REUSE OF COMPONENTS

BUILDING USE — RELOCATION OF WHOLE BUILDING

DISASSEMBLY

DOMAIN OF THE BUILT ENVIRONMENT

WASTE FOR DUMPING

K.4 The four strategies for material reuse in the built environment.

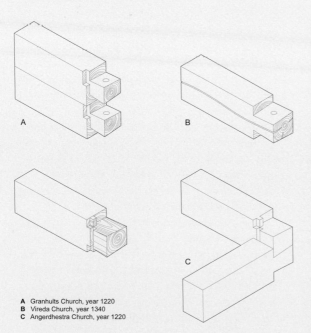

A Granhults Church, year 1220
B Vireda Church, year 1340
C Angerdhestra Church, year 1220

Design for Disassembly is most successful when it allows for maximum flexibility of spatial configuration within a given structure, as this preserves the building structure as a whole. Further to this, designs can be made for whole-building disassembly to enable building systems and subcomponents to be reused in other buildings. Obviously, the individual hierarchies of resource conservation, technical feasibility and economic efficiency may not always align.[8] In such cases a 'layered' design strategy can specify hierarchies and handle the different life cycles of the building elements. Stewart Brand first presented the idea of shearing layers in his 1994 book *How Buildings Learn* (Fig. K.5).[9] The key idea presented by Brand is to technically separate the layers in a building in order to enable changes with minimal use of resources and costs.[10]

The full integration of reuse and recycling with prefabricated industrialised building can be found in work by Philadelphia-based architecture practice Kieran Timberlake Architects. These ideas were first tested in 2006 in the Loblolly House, at Taylors Island, Maryland. Two years later the practice

K.3 Timber jointing techniques seen in Swedish Mediaeval Church buildings demonstrate attitudes toward material re-use or disassembly.

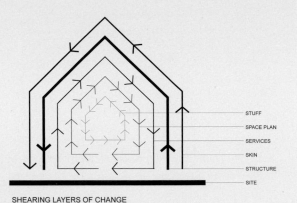

SHEARING LAYERS OF CHANGE
Because of the different rates of change of its components, a building is always tearing itself apart.

K.5 Brand's 'Shearing Layers', referring to a building's layers of permanence and flexibility. The thicker lines denote layers which are hard or costly to change.

developed a second-generation 'assembly/disassembly system' in Cellophane House™, the full-scale pavilion designed for the Home Delivery exhibition at MoMA, New York in 2008. Both projects are based on theories outlined by Stephen Kieran and James Timberlake in their book, *Refabricating Architecture*.[11]

Design strategies based on Design for Disassembly tap into emergent ideas about the circular economy and recycle scenarios in industrial manufacturing, which connect to core systems thinking. Thus they have the potential to be developed into mainstream industrialised manufacturing procedures where materials and building components become part of circular value flows and new sets of economies. However, a move towards Design for Disassembly in construction calls for alternative thinking (business models, building regulations, partnerships etc.) in an industry that is generally known for conservatism. It calls for serious investment and companies willing to develop more exemplary projects from which the wider industry can learn. Ultimately, Design for Disassembly may offer new architectural and construction languages that draw upon the treasures of historical building cultures, while at the same time driving the development of highly advanced industrial solutions.

and 1950s. A solution that maximises strength while saving weight may promise untold benefits for an industry that needs to save precious commodities and floor area through more efficient wall sections. While it is novel and inventive, we might argue that, despite its elegance, this solution is not necessarily innovative because the latter demands *application* and *uptake* in practice.

The approach we have sketched for Problem A is precisely the norm in many R&D approaches in the construction industry, where it is felt that an elegant-*looking* solution or a breakthrough technology will transform the industry. This, as we discussed in Chapter 4, Section 4, is the confusion in thinking that innovation needs to look like invention. Furthermore, it is thought that such innovations today need not only to look inventive, but they also need to be 'disruptive'.

In the current climate of 'tech' industries and start-up culture, 'disruption' has come to mean many things. Increasingly it is used literally – that is, Uber *disrupts* the taxi business. In this sense, disruption could easily be exchanged for 'disturbance'. Originally, 'disruptive innovation' was proposed by Clayton M. Christensen in his now landmark book, *The Innovator's Dilemma* (1997).[12] Christensen describes how disruptive innovations appeared in the marketplace (mainly in technology and machinery industries) and what happened to those markets after their appearance. He noted that disruptive technologies first appeared as a product of *inferior quality* to the widely held or market-leading expectations of the day. These products often possessed the unknown (and, indeed, unknowable) quality of generating *a new market or user groups* that bring with them *new expectations*, not widely known or acknowledged by the market leaders. Entering the market from underneath (not above or from the side), these disruptive innovations impact their industries by being more nimble, by growing market share, and by eventually usurping the market leaders from within – hence the subtitle of Christensen's book, 'When New Technologies Cause Great Firms to Fail'.

We might well ask how such a *disruptive innovation* in housing might come about? To better understand this we first need to realise that disruptive innovation is not the only mode of innovation in Christensen's scheme. The lesser-known category is 'sustaining innovation' which, Christensen tells us, provides incremental improvements on existing models. Applied specifically to industrialised housing, this might mean that making a house cheaper is not disruptive in itself as some companies would contend. In the example above, Uber may be *disturbing* the business model of the taxi industry, even completely replacing it, but it is not *disruptive* in Christensen's strict sense, because it is simply *improving* the level of service that taxis provide by supplying passengers with greater convenience and is, therefore, a sustaining innovation.[13]

The media giant Netflix, is a great example of both types of innovation. The company's initial business offered improved convenience to its customers, allowing them to order DVDs online and have them sent out by post – an example of sustaining innovation. Alongside the traditional high-quality DVD market, Netflix also offered its early subscribers low quality but readily available content for streaming. As we now know, low quality (though on-demand) content was the key disruption offered by Netflix. Having entered the market it was able to continually expand this on-demand content to become the biggest player in a market that did not exist a decade ago. It is now widely regarded as a producer of high-quality media content.

In assessing the innovative quality of the outcomes of the twentieth century's industrialised housing ventures, Bernhardt, Herbert and Davies all identified the leading role played by the mobile/ manufactured home. At the same time as Gropius and Wachsmann were busy failing, Herbert points out the mobile home industry successfully made the leap to full industrialisation and mass production. As Herbert wrote, the success of the industry lay in the understanding that 'industrialized housing is not merely a technological system, but a total system'.[14] Bernhardt went further to spell out the basis of the industry's success as 'a comprehensive nationwide system, a total production-distribution-land development network effectively synchronized with its supporting and regulator environments'.[15] Davies, characteristically, is even more blunt in

his assessment and makes critical reference to Bernhardt's pioneering work on mobile homes:

> Architects, even those interested in mass-produced housing, have mostly ignored the trailer and mobile home, too distracted by the shining example of the automobile to notice what was being towed behind it. And when they have noticed it they have tended, like Bernhardt, to want to change it, to turn it into architecture and make it respectable.[16]

The mobile/manufactured home is a perfect example of Christensen's disruptive innovation: a simpler, low-quality, low-cost product that enters the market from below and through its unique offering creates a new market, new user groups, and ultimately, a whole new industry. In Chapter 6 we return to the potential of a disruptive housing innovation to point out that, like the mobile home industry, disruptive innovation does not always unite opinion, or for that matter, claim to solve all important concerns.

Patterns and Meta-Structure

This book suggests there is a pattern and structure that can help to analyse and improve industrialised housing products, processes and ventures. This pattern requires the inclusion of all constraints and constituent parts, an understanding of their interconnectedness and interdependencies, and a determination of their relative weighting within the total system. This pattern can be likened to a company's DNA, except that it can be modified and improved.

There is a kind of *meta-structure* that governs many aspects of the industrialised house building industry. At the very least, this meta-structure can help us understand, evaluate and visualise both successes and failures at an abstract, structural level. This – we should be very clear – is not a recipe for success or a talisman capable of warding off ineptitude. Rather, it is a process which individuals and companies can apply to test, review, analyse and recast their ventures. Not surprisingly, it is also not complete,

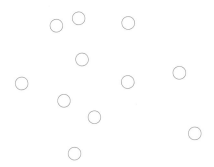

A. Imagine these dots represent all the major areas we need to know about when considering an industrialised housing idea. In our test run, each dot represents a significant part of the total system.

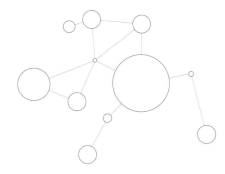

C. As we apply the weightings, some things grow or diminish in importance, some things change colour or plane. This is the role of the 'settings' we have described, also referred to as the objectives or 'ends' of the idea, venture, or company (see Fig. 5.2). So far, our 'areas' have been abstract, but we might apply labels to them.

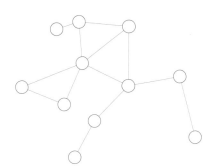

B. Naturally, these different areas will have relationships and dependencies among them. Not all things are contingent on all others; some are highly dependent, others less so. But this diagram suggests all areas are equal, so we might apply some relative weighting to address this.

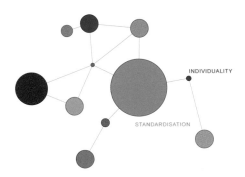

D. For example, we are pursuing a *highly* standardised offering, which, we imagine, will lead to a *diminished* 'individuality', or potential for customisation.

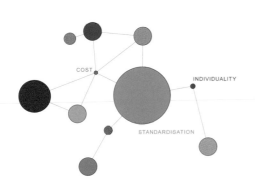

E. Such areas cannot exist in isolation – our highly standardised offering is intended to be *low* cost.

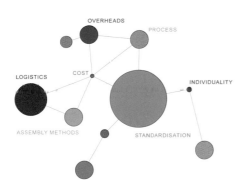

F. And cost, by its nature, is a function of many areas: logistics, assembly and construction method, and overheads, to name a few.

because it is not able to be completed. It serves, rather, as a scaffolding, around which we expect several layers of sophistication to greatly enrich its findings.

In many regards this meta-structure is the same as Kelly's 'complete pattern', Bernhardt's diagrams and Herbert's 'total system'. It is a literal joining of the dots or perhaps what philosophers would term a new *ontology*. Among our group of authors, this meta-structure goes by different names: program, brief, process, platform, recipe, DNA, settings, objectives and constraints, to name a few. What all these various terms and concepts try to capture is the 'total system', which requires integration and synthesis, and whose ultimate goal must be a kind of harmonious, intentional and smooth-running process.

What follows is not a theoretical concept but a 'test-run' diagnostic of sorts. The sequence below is applied to a hypothetical house offering and company.

Start at the End

As we outlined above, every company, venture or offering needs to begin with its settings – a dynamic weighting of criteria. This process needs to start with the 'ends' in mind, suspending the urge to focus on ideas, models and technologies, or the 'means' as we have described them. Having done this, we might see a picture like this emerge:

Diagnostics

Using these settings as the premise of our test run, the series of diagrams left illustrate the application of this model:

How to Apply this Pattern to Problem Solving

Each company, idea, or offering, we propose, has a diagram like this that can describe it. This diagram is a snapshot, a dashboard of sorts that captures the overarching logic and narrative of the business and its offerings, which can be developed quickly. It

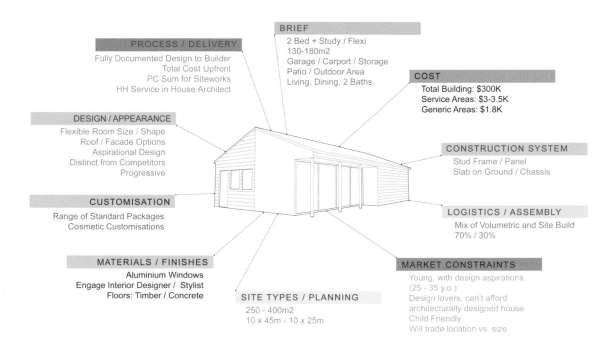

PROCESS / DELIVERY
Fully Documented Design to Builder
Total Cost Upfront
PC Sum for Siteworks
HH Service in House Architect

BRIEF
2 Bed + Study / Flexi
130-180m2
Garage / Carport / Storage
Patio / Outdoor Area
Living, Dining, 2 Baths

COST
Total Building: $300K
Service Areas: $3-3.5K
Generic Areas: $1.8K

DESIGN / APPEARANCE
Flexible Room Size / Shape
Roof / Facade Options
Aspirational Design
Distinct from Competitors
Progressive

CONSTRUCTION SYSTEM
Stud Frame / Panel
Slab on Ground / Chassis

CUSTOMISATION
Range of Standard Packages
Cosmetic Customisations

LOGISTICS / ASSEMBLY
Mix of Volumetric and Site Build
70% / 30%

MATERIALS / FINISHES
Aluminium Windows
Engage Interior Designer / Stylist
Floors: Timber / Concrete

MARKET CONSTRAINTS
Young, with design aspirations
(25 - 35 y.o.)
Design lovers, can't afford
architecturally designed house
Child Friendly
Will trade location vs. size

SITE TYPES / PLANNING
250 - 400m2
10 x 45m - 10 x 25m

5.2 Defining the 'ends' invokes a wide range of 'settings' which must be determined before focusing on the 'means'.

is dynamic and constantly changing, as the various settings do not exist in isolation but in a world of highly contingent forces and circumstances that reflect the changing conditions of housing and business. Such a diagram can illustrate the blockages, paradoxes and wrong thinking in the system, the visualisation of which can help improve the process, make it more coherent and smooth-running. In essence, we believe that such an approach can be learned and applied.

This 'DNA' diagram requires a generalist view, where no single part dominates. We discuss what such a view involves in more detail in Chapter 6 with regard to the future of the professions. When we find a problem or discord, such as individuality versus standardisation, we can acknowledge that there are many reasons that standardisation is inversely proportional to the ability to customise,

and we build in this complexity. But having found such a correspondence, we can do more than simply accept it as a given; we are able to apply effort and time to understanding and perhaps *changing* this relationship. It is in this part of the problem that specialist knowledge and methods are *essential*. The guiding ethos, however, is that having now observed the meta-structure at work and effectively joined the dots, the specialist work of resolving the particular conflict, tension, or discord is carried out against a background that acknowledges this meta-structure and holds it present as constant measure of success. It is through this oscillation between the modes of generalist and specialist that the outcome can be safeguarded from providing the kinds of partial solutions or the highly inventive but ultimately irrelevant solutions outlined above.

Case Study Japan: Sekisui House

Sekisui House is the largest and one of the most well-known of the Japanese prefabricated housing companies. While the emphasis on quality, sustainability, energy-efficiency, and customer service is a common attribute of most of Japan's housing manufacturers (see Japan box, p.93), Sekisui House's attention to these issues places them at the forefront of the national and international industry. Sekisui House is also well known for its high level

of factory automation (see Fig. I.2). The company undertakes wide-ranging research and development on a broad range of topics, including alternative construction systems (steel and timber), earthquake resistance, comfort, environmental systems (solar energy, battery storage, etc.), sustainability, waste reduction through reuse and recycling of building products. Sekisui House's company motto 'Slow and Smart' demonstrates an incremental approach to innovation, and gradual expansion to achieve their current market share.

Sekisui House Ltd was established in 1960 from the housing division of Sekisui Chemical Co. Ltd. Today, the company is recognised as the largest prefabricated housing manufacturer in Japan, producing cumulative sales of 48,245 prefabricated housing units in 2015. Of this total number, 9,591 were steel-framed detached houses and 4,021 were timber-framed detached houses. A further 34,633 were multi-residential housing units.[1] These two construction systems – timber and steel – provide choice to the customer (see Fig. 4.5). Where some

L.1   A Sekisui House display home at their Shizuoka factory site. Sekisui are known for the technological sophistication of their production, advanced performance features, and controlled marketing methods. The design and built form still maintains a familiarity to the mainstream Japanese market.

L.2 The customer sales process at Sekisui House involves a range of selections, notably environmental systems, such as these energy cells, which can be selected as add-on features.

those prescribed in ordinary building regulations. Additionally, Sekisui House has established its own quality standards in order to improve structural resistance, durability and amenities. The company's quality-oriented production contributes towards the delivery of their high 'cost–performance' housing, in which high-tech contemporary features and conveniences were installed first as optional features and later became standard equipment in conventional homes. A recent example is the advancement of the 'Green First Zero'. Initially developed as a conceptual zero emission house for demonstration at the 2008 G8 summit (see Fig. P.2, p.141), these features have been developed to the extent that Green First Zero homes represented 50 per cent of Sekisui House's detached builds in Japan during 2014.[3] Sekisui House's prefabricated housing encompasses high levels of safety and amenities. These homes are not a mere shelter, they provide a living environment with well-controlled room temperature, indoor air-quality and soundproofing. Today, the company fully utilises resource-saving strategies that complement the push to reduce housing emissions through reductions in construction waste. This resulted in the recent establishment of nationwide factory resource management centres and has led to industry-leading standards for the reduction and recycling of construction waste.

Sekisui House offers a high level of customer service. Before entering into a contract to build, extensive information is presented to potential homebuyers through four housing catalogues that communicate the company's business platform and offerings in terms of plans, finishes, components and technology. This emphasis on communication and marketing is central to the company's business model and Sekisui maintains multiple showrooms and design centres. In these facilities, customers are introduced to the general features offered by Sekisui, along with a series of optional products, materials, finishes, and even future R&D products, some of which are not yet available to customers. Here, the heavy investment in R&D has the double function of improving Sekisui's products while also demonstrating the company's continual progress to customers.

producers develop expertise with one material, choice is a key factor in Sekisui House's business model. This approach to customisation is apparent from the construction system to assembly methodology. Described as 'tailored standardisation', Sekisui House's offering sees components and sub-assemblies arranged on-site to meet the individual customer's needs, and contrasts with a number of the other Japanese volumetric builders that lack this degree of design flexibility.[2]

Like other housing manufacturers in Japan, the company adheres to strict quality control accreditations that guarantee higher standards than

Sekisui House also invests heavily in advertising, despite the extremely high costs associated with such campaigns. (It is not unusual for a Japanese housing manufacturer to spend more than three per cent of its annual income on advertising.[4]) Sekisui's strategy is to build a relationship with the client at the earliest possible stage of purchasing a home, and thereby to enhance the consumer's motivation and introduce them to the products and services available. Sekisui House's approach here is similar to other housing manufacturers, who adopt a variety of modes of advertisement to enhance the consumers' trust in their products. Alongside the now ubiquitous online advertising, other modes include local media and newspaper advertising, inserts in monthly or quarterly housing pamphlets, mailouts to rental dwellers, as well as presentations at large companies or to social gatherings. Referrals and testimonials from previous customers are another important source for new clients.

Sekisui House also operates a home amenities experience studio, 'Nattoku Kobo', for the general public. The studio provides a variety of information on housing functions and performance such as lifetime barrier-free design, home security, earthquake and typhoon resistance, energy and space use efficiency, and off-grid power generation. Similar prefabricated housing information centres are spread across Japan, allowing customers to assess the quality of the company's products and learn more

L.3   The finished result of Sekisui House's Shawood timber construction system. A high quality, well-designed and distinctly Japanese living environment.

about its housing options, including examining full-sized products. They function as an exhibition and design consultation base, where experienced staff can make concrete proposals concerning the external appearance and floor plans of standardised, yet customisable, homes using advanced information and communication technologies. The centres allow potential homebuyers to familiarise themselves with the companies and their products, and enable the prefabricator to establish personal contact with customers. This consumer outreach is a prelude to customer relationships that may continue for several decades.

Sekisui House is expanding its operations internationally around the Pacific Rim. These operations go beyond prefabricated single-family house building. Their tripartite business model consists of: built-to-order single-family dwellings, a supplied-housing business that involves renovation and real estate management, and development projects, which are large-scale community developments and apartment buildings.[5] This expanded business model demonstrates the opportunities and complexities involved in a holistic approach to prefabricated house building and show what is possible through a strong and sustained customer focus (see Business Models and Industrialised Construction box, p.57).

L.4   The environmental systems of Sekisui House can be controlled and managed by the home owner, with live readings communicated by their TV. This level of technology is promoted during the sales process.

6 Prefab Housing and the Future of Building

This book has charted a journey through the field of industrialised building. Along the way, significant questions have emerged: What ideas and research preceded current thinking? What are the major landmarks in this field? Where are the barriers and the problems? And what is an appropriate approach to problem solving and innovation for industrialised house building?

Having mapped a path through the complex and uneven terrain of prefabrication, what have we learnt? What areas are ripe for further exploration?

What follows is a list of ten opportunities that capture the findings, recommendations, and ideas for future exploration, in the hope that they will stimulate further research and development, discussion and debate, and thereby help the industry to realise the promise of prefab.

6.1 For over two decades, Swedish builders Lindbäcks have refined an efficient construction system which uses a volumetric timber-frame. This system is able to provide high-performing multi-residential buildings at an accessible price point, with increasing design flexibility.

1 If Sufficiently Broad in Scope, Industrialised Housing Ventures can Play a Role in Solving Housing Affordability

Industrialised house building is ideally placed to combat the problems of housing affordability, but only if it is conceived, designed and operated within an expanded framework like that proposed in this book.

Housing is notoriously complex, and the provision of more affordable housing is seen as a 'wicked' problem. If we are to realise the promise of prefab we need to develop new business models that address the complex factors that have impeded the development of affordable housing to date. These include: building costs, access to affordable land and ensuring the gains in efficiency and the lowering of cost are passed on to end users. Reforming access, supply and the continuing operation of affordable housing requires broad investigation across a range of areas, including finance, development and ownership models, taxation law, regulatory environment, social and cultural factors and, of course, the design, construction and operation of the physical buildings themselves.

Industrialised building has promise precisely because it has the capacity to address these varied constraints in an integrated and strategic manner. It was broad reform across the full spectrum of constraints which allowed the mobile/manufactured home industry to provide disruptive (and affordable) solutions to the housing market. There is much that prefab housing might learn from the *process* (less so the *product*) followed in this related industry.

2   Disruptive Innovation may Initially Appear in a Disreputable Form

Disruptive innovations do not always unite opinion and may not always have positive moral associations. That is, not everyone is likely to agree on what disruptors will look like or if they are even 'good'. And we must remember that not all disruption will follow the model of the near-mythic disruptors, the iPhone or the Tesla electric car.

To achieve disruptive innovation in the housing and property industries we should focus more on the prosaic lessons offered by the mobile/manufactured home industry, or the development of plasterboard and resist (somewhat) the distractions of today's conceptually rich offerings.

Such lessons will allow us to cast the net widely and to keep in mind the key markers that distinguish disruptive innovations from sustaining innovations. This would also enable us to accept that, like mobile homes, disruptive innovation may not unite opinion. It may first appear in a 'disreputable' form. Innovation may come from the bottom, and it may challenge the business model and technical solutions of today's market leaders. Rather than fear such an association, the industry should embrace it.

3   The Future Industrialised Housing Industry will be Driven by a New Generation of Professionals

Not all professions will survive the next wave of technological advances.[1] Those that do will be agile and adept at effective collaboration between areas of expertise and newly devised business models. They will drive the next phase of industrialised building.

In the built environment industries, the next technological wave is likely to include both the now-familiar advances in computation, fabrication and automation, and the yet-to-be-realised outcomes of marrying big data to artificial intelligence.

6.2   Twilight in an American trailer park. The results achieved by the mobile/manufactured home industry show that innovation need not look inventive, and that some disruptive innovation may appear first in a 'disreputable' form.

Tasks that can be made routine and automated will be the first to go but this event will also provide an opportunity for the emergence of a new generation of professionals. Already we see new skills and knowledge emerging in and around the industrialised house building industry. Existing disciplinary boundaries are blurring, and new and strategically distinct competencies are emerging.

The new professionals will not be bound by disciplinary specialisation and the compartmentalisation of risk. Conventional professional and disciplinary frameworks were developed within the specialisation of knowledge, on the one hand, and the compartmentalisation of risk and capital flow within the business model of the construction industry on the other. For these new professions to be sustainable, they must also generate value (particularly value that eludes outsourcing to computational technologies), and they must be profitable. The construction industry currently rewards those who have the most capital or take the most risk. Those who create the most value are arguably rewarded the least.

The new professions have the potential to reverse this situation and some forward-thinking companies have embarked on this path, such as SHoP Architects in New York (see Section 6 in Chapter 4).

Sweden

Sweden is a small country (2017 population approx. 10 million) with a long, sustained and effective history of prefabrication, the result of a fertile mix of geographic, political and cultural circumstances over time. Its history of industrialised building reveals structural and cultural factors that support innovation and embrace the opportunities and challenges inherent in prefabricated systems. Sweden is also unusual for the close and collegial relationship between government, industry and research institutions, which has placed it at

the leading edge of innovation among Western developed nations. Sweden's incremental story of construction industrialisation, nurtured by context and history, demonstrates the range of solutions that are possible when there is time and appetite for change.

With Russia to the east, Germany to the south and the United Kingdom to the west, Sweden's location facilitated its absorption of developments in science, culture and politics during the seventeenth and eighteenth centuries. This new knowledge, combined with vast natural resources in forestry and mining, provided the country with a strong capacity for technological development, especially when severe famines in the late-nineteenth century drove urbanisation.

This history enabled Sweden to develop large-scale prefabrication of houses in response to a housing crisis in the 1920s. Government-led research into housing supported the rapid production of houses through a range of strategies, including pattern books for home-builders, assistance to factories for housing production, and training and education in architecture and engineering schools. By 1930,

1920

1950

1900

1940

1960

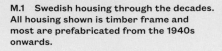

M.1 Swedish housing through the decades. All housing shown is timber frame and most are prefabricated from the 1940s onwards.

Modernism emerged in Sweden as an ideological and stylistic force to underpin these mass-production efforts. World War II saw progress slow as building materials and transportation equipment were required elsewhere, but Sweden's neutral status meant that its industry was one of the few in Europe still fully operational at the end of the war and capable of launching a strong postwar economy.

The housing shortage continued in this postwar period. With new knowledge developed during the war – such as blasting bedrock, using tower cranes and transporting by trucks – the Swedes started building a new society. Government funding supported industrial development, which was underpinned by research. Architectural research brought foreigners to see innovations in suburban planning, studies of housewives and their movements in kitchens, and the architectural theory of housing sight lines and light. Strong ties developed between the manufacturing and construction sectors, and Sweden became an early adopter of modular coordination and standardisation – for example, in window and door measurements and cabinetry. Throughout this period Sweden's reputation in manufacturing grew steadily through companies

like Electrolux, Volvo, ABB, SAAB, IKEA, Sandvik, Ericsson, Atlas Copco, Scania and Husqvarna.

In 1964 the Swedish government made a landmark decision to resolve the great housing shortage, committing to build a million homes in 10 years. Named *Miljonprogrammet* (The Million Homes Program), the legacy of this program still affects how Swedes relate to housing issues in general – and specifically industrialised housing. A shortage of architects created consensus between architects and contractors that design-build contracts were the preferred mode of engagement. Administrative workload was shifted from the architect, with contractors taking control of production decisions. These large contractors were civil engineers in spirit, bringing their knowledge and experience of large-scale structures to bear on housing. Between 1965 and 1975, large-scale, multi-family housing developments were built with the support of the Swedish government in almost every city. The degree of repetition was high and precast concrete technology, combined with timber-framed curtain walls, was a common technique for low-rise, multi-family houses. Steel columns with concrete hollow-core decks were used for high-rise, multi-family structures. These

1970

1990

1980

2000

multi-family housing projects were not enough to meet demand, and one third of the Million Homes Program was realised through single-family homes produced in factories with timber frame elements. As this single-family homes industry thrived in the postwar period, houses were also exported to Germany, Norway and as far as Australia.[1]

The uniform architecture and its universally applicable aesthetics were a perfect fit with the Modern Movement, out of which the Million Homes Program vision had developed. Eventually, however, it led to public protest against the large-scale roll-out of housing estates and, in combination with the oil crisis in the early 1970s, the flurry of industrialisation of Swedish construction came to an abrupt halt. Over the next two decades, small-scale, personalised and decorated houses were in high demand. By 1994, a new economic crisis forced the Swedish government to remove construction subsidies. This saw more than one third of construction companies collapse, among them many producers of single-family dwellings. The entire construction sector was re-structured and housing production was low for over a decade. This stagnation led to a new housing shortage and by 2010 nearly as many homes were required as before the Million Homes Program.

This time around, Swedes were somewhat wary of industrialisation – strong government control and the heavy industrialisation of construction were seen to have resulted in uniform, dull buildings of inferior quality. The new quest was to drive industrialisation to serve the customer through organising product variants, modularisation and a diversity of business models. Inspired by automotive companies, most Swedish industrialised construction companies nowadays have their own expertise in the configuration and development of building systems, in modularisation and organisation of standard designs in platforms, and in product and production development.

This growing customer focus in construction identified the importance of good design as essential to success, in parallel with industrialisation. Today, most single-family home producers have extensive catalogues for customers to choose from, ranging from traditional Swedish houses to 'New England'

style – and even 'Postmodern' (see Fig. 6.11).

In 2015, around 75 prefabricated single-family home manufacturers were active in Sweden. The three largest had a turnover in excess of US$100M, placing them among the 30 largest Swedish construction contractors. Prefabricated timber frame has 95 per cent of the market share in the single-family homes industry. These producers typically receive pre-cut timber, with other materials delivered just-in-time, and use an automated wall production line served by data from a CAD system. Walls, ceilings, floors and roof cassettes or trusses are prefabricated in the factory using precision tools and laser guides. When finished, these elements are covered and delivered by truck to the building site where the house is assembled in two to three days on a precast concrete slab. Construction operations continue through summer and winter.

For multi-family housing, the market penetration for prefabrication is around 50 per cent – that is, half of construction operations are still carried out on-site. The concrete prefabrication industry is strong, with a dozen factories producing precast concrete hollow decks, flat concrete bases, or precast, pretensioned beams. The construction industry has knowledge and experience of handling, assembling, and transporting concrete, including in-situ casted concrete. With a well-trained crew, in-situ casting is just as cost effective as prefabricated elements.

Lessons from the Million Homes Program led to a renewed focus on design, but it also showed that repetition and learning are powerful tools when it comes to increasing quality and workflow. Construction processes have been slowly perfected, and as a result the Swedish construction industry is now highly competitive, producing high-quality houses with a well-paid workforce.

For cost reasons many prefab factories in Sweden are situated in rural areas, often with a former or current connection to a sawmill placed close to forest wood supply. Transportation is usually by truck or boat and costs are usually reasonable. This rural production means the workforce tends to be loyal with good work ethics and a commitment to training. This provides one of the basic conditions for success in industrialisation: the stability to perfect operations combined with innovation to constantly renew the business.

Lately, timber frame has entered the multi-family housing arena. This was enabled by a 1994 regulatory change – prior to this, it was forbidden to erect housing greater than two storeys with a timber frame. By 2016 the market share for timber-framed multi-family housing has risen to 15 per cent.[2] Several of the larger single-family home producers are now entering this market as a consequence of the current discussion on sustainable and environmentally sound construction in Sweden. This involves building houses with good airtightness, low energy use, and a minimised carbon footprint, and is propelled by a strong coupling between industry and the research community. New solutions are developed and tested at universities and research institutes before entering the market, and many Swedish researchers divide their work time between academia and industry. This joint development is supported by Swedish (and European) building codes that allow projects to fulfil functional requirements rather than prescriptive ones. It is up to the supplier to prove that a solution fulfils the demands, which drives the development of new solutions. For the timber industry, this has been extremely beneficial in trying to catch up on the 50- to 100-year lead of the steel and concrete industries.

The success of the Swedish industrialised construction industry depends largely on a cooperative mindset, where learning from other industries is seen as positive. Future challenges for Swedish industrialised construction are found in market segments where uptake of industrialised working methods is low, for example bridge construction and industrial buildings. Another future challenge is found in handling large variation in the production phase to support mass customisation (see The Platform Approach box, p.48). To fully address a market segment, the design and production methods today are either too standardised or too flexible; seeking this balance is the next step for Swedish industrialised construction.

4 Industrialised Housing Companies can Benefit from Vertical Integration

Vertical integration within the construction industry is the sister argument to the new generation of professionals. Vertical integration will allow industrialised house-building companies to operate to their maximum advantage: reducing the compounded margins of the traditional industry; gaining more control over quality; building in more direct and valuable feedback from end users to design and production; and helping to bring about an attitude to R&D that can start the process of long-term and sustainable innovation typical of other manufacturing sectors. Vertical integration can bring about a virtuous cycle where quality increases and cost reductions finally make business sense, allowing the benefits of these to be passed on to end users.

Vertical integration is a different argument to the now common lateral expansion embraced by the large integrated construction and infrastructure consultancies (Fig. 6.4). These companies, such as Arup, have gathered all specialisations 'in house' (see Integrated Building Performance box, p.84). These specialisations have traditionally included design, planning, engineering, project management, legal and IT/documentation services.

As discussed in Chapter 4, Section 10, in relation to change management in the construction industry, few integrated consultancies or construction companies are currently willing to make the jump up or down the pyramid into either manufacturing or development, because they currently see no extra advantage in such a move, only more risk – risk that they have worked hard to avoid.

An example of a company that has achieved a level of vertical integration is Lendlease. Over the past decade, Lendlease has developed a manufacturing capacity in-house in the multi-storey residential building area.[2] This move is facilitated in part by a longstanding tradition within the company for vertical integration. Embedded in the company DNA is the integration of finance, development, construction and property management, on to which the addition of a manufacturing capability is the logical expansion.

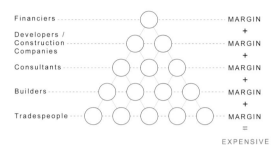

SIMPLIFIED DIAGRAM OF THE CONSTRUCTION INDUSTRY

Financiers .... MARGIN +
Developers / Construction Companies .... MARGIN +
Consultants .... MARGIN +
Builders .... MARGIN +
Tradespeople .... MARGIN = EXPENSIVE

6.3   Each layer of the construction industry adds its own margin.

APPROXIMATE STAKE IN THE OVERALL COST OF A BUILDING

Financiers ....
Developers / Construction Companies ....
Consultants ....
Builders ....
Tradespeople ....

6.4   Large contractors are able to horizontally integrate expertise.

VERTICAL INTEGRATION

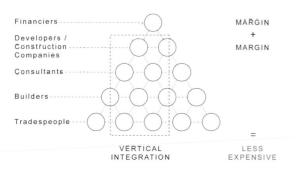

6.5   Some industrialised house builders have the possibility to vertically integrate, straddling the tiers from development to production and thereby reducing the number of margins to the end user.

SUPPLY CHAIN INTEGRATION

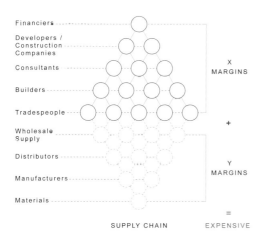

6.6   Not only are margins added to construction projects between tiers of industry, but also in the supply chain from the gathering of raw resources to their installation.

The rationalisation of the construction supply chain alone is ripe for disruptive innovation (Fig. 6.6). Take, for example, a door handle made in China. This unit will be on-sold from the manufacturer to distributors until it eventually reaches the tradesperson who will install it. This shows us that there might be y number of margins on the item before it even reaches the construction site. Then, this is added to x number of margins until it finally reaches the consumer's purse.

Vertical integration can bring about a virtuous cycle that leads to *lower costs* while simultaneously *increasing quality* in design and construction, by undoing the structure that feeds a status quo of high costs and margins on margins.

5   New Business Models and a Whole-of-business Approach are Essential for the Future Success of Industrialised Housing Ventures. These will Rely More on Platforms and on Seeing Housing as a Medium for Connectivity

The ideas introduced above – affordable housing, new professionals, disruptive innovation and vertical integration – all hinge on the articulation of, and seamless integration with, an appropriate business model (see Business Models and Industrialised Construction box, p.57). Here, construction has much to learn from other sectors and advances in business and management theory. Furthermore, to compete on cost, industrialised building companies need to pursue a business model that emphasises a *whole-of-business* approach. This would demonstrate an expanded field of advantages (quality, performance and maintenance), and not just a square metre price of conventional construction.

The competencies associated with business, finance and management are often the missing ingredients of prefab housing ventures. As Kelly insightfully explained in 1951, the prefabrication of houses needs to be treated as 'a complete pattern of operations of which management, design, procurement, production, and marketing are the major subdivisions'.[3] Our case studies show that

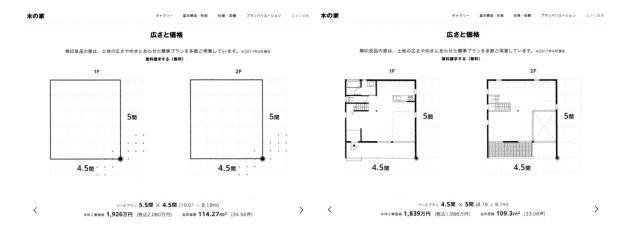

6.7 Increasingly sophisticated online platforms are being developed by industrialised house builders for a range of purposes, not least for customer-engagement. Here, the Muji website allows users to sample the range of plan options which can be achieved by manipulating the overall dimensions of one of their offerings, real-time cost and size figures show the implications of the decision.

the complete integration of all of these areas is essential to the success of industrialised housing ventures. Lars Stehn has outlined the centrality of the often-neglected business model in his formula: *Industrialised Construction = Technical Platform + Business Model.*

Many other dynamic industrial sectors and management teams *start* with the business model,[4] whereas construction shows an often unconscious drift caused by commercial or disciplinary inertia, or the path dependency of companies that have begun ventures with a certain direction and feel the need to continue to recoup 'sunk costs'. Rarely are the needs of the end user or 'the market' revered to the same degree as in, say, consumer electronics or the auto industry. But it is here that some of the new developments and thinking around the overall structure of business models are of interest.

The rise of the sharing economy, the network effects of large, nimble online platforms, and the decentralisation and democratisation of technology have all left indelible impacts on the way companies now strategise, manage and operate businesses. One such example is seen in the move from 'Pipeline' to 'Platform' business models.[5] Platforms are an essential attribute of industrialised house building companies, whether they exist as a series of loosely defined business 'processes' or as highly articulated and integrated IT 'configurators' and 'technical' platforms (see The Platform Approach box, p.48). But platforms as a business model and 'platform thinking' represent slightly different frameworks within which to conceive building and housing ventures. They promise to incorporate a wider framework of connectivity, beyond the sole provision of physical 'hardware'. By connecting myriad 'users' with 'providers', housing has enormous potential to become an aggregator for a whole range of products and services, in ways yet to be fully realised. In such a recast business model, housing has the potential to become a *medium* through which a suite of other flows and connections run.

6 If Companies are Aware of Their Strengths and Weaknesses, the Industrialised Housing Sector can Accommodate Both Large and Small Companies, Where Both Slow and Fast Growth can Occur

There is no single solution, or set of preconditions, for entering the industrialised housing market.

Affordability and Industrialised House Building

Housing affordability is a global issue that confronts many cities and countries. The provision of more affordable housing is often described as a key objective of many industrialised house-building companies, which has led to a focus on cost and become emblematic of early thought on affordable housing. More recently, the view has widened to see the cost of construction as just one piece of a multifactorial problem. Modular, prefabricated, or industrialised housing has an important role to play in the future of affordable housing, and now includes issues such as: improved development time, wider social and economic spin-off benefits, alternative modes of development and financing, reuse and refurbishment of existing housing stock, and more efficient, sustainable and energy-conscious buildings.

Forces are converging to put housing out of reach for increasingly large swathes of urban populations as high-cost cities across the world experience crises in housing affordability.[1] Housing demand is a large factor in this, but the more fundamental causes are incomes not keeping pace with inflation and falling below rental and sales prices, and the cost of construction. More innovative governmental agencies are looking at reducing cost and increasing wages, thereby helping families build wealth while also encouraging denser and more flexible housing options.

The promises of industrialised house building are generally touted as quicker development periods and potentially lower construction costs; and yet many architects and developers have pursued the prefabricated affordable house as an ideology with little market success.[2] Recently, affordable housing has seen a shift in thinking that extends beyond housing provision to include wealth generation, social service provision, skill building and neighbourhood cohesion.[3] Componentised, modular and other efficient building methods are now being positioned as a means of tackling these broader issues, which can be extended to include skill building, local hiring, long-term adaptability and the lowering of a host of life-cycle costs. In terms of the buildings, increasingly high-level energy efficiency certification and proximity to jobs and services are now integral for governmental agencies in selecting development teams and sites.[4] Lower costs, alone, are no longer enough.

Theoretically, the industrialised house-building industry is well positioned for this market, but

N.1   The proposals for digitally prefabricated housing in New Orleans, by MIT and Larry Sass at MoMA's Home Delivery exhibition. This solution demonstrated the possibility to quickly (and cost effectively) rebuild areas of the city affected by Hurricane Katrina.

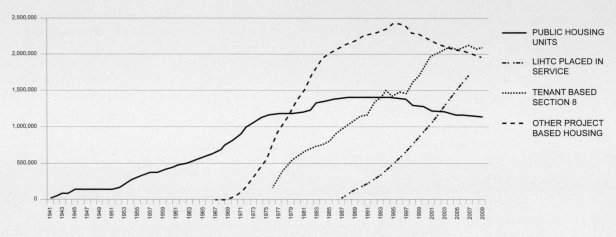

CHANGE OVER TIME IN NUMBER OF RENTAL HOUSING UNITS / HOUSEHOLDS ASSISTED

- PUBLIC HOUSING UNITS
- LIHTC PLACED IN SERVICE
- TENANT BASED SECTION 8
- OTHER PROJECT BASED HOUSING

N.2   In the United States, governments' role in housing provision has trended away from the implementation of its own construction programme, toward incentivising private development. This has created competitive funding streams that increasingly favour lower costs and shorter timeframes.

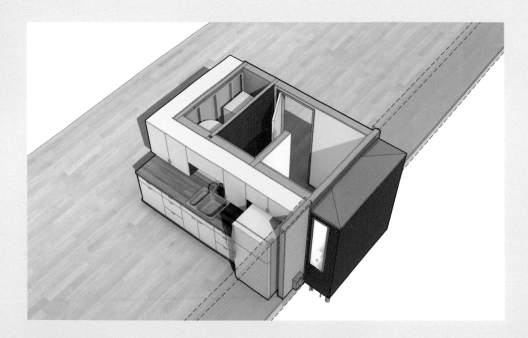

N.3   Modular service pods are increasingly popular, especially for multi-residential developments. The 'Mod-Pod' by Rice Building Workshop builds on this trend seeing these pods as able to incorporate the majority of servicing required for new or existing structures.

has yet to exploit its full potential. Nonetheless, a growing list of projects that show reductions in development costs while also achieving high energy efficiency and quicker completion times is leading to greater interest in modular housing options, and these are increasingly discussed within many affordable housing circles.[5] There are several ways the industry could embed itself in the affordable housing ecosystem and increase its presence in the overall unit provision.

Embedding modular logics into building codes, housing standards and design guidelines is one way to move toward this goal. In the United States the key mechanism for funding affordable housing is the Low-Income Housing Tax Credit (LIHTC) which produces on average 100,000 affordable units per year. This national program is administered at the state level and each jurisdiction creates a point system to select projects to proceed. In this highly competitive process, successful project bids receive tax incentives that can be sold to corporate investors who provide equity that may total more than 50 per cent of the project costs. Lowering construction costs or reducing construction timeframes creates a virtuous cycle in which developments require less subsidy and federal funds are freed to fund more housing units.

Prefabricated, modular and manufactured housing has a unique opportunity within this framework. Unlike earlier governmental housing efforts, the LIHTC program relies on private for-profit and non-profit developers making individual decisions on sites, materials and development partners. Unlike European or Latin American models for affordable housing provision, in the US one housing model, technique or development entity will not drive the market. This provides both a hindrance to specific models or processes becoming ubiquitous, and an opportunity for new modes of thinking to enter the industry. A key benefit of this model is that the competitive nature of the funding streams means successful developments typically become best practices and, over time, are incorporated into the regulatory guidelines.[6] As part of this process many states now award points for cost containment,

energy efficiency and lowering of operating costs, all areas where modular is gaining advantage over traditional building.

Another area where the modular industry and affordable housing intersect is rehabilitation and renovation. Most funds spent in the construction industry revolve around renewing existing structures, which make up the bulk of our housing. In the world of affordable housing, the preservation of units is just as important as new construction – and possibly more so. For cash-strapped housing agencies, focusing on these areas also stretches subsidy dollars further. One good example of incorporating the benefits of modular and prefabricated components into existing structures can be found in Houston, Texas and the work of the Rice Building Workshop. Their 'mod-pod' is a prefabricated fully contained unit that includes all of the wet services and systems of a home and can be slotted into a freestanding structure, or craned up to an existing building (Fig. N.3).

This technique holds the promise of inserting targeted volumetric construction into existing neighbourhoods while also giving buildings the flexibility to change and adapt over time. It provides a hybrid method that sets a path for retrofitting existing neighbourhoods and delivering the benefits of lower costs and greater energy efficiency inherent in prefabricated construction.[7] Here, local workers can participate in the renovations and build skills while also maintaining the fabric of neighbourhoods.

In finance, these techniques would fall under the category of triple bottom line benefits, meaning an investment where a product can provide an economic benefit, achieve social benefits and achieve reductions in energy use and carbon emissions. This finance sector has been growing rapidly, seeking to deploy funds for socially motivated investors.[8] If the modular industry can create the datasets and design the physical components that reduce costs, create the flexibility to confront a variety of neighbourhood conditions and create opportunities for skill building and wealth generation, then gaining acceptance in the affordable housing ecosystem could be in reach.

Industrialised housing requires truly flexible business models that can accommodate both the very large companies capable of achieving vertical integration, and small companies that are organically (and slowly) expanding upstream and downstream along the value chain – and up and down the traditional hierarchy of the construction industry.

Another area awaiting exploration is how companies can resist and overcome the inevitable downturns of the construction industry. The boom–bust logic of construction, particularly residential construction, has historically been unfavourable to industrialised building ventures (see Chapter 4, Section 16). The downturn leaves such businesses holding large standing and operational costs, whereas traditional construction companies (who outsource equipment, manufacturing facilities and staff) have much less exposure, because they downsize in the face of such downturns.

The options for large and small players in this field are dynamic and variable, not fixed. They are more like a golf course than a set of railway tracks along which each venture must travel with set speed and direction. On a golf course, each player has a different handicap – some players can skip a hole, while others take all day to chip out of the sand bunker. Players can overtake a slower party, or head directly to the club house. Importantly, the golf course has room for both large and small groups and can cater to players both fast and slow. This analogy is important because many see the railway (linear, exclusive, limited, pre-determined) as the model and fear groups cluttering their path to the next station, essentially jamming up the line.

The key to coexistence and pluralism in industrialised housing is in each player recognising the inherent potential and limitations of their size, scope and capacity. This is particularly the case with the vexed issue of 'scaling'. Many companies write off inefficiencies in their production system, their lack of uptake, their fit between market and product, an uneconomical cost structure, or outright unprofitability, to the need to 'scale' – and scale quickly! Our research has shown that companies in countries with longstanding traditions in industrialised construction have taken very many years

to develop their approaches and pursued a slow, organic and incremental approach – Sekisui House's 'Slow and Smart' philosophy, for example. Similarly, most successful Swedish companies have taken decades to consolidate their market position. This does not mean that fast growth from a standing start for a company with no tradition or experience in industrialised house building is impossible per se, but rather that that company must pay particular attention to key issues which will sink them if left unattended. To return to our golf analogy, having only driving and putting clubs in the golf buggy does not make it impossible to complete the round, one must simply adjust the style of play and take more time. Similarly, having the widest possible selection and most expensive clubs on the course is no guarantee of winning.

Different companies have different handicaps and can pursue different opportunities. Factors that often go unaddressed and can sink large, fast ventures include: large R&D budgets but with limited time for prototyping and testing; limited scope for integrating techniques and technology with a workforce (and supply chain) unfamiliar with the new approach; and time to ensure regulatory compliance. Such large-format scaling would be very difficult for a small company (close to impossible) but is *more* likely to succeed if the company has the backing of a large organisation or investor pool. Small companies can operate at a scale and volume that would sink large companies precisely because of their efficient cost structure and low overheads. The real problem in this framework comes if a company is not aware of its handicap, that it plays as though it had ten clubs when it only has three, that is: when a company behaves as though it were not bound by the same rules and logic as the rest of the industry.

This model is both a barrier and opportunity. For example, entrant companies, or countries with no longstanding industry, are not necessarily at a disadvantage. The Japanese industry, for example, is seen as highly technologically advanced, with a highly efficient, rationalised, and automated design and production system. Yet this massive investment brings an inevitable inertia and an inability to change, adapt, or be nimble, such as might afflict a large factory geared up to produce houses that cannot be used for anything else and needs a constant pipeline of business. This method may allow for great volume of production but little variability, and is more like an older mode of mass production in the automotive industry which, in many ways, has already been superseded. Conversely, entrant countries with no historical industry can use new technologies, learn existing techniques and avail themselves of the latest thinking, without making the 60-year investment of a Sekisui House. Essentially, this situation suggests that, with the correct thinking, these countries and companies can leapfrog the market leaders who are encumbered by the usual handicaps and legacy issues that both weigh them down *and* provide the foundations for success at the same time.

6.9   London-based, Facit Homes operate in an 'Industry-Lite' mode, with the ability to manufacture their system in a distributed manner.

7   Industry 4.0 vs Industry Lite: Industrialised Housing Ventures must Pay Close Attention to the Partioularities of Housing Before Borrowing from Other Sectors. Inter-Sectoral Learning can then Occur in Two Directions

There are a range of models for industrialisation from other sectors that may be relevant to the housing of the future. Which of these are most appropriate? What attributes do they have? As explained in Chapter 4, ideas imported from car manufacturing – such as mass production and lean production – must be carefully scrutinised for relevance before they are taken prima facie as models for application. They may already be superseded, and may not offer the variability and agility required by any future housing industry.

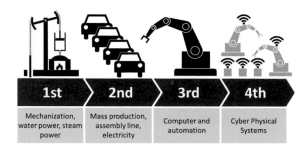

6.8   Industry 4.0 is emerging as the next phase of industrialisation, adding intelligence and connectivity to automated production systems.

A potential model comes in Industry 4.0, which we introduced in Chapter 4. Industry 4.0 is underpinned by new ideas being explored in the manufacturing industries like the now-ubiquitous connectivity of systems and devices, cloud computing, big data, and internet of things. The origins of Industry 4.0 in the car industry and large-scale manufacturing make it 'heavy' in format, big investment, large volume and globally oriented nature. It will hold great value for the giants of the construction industry. But Industry 4.0 does not represent the *only* likely option for future modes of industrial production. Where, we might ask, is *Industry Lite*?

Industry Lite, a concept we have invented here, is perhaps a reform argument to Industry 4.0, one alternative path among many that industrialised house building *could* take. If Industry 4.0 is still 'heavy', what ideas, capacity and benefits should Industry Lite have? These might include: its ability to accommodate large and small companies, that can grow slowly or rapidly; its utilisation of emerging technologies that have the potential to both redistribute industry and bring about a democratisation of its means; and it should also hold the potential for a decentralised and distributed industry implied by these techniques and technologies.

This Lite version of future industry would not require the scale of a Volkswagen, Bosch or Siemens churning out thousands of identical products (as smart as that system may be), but thousands of makers producing targeted products for specific users – as Alastair Parvin of Wikihouse puts it, 'the factory is everywhere'.[6] Such an idea could open up an opportunity for new business models in house building: low overheads could be married to real diversity and flexibility; historical geographical barriers would no longer be the impediment they once were; finally, volume and scaling would also be radically different within this model. Industry Lite might provide an alternative to Industry 4.0's handful of large companies needing to achieve high volumes, by allowing a multitude of companies to produce much lower volumes toward the same gross output.

To date, learning within the construction industry from other sectors has mainly occurred in one direction: by forward-thinking individuals and companies comparing and measuring their efforts against the seemingly constant advances of other sectors. The fusion of design value with market-oriented offerings and the development of new knowledge and thinking around lightweight and highly flexible production systems, are just two ways that Industry Lite and a newly recast mode of industrialised housing could contain valuable lessons for other industrial sectors.

6.10   The Facit 'Chassis', a custom-cut plywood structural system, is able to achieve a range of forms, be simply serviced, and achieve a high thermal, structural and acoustic performance.

Case Study Sweden: BoKlok

BoKlok is a joint venture between two of Sweden's largest and most successful companies: IKEA and Skanska. The IKEA brand has come to symbolise the democratisation of design through mass production, and the joint venture with the international construction giant Skanska appeared to have all the elements necessary to disrupt the traditional house-building industry. These expectations may have been exaggerated, but BoKlok is of interest for its focus on key markets and for the way it has organised its rigid design offerings to suit both that market and a highly refined and process-oriented production system. This has enabled BoKlok to become a market leader in the provision of key worker housing – and to deliver projects in very short timeframes.

When hearing of the joint venture between IKEA and Skanska, journalists instinctively drew parallels with IKEA's design and production techniques for flat-pack furniture.[1] Although the results of the venture have been of great interest, these reported parallels with IKEA homewares are not so straightforward. BoKlok – 'Boo-clook' for the non-Swedish speaker – literally means 'Live Wise'. The idea for the business originated in 1996, when Ingvar Kamprad, founder of IKEA, met Melker Schörling of Swedish construction giant Skanska at a housing fair to discuss a new approach to mass housing. Together they committed to create a housing product that could 'provide better homes for the many', a vision that echoes that of IKEA, and reflects the

O.1 A BoKlok module being installed. Despite the initial reaction to IKEA's involvement allowing for parallels to be drawn with their 'flatpack' furniture, the BoKlok construction system relies on a timber-framed volumetric system.

mostly social-democratic politics of Sweden and the earlier 'Million Homes Program' (see Sweden box, p.120).

BoKlok's mission is to create housing 'for people who want to live in a home of their own, but still have money left at the end of the month'.[2] This targeted statement set clear boundaries for their business model and design parameters for the anticipated product offering (see Business Models and Industrialised Construction box, p.57). Before design work could be undertaken, a finite cost structure

0.2 BoKlok's Classic offering, the 'Älmhult' range.

was established that would drive product development. An imagined, though very accurately defined, client for the initial design was invoked – a single nurse, one child, university-educated, but working for a low wage – and comprehensive modelling was undertaken to understand their typical income and spending commitments. The money they had left over for spending on housing each month became BoKlok's target price.

The early design team consisted of architect Gun Ahlström and IKEA interior designer Madeleine Nobs – who brought customer and design marketing knowledge – and Inger Olsson, a project manager from Skanska who was practised in implementing innovative concepts within traditional construction.

The first project was built in 1997, and by 1998 around 150 dwellings had been constructed. Since 2010, after a decade of proving the business concept, BoKlok has grown the business through greater integration of the value chain and more direct business strategy decisions. The company has expanded from 30 to 300 employees, while the number of projects has similarly grown from 300 units per year in 2010 to over 1000 in 2016.

Early on, the analogies of IKEA moving into construction to produce 'flat-pack' houses were true. Yet, for the most part, BoKlok has produced housing using a volumetric timber-frame construction method. Both construction methods are familiar to Swedish house builders, as the transition to timber volumetric construction mirrors developments among the nation's multi-family house builders.

BoKlok has three product offerings. The Classic, BoKlok's initial design, is very much in the Swedish 'type-house' or 'standard dwelling' tradition, with almost no option for customer choice or customisation.

The Flex provides greater design possibilities for responding to municipal planning concerns while still controlling customisation. This has increased BoKlok's market possibilities fourfold. The third offering is a terrace house, which BoKlok offers in two sizes. Customisation opportunities are limited to choices in the number of bedrooms, a gable or skillion roof and an external finish comprising timber or render finishes.

BoKlok operates across the Nordic region and the company's designs have become technically different in response to varying regulatory requirements and, to a lesser degree, local building traditions. A significant amount of work was undertaken between 2010 and 2015 to establish a 'base logic' BoKlok building system that could operate between countries, thus minimising this variation (see The Platform Approach box, p.48). BoKlok's product development platform has ensured consistency and standardisation while being finely tuned to limit customisation opportunities. This has resulted in the creation of a well-built, fundamentally well-designed, low-cost product, which supports a business model that is highly transparent to their customers.

BoKlok's product-oriented business model, as described and analysed by Jerker Lessing and Staffan Brege, relies on having a strong customer emphasis with a high level of supply chain control.[3] The sole imagined customer profile, used when BoKlok was established, is still a key part of the concept, but there is now a range of imagined customers whom BoKlok revisit and a financial model to keep cost constraints realistic and current. BoKlok's control over its supply chain has allowed the integration of product development, sales and manufacturing, reinforced by long-term relationships with external suppliers to provide a stable business foundation (see Construction Logistics and Supply Chain Management box, p.98).

0.3 The Flex offering. The Flex range offers various cladding and roof forms, adding the capacity for minimal adaption to local conditions and desires. This project is under development in Glasörten, Skåne, Sweden.

While the BoKlok business concept has undergone steady growth, the underlying vision has also evolved 'to create new sustainable homes for the many'. This reflects both IKEA's and Skanska's business visions, which emphasise sustainability and accessibility. The changing vision has also responded to the strong customer focus, which BoKlok acknowledges as essential when pursuing a product-centric business model. Customer experience is driven by a four-pronged emphasis: on low costs, both for purchase and during operation (first-home buyers); smart homes (attractive, spacious homes); sustainability (an increasing business priority); and sales experience (driven by the IKEA

0.4 BoKlok's technical platform results in an offering based on a strictly limited number of modules that can be quickly arranged into many design permutations. This capacity is a great advantage for BoKlok, allowing the company to put forward development proposals in a fraction of the time required in traditional construction projects, without foregoing certainty around costing.

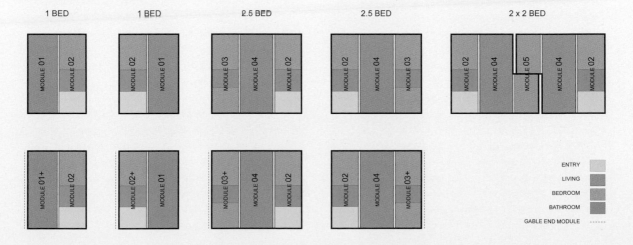

connection). This final point, the sales experience, is BoKlok's critical advantage in the market. The company is able to promote and sell the housing through IKEA – instore customers can sign up to a waiting list and are selected by a lottery. Customers are also offered interior design consultations and store credit for furnishings, adding an extra dimension to the standard sales experience and reducing the demand for customisation of the built product.

BoKlok also supports its business model through a 'cost-advantage strategy', which emphasises speed, predictability and cost control. Site choice is restricted to those that are simple. This limits town planning and design complications, allowing the concept of a project to be developed within a day and the overall development process to be realised in less than half the time typical in Sweden. In Sweden these approvals can take several years to attain, so efforts towards their reduction are of great benefit. Industrialisation of the various processes involved has also allowed construction time to be significantly shortened, while increasing predictability and standardisation. This has placed BoKlok in between the models pursued by its competitors. Some have highly industrialised processes, while others seek high levels of product standardisation – the competition rarely aims for both. The focus on cost is largely achieved through modest design choices in a clearly structured process and product development model, as well as through waste reduction and production efficiency, which have been emphasised in response to Sweden's high labour costs.

While BoKlok was conceived jointly by IKEA and Skanska, there remains a question as to the extent of IKEA's involvement in the physical product, beyond the kitchen and bathroom fittings. As a construction business, BoKlok's foundation was heavily informed by the experiences of Skanska. The design 'settings' for the product were determined by an IKEA interior designer, but the projects rolling out of the factory today say less about brand IKEA and more about typical 'Swedish' housing. This is not a criticism, rather an opportunity for future development and as yet untapped potential that arises when two highly competent and well-respected companies create a joint venture.

8 The Design and Production of Housing is an Exercise in Diversity, Not Similarity. Solutions do not Need to be Complex or 'Closed', and Technology Alone will Not Determine the Products and Outputs of Industrialised Housing Ventures

Prefab housing invokes a complex web of constraints that, if not taken properly into account, can sink new ventures. Throughout this book we have gone to great lengths to demonstrate that although prefab may have appeared as a *simple* problem it is actually much more *complex*. It is for these reasons that the design and production of industrialised housing in the future will be an exercise in diversity, not similarity.

A successful future venture in this area is more likely to revolve around solutions and processes that can produce highly customised, flexible and cost-effective solutions, but only if they respond to the full variety and specificities of housing. Thus, a technologically rich system will only succeed if it can provide truly flexible housing solutions that can accommodate different users, sites, regulations and locations.

A key piece of this puzzle is an integrated platform. This may range from a series of casual systems and processes to a fully integrated IT and technical platform controlling all inputs and outputs from the sales, design, production, installation and operational phases. What matters here is not the attainment of 'full automation' but rather the awareness of, and integration with, all the various areas relevant to a particular business model. Such a system was the promise of Blu Homes and, to a lesser degree, Wikihouse. Many successful Swedish and Japanese companies have already demonstrated the potential of integrated platforms, which take a variety of approaches suited to the particularities of their respective companies.

In working towards the new systems and platforms necessary for smooth running industrialised housing ventures, we should also be wary of repeating the overdetermination of technological solutions that have plagued the history of prefab housing. Industry 4.0 and Industry Lite, for example, are both

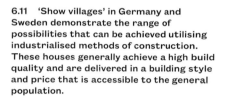

6.11 'Show villages' in Germany and Sweden demonstrate the range of possibilities that can be achieved utilising industrialised methods of construction. These houses generally achieve a high build quality and are delivered in a building style and price that is accessible to the general population.

highly reliant on new technologies. So how can they avoid the problems of the past?

Recent advances in computational design, materials science, additive and subtractive manufacturing, along with digital and automated fabrication technologies, have the combined potential to change *everything*. The path to developing and applying such technology is not straightforward, but nor is technological change an irresistible wave over which we have no agency. To date, these technologies have mostly been used in a highly experimental manner: 'the blue sky' projects to 'print' entire buildings, extreme structures for military applications, or, in the case of many architectural design applications, to carry out formal and material gymnastics intended to stretch and test the limits of imagination or to create landmark buildings. Rarely have these technologies and techniques been put to the service of solving the more prosaic problems discussed in this book – of marrying great design with efficient and quality production. The approach to the integration of technology proposed in this book will assess the value of technology not for its novelty, adherence to misplaced ideas of 'progress',

or science fictions of the 'future', but for its appropriateness in solving the significant problems of the day.

9 Understanding and Incorporating 'Design Value' is Critical to the Future Success of the Industry

A renewed focus on design will emerge from the new mix of technology, business models and recast professional roles described in this book. Quality design can help to save costs, offer more value and convenience to users and play a role in leading market expectations. Much like the success of Apple, where design is central to the ethos of the company, design can also be a lens through which to bring technological and manufacturing solutions into sharper focus, and balance consumer and technical demands. If housing is an exercise in diversity not similarity, the new processes that stand behind this shift need to be imbued with rigorous design value at every step. This would be a more harmonious fusion of conceptual and utilitarian prefab, where companies apply considerable effort to getting the balance between both modes of operation right for their target markets.

But this bright future for industrialised housing that has 'design value' at its core also has a darker, more meagre *Doppelgänger*. This alternative, shadow path is one where an ethos of *Existenzminimum* (minimally acceptable needs for living) holds sway. *Existenzminimum* suggests a future where rising

6.12 An example of Baufritz's 'Alpenchic' range. The high performance, premium construction system is highly adaptable and customisable.

costs are lowered by reducing houses to the minimum acceptable floorspace, where every fixture, finish, or material is examined and exchanged for one of lower cost. Patterns of use might be analysed to enable the bare minimum required. This would be a complete and rational system, a smooth-running machine with little room for design, artistry or expression.

This is an extreme 'lean production' version of prefab, where all processes and products are evaluated so that any waste can be excluded. Unlike auto manufacturing, in housing this approach looks rather different and even a little menacing. Value Engineering (VE) in construction is often used as a euphemism for cutting costs from a project, usually by taking out easily removed features or parts that make for large savings. Apart from removing cost, VE can also risk removing anything vaguely special from a design. Within this parallel 'dark' future for prefab there is a strong risk that, through the eyes of the value engineer, design looks like waste.

It is for these reasons that industrialised housing companies recognise the value in design, and that it be hardwired into their endeavour and not considered as an afterthought. Ultimately, this discourse around design value is also at the heart of the distinction between *conceptual* and *utilitarian* prefab, and can strike a new balance that can leverage the best of both types.

10   A Successful, Future-oriented Industrialised Housing Industry Demands New Approaches to Research and Development, Which Move from Product to Process, from Conceptual Purity to Imperfect Application

If the advances in construction outlined in this book are to be made, new approaches to R&D are required. Currently, construction has one of the lowest levels of investment in R&D of any major sector.[7] This future attitude toward R&D should reflect the particularities and specificities of housing we have discussed. The old approach – where a company starts with a stand-out idea or concept, or where a business model is parachuted in because it has worked elsewhere – should, by now, give us cause for caution.

This move is a change in focus, from a *product-driven* approach to a *process-driven* approach. Companies and individuals need to move away from a line of thinking that revolves around the strategy of the *winning product*, which, it is felt, has the power – through the sheer ingenuity of its conception – to bend the market towards it. There is nowhere more important for this lesson to be learned than in the R&D operations of such ventures.

Other parts of this changing attitude to R&D need to involve a move away from the partial-solution logic outlined in Chapter 4 towards the end-to-end, integrated solutions required to achieve innovation through application and uptake. This is perhaps best embodied through Steve Jobs' well-known maxim 'Real CEOs ship' – meaning, it is easy to be a perfectionist, or focus endlessly on details or particular parts of the problem at hand, but it is only through the act of 'shipping' or, in our case, implementing a particular solution that the full range of inputs and lessons will be learned. This is exactly the lesson that the Minimum Viable Product (MVP) teaches us. Prototype early and often, as Tim Brown has suggested, and take the product to market as soon as practically possible, avoiding at all costs R&D that is insulated from real-world conditions and problems.

Environmental Systems

Pressures on construction to become more 'sustainable' are increasing, and consumers now demand buildings that can actively save money over their life cycle through lowering energy use (see Life Cycle Analysis box, p.143). Japan is a critical case in point for this field, having one of the most developed and sophisticated markets in the world (see Japan box, p.93). In recent years the number and types of environmental systems available to the Japanese market have risen, and these systems are now widely deployed. Environmental systems play a particularly important role in industrialised house building, because, unlike other building applications, industrialised processes require a lengthy period of planning, testing and R&D before any building is constructed on site. This process is conducive to the successful integration of environmental systems into housing products, whereas traditional construction with its project-to-project approach makes such planning and pre-design testing difficult.

Japan's leading role in the development and integration of environmental systems in buildings can be traced to a series of factors, including: a large and established national prefabricated housing industry; an extensive hi-tech manufacturing base with commensurate investment in R&D; and finally, the country's peculiar climate, which offers an enormous range of climate zones from north to south, along with vast extremes in a single location, where summers are hot and humid, yet winters in the same location are sub-zero and snowy. This confluence of factors provides the foundations of an industry focused on user comfort, high-performance building systems and a culture of implementing sophisticated R&D.

Perhaps the most recognisable and now widely adopted environmental system to emerge in recent decades is the solar photovoltaic panel. Japan's leading housing manufacturers helped create a new market for residential solar photovoltaic (PV) power-generating systems, developing all-electric houses with energy fully or partially supplied by micro-power generation systems.[1] To further meet the societal demand for environmental sustainability in housing, Japanese manufacturers have successfully commercialised low energy, mass-customised homes. These peg the operating energy cost and carbon dioxide (CO_2) emissions at low or zero with the support of installed renewable-energy technologies. The companies producing these prefabricated housing products have been able to exploit the opportunity to invest in environmental systems integration precisely because of the repetitive nature of their business models. These allow for the amortisation of the heavy investment in R&D over a multi-year rollout.

For example, Sekisui Heim aims to develop a business that focuses on the production of high performance and value-added housing products that integrate their modular construction system technologies with a range of environmental systems. In April 2004, Sekisui Heim launched a new net zero-energy-cost home, called Parfait AE. Added features include: thermal barrier-free systems applied to the foundation and floors, a passive ventilation heat-blocking system for the high heat dissipation skylight, and heat-blocking screens that control the amount of sunlight. The company has also collaborated with Sumitomo Trust and Banking to develop a new housing loan that favours homebuyers who purchase a house equipped with high-capacity PV systems. Sekisui Heim explains that 'the higher the power generating capacity of [the] photovoltaic generator, the lower the loan's interest rate'.[2] The rate was estimated to go as low as 2.8 per

P.1 PanaHome City Seishin-Minami, 100
houses near Kobe. Each house is fitted with
an integrated 3kWh power system.

cent, comparing favourably with long-term fixed-rate bank loans. This industry partnership with a bank is novel, and demonstrates a commitment to addressing sustainability concerns by enhancing the economic appeal of their PV solar homes, and to providing a financial solution that enables this. With cumulative sales of over 85,000 solar homes to date, the company is widely recognised as the largest modular manufacturer of net zero-utility-cost housing in Japan.

The experience of Sekisui Heim is emblematic of many Japanese housing companies, including Sekisui House, Misawa Homes and PanaHome. Misawa Homes began research in 1980 on the development of its own zero-energy housing prototype. In 1998, it successfully developed the world's first zero-energy home – HYBRID-Z equipped with PV integrated roof systems.[3] PanaHome, formerly the National House Industrial Co. Ltd, has been operating since 1963 as a housing company within the Panasonic Group. Today, the company produces steel-frame panels that are applied to its industrialised mass custom homes through highly automated production lines. In line with this state-of-the-art automation system, the company has also been at the forefront of solar community developments (see Fig. P.1), which is not surprising given the Panasonic Group's interests in energy production and storage, along with its enormous air-conditioning presence.

The PanaHome-city Seishin Minami, a prefabricated housing estate development near Kobe, dates from 2004 and comprises over a hundred PV mass-customised homes. In 2009, the development was selected as one of 100 excellent regional projects that introduced new types of energy promoted by the Ministry of Economy, Trade and Industry, and the New Energy and Industrial Technology Development Organization. PanaHome then developed the 'Casart' range of zero-energy housing from joint industry-academic research projects: these integrate passive design with solar panels, a home management system and a lithium-ion fuel cell.

A similar case is that of Sanyo Homes, established in 1969 as Kubota House. The company's core business concept of 'Eco & Safety' aims to enhance their housing performance in terms of local power generation, energy efficiency, and earthquake resistance and emergency measures. The company is thriving from having integrated SANYO HIT solar cells in its mass custom homes. These cells have the world's highest energy conversion efficiency of 23 per cent. Sanyo Homes also integrates solar water-heating panels into its houses along with an air-source heat pump that aims to control and secure the supply of domestic hot water regardless of the weather conditions.

P.2 Sekisui House's first zero CO_2 emission house, launched at the 2008 G8 Summit.

Sekisui House (see Box) is committed to developing zero-carbon-emission housing based on the company's Action Plan 20, which aimed to introduce a variety of energy-efficient housing measures.[4] In conjunction with the G8 Hokkaido Toyako Summit held in July 2008, Sekisui House announced their Zero Emission House (see Fig. P.2). This single-storey steel-structure prefabricated house had a

P.3 An example of Sekisui Heim's sub-floor climate control system, utilising the thermal energy stored in the site installed concrete slab and trapped under their volumetric installations, then circulated and vented by duct work.

P.4   A range of organisations in Japan are involved in the research and development of innovative technology in response to environmental concerns. Here, the Taisei Corporation's Technology Centre in Yokohama utilises their own integrated Solar PV glass units on the facade.

total floor area of approximately 200m² and featured a 14.5kWp capacity photovoltaic power generation system, energy-efficient lighting, a household fuel cell and energy-saving domestic appliances.

Today, Sekisui House markets a house called Green First Hybrid, which is equipped with an integrated roof tile/PV panel, and a fuel cell in addition to a lithium-ion battery, with an energy storage capacity ranging from 4.6kWh to 9.3kWh. The house is also designed so it can import electricity from an electric car parked at the house, which could be used, for example, in the case of a blackout. The company claims that the daily electricity use of a house can be covered by the electricity imported from an electric car with a 24kWh energy storage battery.

In addition to implementing passive-design techniques for the reduction of domestic energy demand and active renewable-energy technologies for micro-power generation, Japanese housing manufacturers have demonstrated a leading advantage in the implementation of environmental systems. Energy efficiency is promoted by installing home energy management systems (HEMS) in prefabricated homes. HEMS help visualise domestic energy use and power generation patterns and manage the energy consumption of electrical appliances in the home. With Google's investment in home technologies, such as Nest, it seems that increased integration of environmental systems and their control in homes is inevitable. Decades of attention to these areas in Japan mean that Japan's housing manufacturers are technically capable of delivering net zero energy housing, thereby positioning the industry to meet the nation's housing code mandating zero net energy, which will come into effect by 2020.

Life Cycle Analysis

Buildings are responsible for significant energy consumption and the consequential generation of greenhouse gas (GHG) emissions. Existing buildings consume more than 40 per cent of the world's total primary energy and account for 24 per cent of global carbon dioxide (CO_2) emissions. Against a background of climate change and global warming, it is important to attempt to reduce the energy use and carbon footprint in buildings. Because of the heavy emphasis on planning, design and logistics at the beginning of the process, industrialised house building has a unique opportunity to capture a large portion of the benefits of life cycle analysis, especially when compared to traditional design and construction practices.

The ideas behind life cycle analysis (LCA) emerged in the late 1960s through forerunners such as resource environmental profile analyses (REPAs).[1] Initially LCA focused on energy analysis due to oil shortages, with multi-criteria systematic analysis increasing by the mid-1980s.[2] Early methods only considered the embodied energy in the materials, or the energy needed during the operational phase of a building's life cycle, but in recent decades these phases have been progressively expanded to include the manufacturing phase, construction phase, maintenance, end-of-life and all interrelated transportation.

Other factors were eventually added to the LCA method. Cradle-to-grave analysis includes all phases of a product's life – the extraction of raw materials, the production of components and related materials, their use and maintenance, and waste removal or recycling.[3] LCA is often considered as a cradle-to-grave approach in the evaluation of environmental performance. Today there is a growing body of literature comparing the energy and carbon embodied in buildings that use different construction systems and alternative materials. Reducing the energy demand and CO_2 emissions attributed to buildings is an important goal for government climate policy.[4]

The most critical decisions regarding building efficiency in terms of minimising life cycle environmental impacts and energy consumption are often made at the beginning of the design process. Early decisions thus significantly influence the life cycle energy performance of the building (see Fig. Q.2). The availability of data in the initial stages of design is a major problem for designers. A huge amount of data and a certain degree of expertise in the field are required to carry out LCA. Furthermore, building plans, including details of external walls, partitions, slabs, roof, as well as the selected cladding system, need to be well defined if LCA is to be carried out accurately upfront. Figure Q.3 illustrates the most effective parameters for a building's LCA.

There are a number of software tools to help architects and building designers quantify a building's

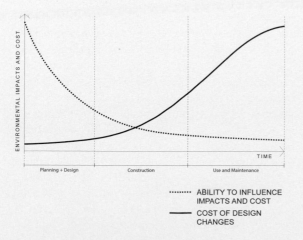

Q.1   Design-decision making has a greater impact at the beginning of the project. This key advantage meshes well with the process behind industrialised construction methods, which require substantial upfront design and planning.

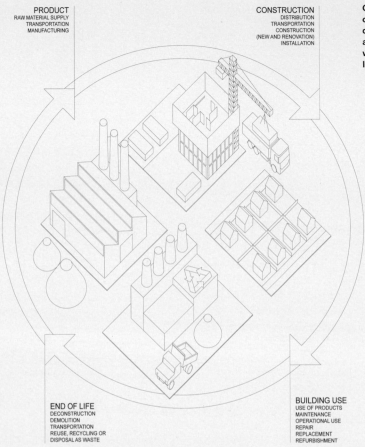

PRODUCT
RAW MATERIAL SUPPLY
TRANSPORTATION
MANUFACTURING

CONSTRUCTION
DISTRIBUTION
TRANSPORTATION
CONSTRUCTION
(NEW AND RENOVATION)
INSTALLATION

END OF LIFE
DECONSTRUCTION
DEMOLITION
TRANSPORTATION
REUSE, RECYCLING OR
DISPOSAL AS WASTE

BUILDING USE
USE OF PRODUCTS
MAINTENANCE
OPERATIONAL USE
REPAIR
REPLACEMENT
REFURBISHMENT

Q.2 An holistic consideration of construction expands the realm of the design team from a building's construction and use to include the impacts associated with sourcing of materials and their end of life processing.

environmental impact. However, the data-intensive nature of these software platforms and the traditional LCA method can make them uneconomical, inaccessible and too time-consuming for designers, particularly in the early design stage when the building form and fabric are fluid.[5] Conventional buildings involve a complex process from the multi-stage conceptualisation, programming, preliminary design and final design to construction. As a result, architects, designers and engineers rarely employ these powerful software platforms in the design of traditional buildings due to their complexity and their requirement of highly detailed inputs that are usually only available once the design phase is complete.

Prefabricated, modular, or industrialised building provides a unique opportunity to quantify and qualify all the design priorities relevant when designing an LCA-friendly building (see Integrated Building Performance box, p.84). The individual modules or components of a building, which are made in a factory and then transported to construction sites for final assembly, emerge only after a long pre-design process. This has the potential to allow more time and effort for energy- and material-efficient design during the architectural and design decision-making stages. Collecting life cycle inventory data for numerous materials and processes is cost-effective in an industrialised building context as it can be amortised and repeated over a large number of installations, projects and individual buildings.[6]

Industrialised building methods make environmental performance improvements possible for every phase of a building's life cycle from manufacturing to the end of life. The major phases for consideration are:

1. Construction phase

The longer early design phase of prefabrication enables designers to apply quantitative and qualitative analysis of material selection, which results in the application of more environment-friendly materials. Moreover, material selection can be prioritised with the aid of LCA tools. The multi-functionality in the building's envelope system can integrate the complex piping systems for solar thermal panels, natural ventilation, HVAC and energy management, or any other specific technical requirements. The overall cost-effectiveness will very likely increase as a consequence, particularly if compared to traditional, one-off building. Importantly, the development of models and construction technologies can lead to decreased carbon emissions by optimising raw materials in the manufacturing process.[7]

2. Use Phase

In operational and maintenance phases, several positive benefits can be achieved by using prefabrication systems. Supervised factory conditions, quality controls and more precise production processes lead to a better build quality, resulting in reduced operational energy demands during the use phase and lower maintenance costs. In addition to new building modules or components, the application of prefabricated modular systems to retrofitting existing buildings can significantly increase a building's thermo-acoustic performance, and minimise the usual disturbances of conventional building refurbishment.

3. Disposal Phase

The positive impact of waste reduction achieved by prefabrication is an area of growing research interest, where some energy-efficient solutions are only possible within a more industrialised approach to design and construction (see Design for Disassembly box, p.106). One study from Hong Kong shows a saving in construction waste of up to 52 per cent.[8] Figure Q.3 highlights some of the prefabrication benefits for various phases of a building's life cycle in terms of reducing environmental impacts.

Off-site and industrialised methods of construction have an important role to play in improving the environmental impact of construction, despite the challenges that exist in measuring the difference in impact compared to traditional methods.[9] The provision of LCA-friendly buildings is a major challenge in both developing and industrialised countries. Addressing climate change and other environmental issues is an important and urgent objective for the construction industry, especially in a context where most industrialised nations are moving towards mandating net zero-energy buildings by 2030–50.

MINIMISING ENVIRONMENTAL IMPACT:

CONSTRUCTION (MANUFACTURING / ON-SITE)	OPERATION + MAINTENANCE	DISPOSAL
PRECISE CUTTING + MEASURING Less waste material Less transportation	MATERIAL THERMAL PROPERTIES ASSESSMENT	ON-SITE DISMANTLING POSSIBILITY
STORE IN CONTROLLED ENVIRONMENT Less waste material Less material damage	BETTER AIR TIGHTNESS MINIMISE THE REPLACEMENT IMPACTS	MODULAR DESIGN Maximises the possibility of reusing
FASTER CONSTRUCTION TIME Less on-site opertation energy demands		INDUSTRIALISED ASSEMBLY PROCESS Maximises the capability of recycling
INTEGRATE ALL INSULATION LAYERS Less material consumption		

Q.3   Processes of industrialised construction, shown here in three phases of building construction, operation, and disposal, can have clear and beneficial impacts on a building's life cycle cost, and help reduce its environmental impact.

6.13   In Los Angeles, the Star Apartments
provide housing to 100 formerly homeless
tenants. Designed by Michael Maltzan
Architecture, the apartments were
commissioned by the Skid Row Housing
Trust and built using a volumetric system
which stacks the apartments over an
existing two-storey structure which
was redesigned to provide community
facilities.

Conclusion

The chief aims of this book are to show the promise of prefab, the complexities standing behind it, and to sketch out potential paths through this uneven, rocky landscape. We have argued that it is only through a deeper understanding of this complexity that we can avoid the wrong thinking of past failed ventures. Likewise, the multifactorial interdependencies at play in housing and the attempts to industrialise it must be taken into account if lasting or substantial innovation is to be made. We illustrated this complexity in the form of a meta-structure or total pattern of operations at the end of Chapter 5, which, if grasped, can help analyse problems and unlock new potential. In pursuing these objectives, through both traditional scholarship and applied research with industry, new ways of thinking about problems have emerged. We think this will also benefit other areas beyond our immediate study of industrialised house building.

Our book has also attempted to address some of the widespread misconceptions in the field. We need to acknowledge, once and for all, that despite some lofty claims and a handful of high-performing companies, prefab has never really lived up to its expectations. To unlock its future potential we need to adopt a different mindset. This should aim to restore the balance between process and product, content and form, prose and poetry, and substance and style. It is a mindset that places more value on understanding the problem than finding stand-out (though off-target) solutions, and values results and service over ideas and concepts. And finally, it points to a greater historical awareness and argues for a criticality towards the sparkle of the new.

We cannot predict the future. But we hope to put forward a framework to help our readers navigate a viable path in the direction of the future.

The key questions in this process become: How do we bring utilitarian and conceptual prefab into a more productive harmony? How should we channel our efforts to put invention at the service of innovation? Is there a place for poetry among the prosaic worlds of housing and construction? And where is the happy medium between problem solving and solution finding? Answers do not come easily, but we hope it is of some comfort to note that our future view of industrialised housing is not reached by one path available only to a select few. Like the golf course metaphor, there are many paths and many possible outcomes.

Each path involves a series of complex and inter-related trade-offs. Every process needs a product and every product needs a process. Likewise, utilitarian prefab would be a monstrosity, a modern-day Frankenstein, were it not for the redeeming qualities of conceptual prefab. Industry would be meaningless if it delivered no value to its customers. And so, our discussion of product and process returns to and can be informed by other classic dichotomies and their inherent tensions and potentials. The balance between art and science, architecture and building, technology and culture.

Notes

1 Introduction

1 Residential design and construction has not only remained relatively stable but has shown little improvement in productivity. See Ryan E. Smith's *Prefab Architecture*, Chapter 4, 'Principles', for discussion of construction productivity in the United States, which decreased between 1964 and 2004 while other industries more than doubled. This experience is mirrored in Australia; Will Chancellor notes construction productivity has remained close to stagnant there between the mid-1980s and 2012. Other reports, such as the UK's Egan report, noted that productivity in the UK construction industry had actually *increased* faster than the economy as a whole, but also noted that there was room for improvement and learning from other sectors. For reasons that will become clear below, we think that, owing to the complexities of the industry, this data needs to be assessed within a wider context. See Ryan E. Smith, *Prefab Architecture: A Guide to Modular Design and Construction* (Hoboken, NJ: John Wiley, 2010); Will Chancellor, 'Drivers of Productivity: A Case Study of the Australian Construction Industry', *Construction Economics and Building* 15, no. 3 (2015): 85–97; and John Egan, *Rethinking Construction* (London: HMSO, 1998).

2 Gilbert Herbert, *The Dream of the Factory-Made House* (Cambridge, MA: MIT Press, 1984), 3.

3 Walter Gropius, 'Gropius at Twenty-Six', *Architectural Review* 773, no. 130 (1961): 50.

4 Burnham Kelly, *The Prefabrication of Houses: A Study by the Albert Farwell Bemis Foundation of the Prefabrication Industry in the United States* (Cambridge, MA: MIT Press, 1951), 4.

5 Smith, *Prefab Architecture*, xi.

6 Chris Knapp, 'The End of Prefabrication', *Australian Design Review* (October 2013), http://www.australiandesign-review.com/features/35295-the-end-of-prefabrication.

7 Allison Arieff, *Prefab* (Salt Lake City: Gibbs Smith, 2002), 4.

8 Allison Arieff, 'Prefab Lives!', *The New York Times*, 23 May 2013, http://opinionator.blogs.nytimes.com/2013/05/23/prefab-lives/?_r=0.

2 Foundations in Literature

1 TalkBack Productions (UK), *Grand Designs*, 'The Computer-cut House, Hertfordshire', Season 12 (2012), Episode 2; TalkBack Productions (UK), *Grand Designs*, 'Customised German Kit House: Revisited', Season 8 (2008), Episode 9.

2 Arnt Cobbers, Oliver Jahn and Peter Gössel (eds.), *Prefab Houses* (Cologne: Taschen, 2010); and Loft

Publications (eds.), *Prefab Architecture* (Barcelona: FKG, 2012).

3 For a commentary on Japanese mass-produced prefabricated housing, see Mathew Aitchison, '20 Shades of Beige: Lessons from Japanese Prefab Housing', *The Conversation*, 1 October 2014, https://theconversation.com/20-shades-of-beige-lessons-from-japanese-prefab-housing-31101 (accessed 9 May 2017).

4 Allison Arieff, 'Prefab, Proven', *Dwell*, 19 October 2009, https://www.dwell.com/article/prefab-proven-30e7a2c0 (accessed 27 October 2016).

5 Joseph Tanney and Robert Luntz, *Modern Modular: The Prefab Houses of Resolution: 4 Architecture* (New York: Princeton Architectural Press, 2013). Many thanks to Joe Tanney for speaking with me during the research for this book.

6 A selected bibliography of these works includes: Kelly, *The Prefabrication of Houses*; Arthur Bernhardt, *Building Tomorrow: The Mobile/Manufactured Housing Industry* (Cambridge, MA: MIT Press, 1980); Herbert, *The Dream of the Factory-Made House*; Arieff, *Prefab*; Colin Davies, *The Prefabricated Home* (London: Reaktion, 2005); and Barry Bergdoll and Peter Christensen, *Home Delivery: Fabricating the Modern Dwelling*, ed. Ron Broadhurst (New York: Museum of Modern Art, 2008).

7 Jerker Lessing, 'Industrialised House-building: Concept and Processes' (Licentiate Thesis: Lund University, 2006); Carina Unger, 'Industrialised House Building: Fundamental Change or Business as Usual?' (PhD Thesis: Royal Institute of Technology, Stockholm, 2006); Jerker Lessing and Staffan Brege, 'Business Models for Product-oriented House-building Companies – Experience from Two Swedish Case Studies', *Construction Innovation* 15, no. 4 (2015): 449–72; Staffan Brege, Lars Stehn and Tomas Nord, 'Business Models in Industrialized Building of Multi-storey Houses', *Construction Management and Economics* 32, nos. 1–2 (2014): 208–26.

8 Gustav Jansson, 'Platforms in Industrialised House-Building' (PhD Thesis: Luleå University of Technology, 2013); Henric Jonsson and Martin Rudberg, 'Classification of Production Systems for Industrialized Building: A Production Strategy Perspective', *Construction Management and Economics* 32, nos. 1–2 (2014): 53–69; Patrik Jensen, 'Configuration of Platform Architectures in Construction' (PhD Thesis: Luleå Technical University, 2014).

9 Gunnar Asplund, Wolter Gahn, Sven Markelius, Gregor Paulsson, Eskil Sundahl and Uno Ahren, *Acceptera* (Stockholm: Tiden, 1931).

10 Carl Ekbrant, *Miljonprogrammet i bostadsbyggandet: fortsättningen på 1946 års program* (Gävle: Swedish Institute for Building Research, 1983).

11 Helena Lidelöw, Dan Engström, Jerker Lessing and Lars Stehn, *Industriellt husbyggande* (Lund: Studentlitteratur, 2015).

12 Kurt Junghanns, *Das Haus für alle: zur Geschichte der Vorfertigung in Deutschland* (Berlin: Ernst und Sohn, 1994).

13 Shigeaki Iwashita, 'Production Integration in Japanese Housing', *Habitat International* 14 (1990): 235–43; James Barlow and Ritsuko Ozaki, 'Building Mass Customised Housing through Innovation in the Production System: Lessons from Japan', *Environment and Planning A* 37, no. 1 (2005): 9–20; Tomonari Yashiro, 'Conceptual Framework of the Evolution and Transformation of the Idea of the Industrialization of Building in Japan', *Construction Management and Economics* 32, nos. 1–2 (2014): 16–39; Masa Noguchi, 'The Effect of the Quality-Oriented Production Approach on the Delivery of Prefabricated Homes in Japan', *Journal of Housing and the Built Environment* 18, no. 4 (2003): 353–64.

14 Ikebe Yo (ed.), *Product Development of Housing Industry* (Kashima: Kashima Laboratory Publishing Association, 1971) Japanese language.

15 David M. Gann, 'Construction as a Manufacturing Process? Similarities and Differences between Industrialized Housing and Car Production in Japan', *Construction Management and Economics* 14, no. 5 (1996): 437–50; James Barlow et al., 'Choice and Delivery in Housebuilding: Lessons from Japan for UK Housebuilders', *Building Research & Information* 31, no. 2 (2010): 134–45; William Johnson, 'Lessons from Japan: A Comparative Study of the Market Drivers for Prefabrication in Japanese and UK Private Housing Development' (Master's Thesis, University College London, 2007).

16 Robert Kronenburg, *Architecture in Motion: The History and Development of Portable Building* (London: Routledge, 2014); Arieff, *Prefab*; Arieff, 'Prefab Lives!' See also Sherri Koones' 'Prefabulous' range of publications, for example: Sherri Koones, *Prefabulous Small Houses* (Newtown, CT: The Taunton Press, 2016); Sheri Koones, *Prefabulous + Sustainable: Building and Customizing an Affordable, Energy-Efficient Home* (New York: Harry N. Abrams, 2010).

17 Andreas Vogler, *The House as a Product* (Amsterdam: IOS Press, 2015); Sergi Costa Duran, *New Prefab* (Barcelona: Loft, 2008); Mark Anderson and Peter Anderson, *Prefab Prototypes: Site-specific Design for Offsite Construction* (New York: Princeton Architectural Press, 2006).

18 Stephen Kieran and James Timberlake, *Refabricating Architecture: How Manufacturing Methodologies are Poised to Transform Building Construction* (New York: McGraw-Hill, 2004).

19 Robert Corser (ed.), *Fabricating Architecture: Selected Readings in Digital Design and Manufacturing* (New York: Princeton Architectural Press, 2010); Branko Kolarevic (ed.), *Architecture in the Digital Age: Design and Manufacturing* (New York: Spon Press, 2003); Fabio Gramazio, Matthias Kohler and Jan Willmann, *The Robotic Touch: How Robots Change Architecture* (Zürich: Park Books, 2015); Alfredo Andia and Thomas Spiegelhalter, *Post-Parametric Automation in Design and Construction* (Norwood, MA: Artech House: 2015); Thomas Bock and Thomas Linner, *Robotic Industrialization: Automation and Robotic Technologies for Customized Component, Module, and Building Prefabrication* (Cambridge: Cambridge University Press, 2015).

20 Mark Lawson, Ray Ogden and Chris Goodier, *Design in Modular Construction* (Boca Raton, FL: CRC Press, 2014); Gerald Staib, Andreas Dörrhöfer and Markus Rosenthal, *Components and Systems: Modular Construction – Design, Structure and New Technologies* (Basel: Birkhäuser, 2013); Ulrich Knaack, Sharon Chung-Klatte and Reinhard Hasselbach, *Prefabricated Systems: Principles of Construction* (Basel: Birkhäuser, 2012); Cornelia Dörries and Sarah Zahradnik, *Container and Modular Buildings: Construction and Design Manual* (Berlin: DOM Publishers, 2016); Leonard R. Bachman, *Integrated Buildings: The Systems Basis of Architecture* (New York: John Wiley & Sons, 2003).

21 Nick Blismas (ed.), *Off-site Manufacture in Australia: Current State and Future Directions* (Brisbane: Cooperative Research Centre for Construction Innovation, 2007); Robert Hairstans, Sean Smith, Fausto Sanna and Russell MacDonald, *Strategic Review of the Offsite Construction Sector in Scotland Summary Report* (Edinburgh: The Scottish Government, 2013), available at http://www.gov.scot/ Resource/0041/00415799.pdf (accessed 9 May 2017); Mark Phillipson, *DTI Construction Industry Directorate Project Report: Current Practice and Potential Uses of Prefabrication* (Watford, UK: Building Research Establishment, 2003); National Audit Office, *Using Modern Methods of Construction to Build Homes More Quickly and Efficiently* (London: UK Government, 2005).

22 Robert Hairstans, *Building Offsite: An Introduction* (Edinburgh: Edinburgh Napier University, 2014), available at http://www.buildoffsite.com/content/uploads/2015/06/ Building_Offsite_An_Introduction.pdf (accessed 9 May 2017); Hairstans et al., *Strategic Review of the Offsite Construction Sector in Scotland*; The National Audit Office, *Using Modern Methods Of Construction to Build Homes More Quickly and Efficiently* (London: UK Government, 2005); Ryan E. Smith, *Permanent Modular Construction: Process, Practice, Performance* (Charlottesville, VA: Modular Building Institute, 2015); The Modular Building Institute, *Improving Construction Efficiency & Productivity with Modular Construction* (Charlottesville, VA: Modular Building Institute, 2015); Andrew Hartley and Alex Blagden, *Current Practices and Future Potential in Modern Methods of Construction* (Oxford: Waste & Resources Action Programme, 2007); Harvey Bernstein, John Gudgel and Donna Laquidara-Carr, *Prefabrication and Modularization: Increasing Productivity in the Construction Industry* (Bedford, MA: McGraw Hill Construction, 2011); The Boston Consulting Group, *Shaping the Future of Construction: A Breakthrough in Mindset and Technology* (Geneva: World Economic Forum, 2016); Grant Daly, *Prefabricated*

Housing Australia: Skill Deficiencies and Workplace Practice (Camberwell, Vic.: International Specialised Skills Institute, 2009).

23 Kelly, *The Prefabrication of Houses*.

24 Albert Farwell Bemis and John Ely Burchard, *The Evolving House*, 3 vols (Cambridge, MA: The Technology Press, MIT, 1936). After Bemis' death in 1936, Burchard had been the first director of the housing research centre at MIT that had been funded by the foundation established by Bemis' family in 1938. Kelly took over the directorship of the centre from Burchard in 1945, which he held until 1960.

25 Kelly, *The Prefabrication of Houses*, xi. Italics by the authors.

26 Bernhardt, *Building Tomorrow*.

27 ibid., 503.

28 Arthur D. Bernhardt, 'The Building Sector Tomorrow, or Mobile Homes – A Housing Alternative', R.O. Smee Memorial Lecture, 28 June 1977. A copy of Bernhardt's lecture in Australia is held by Sydney University Library.

29 Gilbert Herbert, *Pioneers of Prefabrication: The British Contribution in the Nineteenth Century* (Baltimore, MD: Johns Hopkins University Press, 1978); and Herbert, *The Dream of the Factory-Made House*.

30 Davies, *The Prefabricated Home*.

31 ibid., 69–87.

32 Bergdoll and Christensen, *Home Delivery*.

33 Barry Bergdoll, 'Home Delivery: Viscidities of a Modernist Dream from Taylorized Serial Production to Digital Customization', in Bergdoll and Christensen, *Home Delivery*, 12–26.

34 Smith, *Prefab Architecture*.

35 Burchard in Kelly, *The Prefabrication of Houses*, x.

3 Utilitarian Prefab, Conceptual Prefab, or a Third Way

1 See Herbert, *Pioneers of Prefabrication*; and Judith Ainge, 'Walls of Iron: Nineteenth Century Prefabricated Iron Buildings in Australia' (PhD dissertation, University of Sydney, 2017).

2 Mathew Aitchison, 'Back to the Future: FIFO, Mining and Urbanisation in Australia', in *Out of Place: Occasional Essays on Australian Regional Communities and Built Environments in Transition: Gwalia*, eds Philip Goldswain, Nicole Sully and William M. Taylor (Crawley, WA: UWA Publishing, 2014), 267–301; Mathew Aitchison, 'Dongas and Demountables: Four Observations Concerning Prefabricated Housing', in *Proceedings of the Society of Architectural Historians, Australia and New Zealand: 31, Translation*, ed. Christoph Schnoor (Auckland: SAHANZ and Unitec ePress; and Gold Coast, Qld: SAHANZ, 2014): 401–11; Mathew Aitchison, 'The Experience of Australian Mining: Buildings, Planning and Urbanization', in *The Architecture*

of Industry: Changing Paradigms in Industrial Building and Planning, ed. Mathew Aitchison (Farnham: Ashgate, 2014), 163–94.

3 Ben Slee, 'Improving the thermal performance of the New South Wales Demountable Classroom: A design-led research thesis' (PhD dissertation, University of Sydney, 2017).

4 Of this project, Le Corbusier wrote:
My intention was to illustrate how, by virtue of the selective principle (standardization applied to mass-production), industry creates pure forms; and to stress the intrinsic value of this pure form of art that is the result of it. Secondly to show the radical transformations and structural liberties reinforced concrete and steel allow us to envisage in urban housing – in other words that a dwelling can be standardized to meet the needs of men whose lives are standardized. And thirdly to demonstrate that these comfortable and elegant units of habitation, these practical machines for living in, could be agglomerated in long, lofty blocks of villa-flats. The 'Pavillon de l'Esprit Nouveau' was accordingly designed as a typical cell-unit in just such a block of multiple villa-flats.
Extract from Le Corbusier, *Oeuvre complète*, volume 1, 1910–29, 104.

5 See the chapter on 'Authorship', in Davies, *The Prefabricated Home*, 88–106.

6 Manfredo Tafuri, *Architecture and Utopia: Design and Capitalist Development* (Cambridge, MA: MIT Press, 1976).

7 Elsewhere, some of us have speculated in regard to the culture of these disciplines. See Mathew Aitchison and John Macarthur, 'Prefabricated Housing in Architectural Culture', in *Offsite Architecture: Constructing the Future*, eds Ryan E. Smith and John D. Quale (Abingdon: Routledge, 2017), 77–89.

8 Paul Adamson and Marty Arbunich, *Eichler: Modernism Rebuilds the American Dream* (Salt Lake City: Gibbs Smith, 2002); Paul Adamson, 'California Modernism and the Eichler Homes', *The Journal of Architecture* 6, no. 1 (2001): 1–25; Annmarie Adams, 'The Eichler Home: Intention and Experience in Postwar Suburbia', *Perspectives in Vernacular Architecture 5, Gender, Class, and Shelter* (1995): 164–78.

9 Walter Isaacson, *Steve Jobs* (London: Little Brown, 2011), 6.

10 See discussion in Chapter 1 of Gropius' 1910 proposal.

11 As Herbert's *The Dream of the Factory-Made House* is still the best account of this pivotal moment in the history of large-scale prefabrication in English-speaking, industrialised countries, it remains the key text for the following discussion.

12 Konrad Wachsmann, *Wendepunkt im Bauen* (Dresden: Verlag der Kunst, 1989).

13 Herbert, *The Dream of the Factory-Made House*, 243–45.

14 ibid., xii–xiii.

15 For a more recent account of the historical and creative context of the Packaged House and its reliance on systems theory and problems around closed building systems in the mid-twentieth century, see: Alicia Imperiale, 'An American Wartime Dream: *The Packaged House* System of Konrad Wachsmann and Walter Gropius,' in, *Offsite: Theory and Practice of Architectural Production*, eds Ryan E. Smith, John Quale, and Rashida Ng (Proceedings of the ACSA conference in Philadelphia, Fall 2012): 39–43.

16 Herbert, The *Dream of the Factory-Made House*, 307.

17 ibid., 308–9.

18 ibid., 307.

19 ibid., 310.

20 ibid., 302.

21 ibid., 321.

22 ibid., 323.

23 For a discussion of the Lustron company see Herbert, *The Dream of the Factory-Made House*, 321–23.

24 ibid., 321–23.

25 ibid., 238.

4 Barriers to the Uptake and Success of Prefab Housing

1 David Donnison, *The Government of Housing* (Harmondsworth: Penguin, 1967), 294, cited in Barry Russell, *Building Systems, Industrialization, and Architecture* (London: John Wiley and Sons, 1982), 187.

2 Donnison, *The Government of Housing*, 294.

3 Refer to note 1 in Chapter 1 regarding stagnant productivity in the construction sector.

4 See, for example, Herbert, *Pioneers of Prefabrication*.

5 This territory has been explored by others; see Staib, Dörrhöfer and Rosenthal, *Components and Systems*; Hairstans, *Building Offsite*.

6 Terminology translation also accessed from the Japan Prefabricated Construction Suppliers and Manufacturers Association website: http://www.purekyo.or.jp/structure.html (accessed 21 March 2017).

7 Lessing, 'Industrialised House-building'; Brege, Stehn and Nord, 'Business Models in Industrialized Building of Multi-storey Houses'.

8 With thanks to Dan Engström and Helena Lidelöw for discussion of Swedish construction terminology and culture.

9 https://www.bluhomes.com/fact-sheet (accessed 13 January 2017).

10 See, for example, capital raised: in 2012, https://www.bluhomes.com/news/press-release/blu-homes-raises-25-million-in-additional-capital; in 2013, https://www.bluhomes.com/news/press-release/blu-homes-raises-over-65-million; in 2015, https://www.bluhomes.com/news/press-release/blu-homes-raises-additional-35-million-meet-demand-its-premi-um-prefab-homes (accessed 13 January 2017).

11 https://www.bluhomes.com/our-vision (accessed 13 January 2017).

12 See Alastair Parvin, *Architecture for the people, by the people* (TED Talk, 2013), Online video, 13:11, https://www.ted.com/talks/alastair_parvin_architecture_for_the_people_by_the_people (accessed 13 January 2017).

13 Although the explosion of interest in digital and automated fabrication in this decade precludes identifying any definitive 'origin' for these techniques, a notable figure in the field has been Professor Larry Sass of MIT, seen in his contribution to MoMA's 2008 exhibition 'Home Delivery'.

14 These issues are canvassed in detail in Mathew Aitchison, 'A House is not a Car (Yet)', *Journal of Architectural Education* 71, no. 1 (2017): 10–21.

15 We expect that new industrialised housing ventures will set about emulating what Industry 4.0 has done for the Volkswagen Group. See Volkswagen Group, 'Industry 4.0 in the Volkswagen Group', *YouTube*, 20 August 2015. https://www.youtube.com/watch?v=JTl8w6yAjds (accessed 27 July 2016).

16 For a summary overview of the Japanese industry, see Aitchison, '20 Shades of Beige'.

17 Smith, *Prefab Architecture*, 64.

18 Greg Pasquarelli, Presentation at '*Risk*', National Architecture Conference. Australian Institute of Architects, 14–16 May 2015.

19 Barlow et al. define a range of customisation options that typically exist in industrialised house building operations. Using Japan as an example, their study reveals that the results of 'customisation' are limited. They use other terms to describe this: 'segmented standardization', 'customized standardization', and 'tailored customization'. See James Barlow, Paul Childerhouse, David Gann, Severine Hong-Minh, Moh Naim and Ritsuko Ozaki, 'Choice and Delivery in Housebuilding: Lessons from Japan for UK Housebuilders', *Building Research & Information* 31, no. 2 (October 2010): 134–45.

20 https://theconversation.com/what-construction-jobs-will-look-like-when-robots-can-build-things-63263 (accessed 23 March 2017); Thuy Duong Oesterreich and Frank Teuteberg, 'Understanding the Implications of Digitisation and Automation in the Context of Industry 4.0: A Triangulation Approach and Elements of a Research Agenda for the Construction Industry', *Computers in Industry* 83 (2016): 121–39; Thomas Bock and Silke Langenberg, 'Changing Building Sites: Industrialisation and Automation of the Building Process', *Architectural Design* 84, no. 3 (2014): 88–99.

21 Dan Engström and Lars Stehn, 'Design Creating Value for Systems Building of Housing', *Construction Innovation* 14, no. 2 (2014): 138–44.

22 US Department of Housing and Urban Development, *HUD – Manufactured Housing and Standards – Alternative*

Construction Introduction, https://portal.hud.gov/hudpor-tal/HUD?src=/program_offices/housing/rmra/mhs/faqs (accessed 6 February 2017); Hairstans, *Building Offsite*.

5 A Problem-Solving Approach for Industrialised House Building

1 The Australian government, for example, has developed a six-digit Field of Research (FoR) code classification system. There are 22 broad areas and several hundred subsections under these. See http://www.abs.gov.au/Ausstats/abs@.nsf/latestproducts/6BB427AB9696C-225CA2574180004463E?opendocument (accessed 18 January 2017).

2 Horst W.J. Rittel and Melvin M. Webber, 'Dilemmas in a General Theory of Planning', *Policy Sciences* 4 (1973): 155–69.

3 David Adams, 'The "Wicked Problem" of Planning for Housing Development', *Housing Studies* 26, no. 6 (2011): 951–60.

4 Compare, for example, the Japanese companies Misawa and Sekisui House. Each company has a different construction system to the other, and, in the case of Sekisui House, multiple construction systems within the same company. Similarly, compare the big Swedish and Norwegian companies Peab, BoKlok, NCC, and Veidekke. Each company has a radically different construction system, which uses different materials. See, Duncan W. Maxwell and Mathew Aitchison, 'Lessons from Sweden: How Australia Can Learn from Swedish Industrialised Building', Proceedings of the *2016 Modular and Offsite Construction Summit* (Edmonton: University of Alberta, 2016), 190–97.

5 Kelly, *The Prefabrication of Houses*, xi.

6 Michael Gibbons, Camille Limoges, Helga Nowotny, Simon Schwartzman, Peter Scott and Martin Trow, *The New Production of Knowledge: The Dynamics of Science and Research in Contemporary Societies* (London: Sage, 1994).

7 ibid., vii.

8 See Murray Fraser (ed.), *Design Research in Architecture: An Overview* (Abingdon: Routledge, 2013). See also Mathew Aitchison, 'Design Research in Architecture: An Overview' (Book Review), *The Journal of Architecture* 21, no. 2 (2016): 308–312.

9 Tim Brown, *Change by Design: How Design Thinking Transforms Organizations and Inspires Innovation* (New York: Harper Collins e-books, 2009).

10 Roger Martin, *The Opposable Mind: Winning Through Integrative Thinking* (Boston: Harvard Business School Press, 2007).

11 For the Theory of Constraints, see Eliyahu M. Goldratt and Jeff Cox, *The Goal: A Process of Ongoing Improvement*, 2nd ed. (Aldershot: Gower, 1993).

12 Clayton M. Christensen, *The Innovator's Dilemma: When New Technologies Cause Great Firms to Fail* (Boston, MA: Harvard Business Review Press, 1997).

13 Much closer to the original disruptive innovation is Uber's 'ride share' modality. Ride share, like carpooling, offers less 'convenience' because it is neither a direct route nor entirely private. Yet ride share offers these services at radically lower prices than its conventional taxi replacement. Greg Lindsay, 'What if Uber kills off public transport rather than cars?', *The Guardian*, 13 January 2017, https://www.theguardian.com/sustainable-business/2017/jan/13/uber-lyft-cars-public-transport-cities-commuting (accessed 23 March 2017).

14 Herbert, *The Dream of the Factory-Made House*, 321.

15 Bernhardt, *Building Tomorrow*, quoted in Herbert, *The Dream of the Factory-Made House*, 321.

16 Davies, *The Prefabricated Home*, 85.

6 Prefab Housing and the Future of Building

1 See section 2.8 in Richard and Daniel Susskind, *The Future of the Professions: How Technology will Transform the Work of Human Experts* (Oxford: Oxford University Press, 2015).

2 Disclosure: Mathew Aitchison and the Innovation in Applied Design Lab at the University of Sydney is carrying out a research project with Lendlease and its subsidiary DesignMake in this area. Many thanks to Daryl Patterson for his support and advice throughout the preparation of this book.

3 Kelly, *The Prefabrication of Houses*, xi.

4 See Simon Sinek, *Start with Why: How Great Leaders Inspire Everyone to Take Action* (New York: Penguin, 2011).

5 See special in the *Harvard Business Review*, April 2016, 'How Platforms Are Reshaping Business'. Many thanks to David Hartigan for passing on this article and for the discussion of pipeline vs platform business approaches.

6 Parvin, *Architecture for the people, by the people*. See also the concept by Swedish giant, Skanska, of Flying Factories: Tom Ravenscroft, 'Skanska's "flying factories" take off in Slough', *CM Newsletter*, 2 October 2015, http://www.constructionmanagermagazine.com/on-site/has-skanska-se2en-fu3ture-offsite-slo2ugh/ (accessed 24 March 2017).

7 The 2016 EU Industrial R&D Investment Scoreboard shows that of the top 2500 R&D investors globally, 69 (2.8%) were from the construction sector, with their investment totalling €11billion of a €696billion total (equal to 1.6%, despite construction totalling around 10% of global GDP) http://iri.jrc.ec.europa.eu/scoreboard16.html (accessed 10 March 2017).

Notes for Text Boxes

Assembly and Construction Methods for Industrialised House Building

1 Louis Sullivan, 'The Tall Office Building Artistically Considered', *Lippincott's Magazine*, March 1896. Le Corbusier, *Vers une architecture* (Towards an Architecture), originally published in *L'Esprit nouveau*, 1923.

2 See, for example, Gustav Jansson, 'Platforms in Industrialised House-Building' (doctoral dissertation, Luleå University of Technology, Sweden, 2013).

3 For a longer glossary of terms, please see: http://www.forestryscotland.com/media/320961/building_offsite_an_introduction.pdf (accessed 10 May 2017).

4 N. John Habraken, 'Open Building as a Condition for Industrial Construction', *ISARC2003 The Future Site*, Eindhoven, 21–24 September 2003, 37–42, https://pure.tue.nl/ws/files/2466647/570755.pdf (accessed 16 May 2017).

Digital and Automated Fabrication

1 Nick Dunn, *Digital Fabrication in Architecture* (London: Laurence King Publishing, 2012), 20.

2 Karl L. Wildes and Nilo A. Lindgren, *A Century of Electrical Engineering and Computer Science at MIT, 1882–1982* (Cambridge, MA: MIT Press, 1985); Luca Caneparo, *Digital Fabrication in Architecture, Engineering and Construction* (New York: Springer, 2013).

3 William J. Mitchell, *Computer-Aided Architectural Design* (New York: Van Nostrand Reinhold, 1979).

4 Y. Miyatake, 'Smart System: A Full Scale Implementation of Computer Integrated Construction', in *The 10th International Symposium on Automation and Robotics in Construction (ISARC '93)*, Houston, 1993.

5 Lisa Iwamoto, *Digital Fabrications: Architectural and Material Techniques, Architecture Briefs* (New York: Princeton Architectural Press, 2009).

6 Rohana Mahbub, 'An Investigation into the Barriers to the Implementation of Automation and Robotics Technologies in the Construction Industry' (PhD Thesis, Queensland University of Technology, 2008).

7 Joshua Bard, Madeline Gannon, Zachary Jacobson-Weaver, Michael Jeffers, Brian Smith and Mauricio Contreras, 'Seeing Is Doing: Synthetic Tools for Robotically Augmented Fabrication in High-Skill Domain', in *ACADIA 14: Design Agency, Proceedings of the 34th Annual Conference of the Association for Computer Aided Design in Architecture (ACADIA)*, Los Angeles, 2014.

8 Branko Kolarevic, *Architecture in the Digital Age: Design and Manufacturing* (New York: Spon Press, 2003).

9 Fabio Gramazio, Matthias Kohler and Jan Willmann, *The Robotic Touch: How Robots Change Architecture* (Zurich: Park Books, 2014); Behrokh Khoshnevis, 'Automated Construction by Contour Crafting: Related Robotics and Information Technologies', *Automation in Construction* 13, no. 1 (2004): 5–19.

USA

1 This is supported by a discrete building regulation, the Housing and Urban Development Code (HUD Code c. 1976), which is distinguished by reduced quality standards and inclusion of a permanent wheeled chassis for ease of transport.

2 Modular Building Institute, *Permanent Modular Construction Annual Report 2011*, http://www.modular.org/documents/document_publication/2011permanent.pdf (accessed 22 December 2016).

3 See NRB Inc. in Pennsylvania (https://www.nrb-inc.com), and Silvercreek Industries in California (http://silver-creek.net).

4 See SCRA *Oversize/Overweight Permit Manual*, compiled October 2012, http://permits.scranet.org/wp-content/uploads/2012/10/SCRA_PM_1012.pdf.

5 The Modular Building Institute (http://modular.org) and the National Institute of Building Sciences, Off-site Construction Council (http://www.nibs.org/oscc) over the past few years have produced industry and market research to fill this void, but there is much more to be gathered and analysed.

6 http://www.modular.org.

7 'PMC Summary', *Modular Advantage* vol. 3Q (August 2016): 38.

8 *Permanent Modular Construction Annual Report 2014*, 18.

9 Ryan E. Smith, Peter L. Gluck, Chris Sharples, Mimi Hoang and James Garrison, 'New York Modular', *Journal of Architectural Education* 71, no. 1 (2017): 109–17.

10 'Prefab, Proven', *Dwell Magazine* 5, no. 2 (December 2014): 113–23.

11 Dennis R. Michaud, 'Foldable Building Units', US Patent No. 8,739,475 B2, 3 June 2014; Elizabeth Rothwell, Kevin Deng and Dennis Michaud, 'Buildings Formed from Complementary Building Modules, and Methods for Building Same', US Patent Application 13/877,096, filed 30 September 2011.

12 Jared Levy and Gordon Stott, 'Modular Housing', US Patent Application US 2011/0162293 A1, 7 July 2011.

13 http://www.may8consulting.com/pub_14.html.

14 The many bespoke modular builders for high-end residential include Method Homes (Seattle), Living Homes (Los Angeles) and Irontown Homes (Salt Lake City). The mayors of San Francisco and Boston encourage modular construction in their cities.

The Platform Approach

1 Alvin P. Lehnerd and Marc H. Meyer, *The Power of Product Platforms* (New York: Simon and Schuster, 1997), 2.

2 W.L. Moore, J.J. Louviere and R. Verma, 'Using Conjoint Analysis to Help Design Product Platforms', *Journal of Product Innovation Management* 16, no. 1 (1999): 29; Javier P. Gonzalez-Zugasti, Kevin N. Otto and John D. Baker, 'Assessing Value in Platformed Product Family Design', *Research in Engineering Design* 13, no. 1 (12 July 2001): 30.

3 Timothy W. Simpson, Jonathan R. Maier and Farrokh Mistree, 'Product Platform Design: Method and Application', *Research in Engineering Design* 13, no. 1 (27 July 2001): 2–22.

4 David Robertson and Karl Ulrich, 'Planning for Product Platforms', *Sloan Management Review* 39, no. 4 (July 1998): 19–31.

5 Patrik Jensen, 'Configuration of Platform Architectures in Construction' (Luleå Technical University, 2014), http://urn.kb.se/resolve?urn=urn:nbn:se:ltu:diva-26587.

6 Gustav Jansson, 'Platforms in Industrialised House-Building' (Luleå University of Technology, 2013), http://urn.kb.se/resolve?urn=urn:nbn:se:ltu:diva-18777.

7 Gustav Jansson, Helena Johnsson and Dan Engström, 'Platform Use in Systems Building', *Construction Management and Economics* 32, no. 1 (February 2014): 70–82.

8 Jerker Lessing, 'Industrialised House-Building: Concept and Processes' (Department of Construction Sciences, Lund University, 2006), http://lup.lub.lu.se/record/929318.

9 Christian Thuesen and Lars Hvam, 'Efficient On-Site Construction: Learning Points from a German Platform for Housing', *Construction Innovation* 11, no. 3 (2011): 338–55.

10 Marshall Van Alystne, Geoffrey G. Parker and Sangeet Paul Choudary, 'Pipelines, Platforms, and the New Rules of Strategy', *Harvard Business Review* 94, no. 4 (April 2016): 54–62.

Business Models and Industrialised Construction

1 Charles Baden-Fuller and Mary S. Morgan, 'Business Models as Models,' *Long Range Planning* 43, no. 2 (2010): 156–71; Alexander Osterwalder and Yves Pigneur, 'Clarifying Business Models: Origins, Present and Future of the Concept', *Communications of the Association for Information Systems* 16, no. 1 (2005): 1–25.

2 The first evaluation of business models in the context of industrialised building in Sweden is Staffan Brege, Lars Stehn and Tomas Nord, 'Business Models in Industrialized Building of Multi-storey Houses', *Construction Management and Economics* 32, nos. 1–2 (2014): 208–26.

3 Jerker Lessing and Staffan Brege, 'Business Models for Product-oriented House-building Companies – Experience from Two Swedish Case Studies', *Construction Innovation* 15, no. 4 (2015): 449–72.

4 Brege, Stehn and Nord, 'Business Models in Industrialized Building'.

5 Matilda Höök, Lars Stehn and Staffan Brege, 'The Development of a Portfolio of Business Models: A Longitudinal Case Study of a Building Material Company', *Construction Management and Economics* 33, no. 5–6 (2015): 334–48.

6 Jerker Lessing, Lars Stehn and Anders Ekholm, 'Industrialised House-building – Development and Conceptual Orientation of the Field', *Construction Innovation* 15, no. 3 (2015): 378–99.

7 Lessing and Brege, 'Business Models for Product-oriented House-building Companies'.

8 Helena Johnsson, 'Production Strategies for Pre-engineering in Housebuilding: Exploring Product Development Platforms', *Construction Management and Economics* 31, no. 9 (2013): 941–58.

9 John Henrik Meiling, Marcus Sandberg and Helena Johnsson, 'A Study of a Plan-Do-Check-Act Method Used in Less Industrialized Activities: Two Cases from Industrialized Housebuilding', *Construction Management and Economics* 32, no. 1–2 (2014): 109–25.

10 Gustav Jansson, Helena Johnsson and Dan Engström, 'Platform Use in Systems Building', *Construction Management and Economics* 32, no. 1–2 (2014): 70–82.

11 Höök, Stehn and Brege, 'The Development of a Portfolio of Business Models'.

12 Mattias Hallgren, Jan Olhager and Roger G. Schroeder, 'A Hybrid Model of Competitive Capabilities', *International Journal of Operations & Production Management* 31, no. 5 (2011): 511–26.

Case Study USA: Simplex Homes

1 This section draws on research undertaken from 2009 to 2016 that includes a media literature review of Simplex Homes, multiple factory visits and interviews with factory personnel and partnering architect Joseph Tanney of Resolution: 4 Architects in New York City. See Ryan E. Smith, *Prefab Architecture: A Guide to Modular Design and Construction* (Hoboken, NJ: John Wiley & Sons, 2010), 258–62; and Ivan Rupnik, 'Mapping the Modular Industry', in *Offsite Architecture: Constructing the Future*, eds Ryan E. Smith and John D. Quale (Abingdon: Routledge, 2017), 70–91.

2 These dimensions are outlined in a Simplex Homes design parameters sheet provided by Jason Drouse, Multi-Family and Commercial Accounts Manager for Simplex Industries, Inc., June 2016.

3 See http://www.simplexhomes.com/about-us.asp for more information on sister and affiliate companies to Simplex Homes.

4 See http://www.simplexhomes.com/Bio-Patrick_Fricchione_Jr.asp (accessed 20 December 2016).

Notes

Computational Design

1 Christopher Alexander, *Notes on the Synthesis of Form* (Cambridge, MA: Harvard University Press, 1964); Doug Lea, 'Christopher Alexander: An Introduction for Object-Oriented Designers', *Software Engineering Notes* 19, no. 1 (1994): 39–46.

2 George Stiny and James Gips, 'Shape Grammars and the Generative Specification of Painting and Sculpture', in *IFIP Congress 71*, Ljubljana, Yugoslavia, 1971.

3 Larry Sass and Marcel Botha, 'The Instant House: A Model of Design Production with Digital Fabrication', *International Journal of Architectural Computing* 04, no. 4 (2006), 109–23.

4 Jon Broome, 'The Segal Method: Special Issue', *Architect's Journal* 183, no. 45 (1986): 31–68.

5 Kostas Terzidis, *Algorithmic Architecture* (Oxford: Routledge, 2006).

6 Robert Doe and Mathew Aitchison, 'Multi-Criteria Optimisation in the Design of Modular Homes – from Theory to Practice', paper presented at the 33rd Annual Conference of Education Research in Computer Aided Design in Europe (eCAADe15), Vienna University of Technology, Austria, 2015.

7 Daniel Davis, Jane Burry and Mark Burry, 'Untangling Parametric Schemata: Enhancing Collaboration through Modular Programming', in *Designing Together – CAAD Futures 2011* (Liège: Les Editions de l'Université de Liège, 2011).

8 Robert Aish, 'DesignScript: Scalable Tools for Design Computation', in *eCAADe31* (Delft, Netherlands, 2013).

9 Mario Carpo, *The Alphabet and the Algorithm* (Cambridge, MA: MIT Press, 2011).

10 Patrik Jensen, Thomas Olofsson and Helena Johnsson, 'Configuration through the Parameterization of Building Components', *Automation in Construction* 23 (2012): 1–8.

Integrated Building Performance

1 Sir Ove Arup, 'The Key Speech', 9 July 1970. http://publications.arup.com/publications/o/ove_arups_key_speech (accessed 16 May 2017).

Japan

1 According to a housing survey conducted in 1997 by the Government Housing Loan Corporation in Japan, the average initial cost of a conventional home was estimated at 175,404 JPY per square metre and a prefabricated home was at 190,033 JPY per square metre. See Masa Noguchi, 'The Effect of the Quality-oriented Production Approach on the Delivery of Prefabricated Homes in Japan', *Journal of Housing and the Built Environment* 18, no. 4 (2003): 353–64.

2 James G. Sackett, *Japan's Manufactured Housing Capacity: A Review of the Industry and Assessment of Future Impact on the U.S.* (Saint Louis: Energy Design Resources, 1986).

3 Japan Prefabricated Construction Suppliers and Manufacturers Association (JPA), *Japan Prefabricated Construction and Suppliers and Manufacturers Association* (Tokyo: JPA), http://www.purekyo.or.jp.

4 ibid.

5 Masa Noguchi, 'Enhancement of Industry Initiative through the Zero-energy Mass Custom Home Mission to Japan Experience towards Commercialisation', *International Journal of Mass Customisation* 4, no. 1/2 (2011): 106–21.

6 Masa Noguchi and Avi Friedman, 'Manufacturer-User Communication in Industrialised Housing in Japan', *Open House International* 27, no. 2 (2002): 21–29.

7 See note 1 above.

Construction Logistics and Supply Chain Management

1 Christine M. Harland, 'Supply Chain Management: Relationships, Chains and Networks', *British Journal of Management* 7, no. s1 (1996): S63–S80; Douglas M. Lambert and Martha C. Cooper, 'Issues in Supply Chain Management', *Industrial Marketing Management* 29, no. 1 (2000): 65–83.

2 Martin Christopher, *Logistics and Supply Chain Management*, 4th ed. (Edinburgh Gate: Prentice Hall, 2011); John T. Mentzer, William DeWitt, James S. Keebler, Soonhong Min, Nancy W. Nix, Carlo D. Smith and Zach G. Zacharia, 'Defining Supply Chain Management', *Journal of Business Logistics* 22, no. 2 (2001): 1–25.

3 Council of Supply Chain Management Professionals (CSCMP), *Supply Chain Management Definitions and Glossary*, 2013, http://bit.ly/1sYBIlP (accessed 26 February 2016).

4 Vrijhoef and Koskela identified four roles. Ekeskär and Rudberg later refined these definitions and added a fifth role. See Ruben Vrijhoef and Lauri Koskela, 'The Four Roles of Supply Chain Management in Construction', *European Journal of Purchasing & Supply Management* 6, no. 3–4 (2000): 169–78; and Andreas Ekeskär and Martin Rudberg, 'Third-party Logistics in Construction: The Case of a Large Hospital Project', *Construction Management & Economics* 34, no. 3 (2016): 174–91.

5 Micael Thunberg and Fredrik Persson, 'Using the SCOR Model's Performance Measurements to Improve Construction Logistics', *Production Planning and Control* 25, no. 13 (2014): 1065–78; Micael Thunberg, Martin Rudberg and Tina Karrbom-Gustavsson, 'Categorising On-site Problems: A Supply Chain Management Perspective on Construction Projects', *Construction Innovation: Information, Process, Management* 17, no. 1 (2017): 90–111.

client interaction 59
climate change 143, 145
climate control system, subfloor *141*
closed system 90–1
CNC (computer numerically controlled) cutting files *34*
CNC (computer numerically controlled) equipment 33
CNC (computer numerically controlled) machining 77
CNC (computer numerically controlled) plywood carcass, assembly of *71*
colonial settlements 37
Colonial Settlers hut 22
Columbus, Ohio 55
commercial modular construction 41
commonality 25
community developments 117
competence extension 60
competence redeployment 60
complete pattern 29, 102, 113
Component Manufacture and Sub-assembly (CM&SA) production system 100
component standardisation 94
computational design 33, 75–7, 137
'computerised design' 76
conceptual prefab 37, 43–5, 71–2, 137, 138, 147
concrete 28, 88, 122
concrete-based medium-rise building systems 28
concrete base with infill wall 26
concrete column joint 109
concrete hollow decks 28
concrete house, single-pour *44*
concrete sandwich panel *26*
concrete systems 40
Connect Homes 41–2
connectivity 126, 131
consistency 134
construction and infrastructure consultancies 124
construction phase 145
construction project domain *58*, *59*
construction subsidies 122
construction system, Lindbäcks 118
construction timeframes 128, 129
construction waste, reduction 116
Contour Crafting process 36
contractors 121
Cornerstone Building Solutions 68
cost 53–4, 89–90, 122, 124, 125, 129; BoKlok homes 133–4, 135, 136; and *Existenzminimum* 138
cost-advantage strategy 136
cost efficiency 60
cost–performance housing 116
cost-performance marketing and sales strategy 96
cradle-to-grave analysis 143
cross-laminated timber 28, *87*
Crowther, Philip 109
customer experience 135

customer profile 134
customer service 116
customisation 13, 78–80, 100, *101*, 116, 134, 136
cut-sheet algorithm 34, 82

Daiwa House 93, 94
Dassault 77
Davies, Colin 31, 44, 74, 111
Deluxe Building Systems 42
demountable school classrooms 38
design 122, 133, 136, 143–4
design-build contracts 121
designers 92
design flexibility 118
Design for Disassembly 106–10
design research 103, 104
design thinking 103
design value 132, 137–8
detached houses 115
developers 87
digital technologies 33–6, 50, 70, 72, 137
'Dilemmas in a General Theory of Planning' (Rittel and Webber) 98
disciplines 92
disposal phase 145
'disreputable' form 119
disruption 110
disruptive innovation 106, 110–11, 119, 125
distinctiveness 25
diversification 69
diversity 80, 132, 136
domestic energy demand, reduction of 142
domestic hot water 141
'Donga' camps 38
Donnison, David 61, 62
dormitories 69
downturns 130
The Dream of the Factory-Made House: Walter Gropius and Konrad Wachsmann (Herbert) 31, 51–2
drywall 72
Dualit toaster *107*
Dwell 15, 22, 22–3, 41, 43; 'Home Design Invitational' 23
Dymaxion House *43*

'Eco & Safety' 141
'Ecocapsule' *43*
economic benefit 129
Edison, Thomas 44
efficiency 63, 136
efficiency capability 60
Eichler houses 46, 47, *47*, 51
Eichler, Joseph 47
Ekbrant, Carl 24
electricity imported from an electric car 142
Electrolux 121

the 'ends' 2, 45, 92, 104, 112, 113, *114*
ends and means 64–5, 70, 72, 97, 104
energy 96, 140, 141; efficiency 127, 129, 142; reduction of demand 142; use 86, 143
energy cells *116*
energy conversion efficiency 141
engineering capability 59
engineers 86, 87
En L'An 2000 – Chantier de construction électrique (Villemard) 33, *34*
entrepreneurs 92
environmentally sound construction 123
environmental performance 13, 144–5
environmental systems 139–42; of Sekisui House *117*
environment, impact on 106–7
Ericsson 121
European Commission 106–7
European Eastern Bloc countries 88
European regulations 88
The Evolving House (Bemis and Burchard) 29
Existenzminimum 137–8

Fachidiot 97
Facit 'Chassis' *132*
Facit Homes 36, *131*
factory automation 115
factory-built housing 16
family homes 27–8
FC+Skanska Modular 42
Fertighaus 64
finance 89; risks 82–3
fire 86
fire safety 84
fire testing conducted on cross-laminated timber 87
The Fisher Island House, New York *18*
flat-pack furniture 133
flat-pack houses 134
flat-pack systems 15, 25, 26, 27
Fleetwood, Western Australia 37, *38*
The Flex 134, 135
flexibility 25, 60, 101, 109, 118, 132, 136
floors 26, 122
folding technology 41, 65
Forest City Realty Trust 42
Foster and Partners 33
Frazer, John 76
free-bearing floor elements 26
Fricchione, Patrick Jr 66, 69
Fuller, Buckminster 43, 106
functionalist movement 23
Futuro 43

G8 Hokkaido Toyako Summit, 2008 141
Gehry, Frank 33
Gehry Technologies 35

General Motors 48, 74
General Panel Company 31, 46, 51–6, 64, 70; test house 52
German language 64
Germany 24, 28, 50, 122, 137
Gibbons, Michael 102
Gidoni, Elsa 53
Gips, James 76
Glasörten, Skåne, Sweden 135
golf 115
Google 142
Gothenburg, Sweden 26
The Government of Housing (Donnison) 61, 62
Grand Designs 21
Grasshopper 77
green building 96; *see also* environmental systems
greenfield housing estates 88
Green First Hybrid 142
Green First Zero 116
greenhouse gas (GHG) emissions 143
Gropius, Walter 14, 54, 64, 111; and the Packaged House 31, 51, 52, 53, 56

Haney, Bill 41
Das Haus für alle: Zur Geschichte der Vorfertigung in Deutschland (Junghanns) 24
HEMS (home energy management systems) 142
'The Henry Ford Syndrome' 13, 15, 74, 92
Herbert, Gilbert 31, 51, 52–5, 82, 102, 111, 113; and analogy to car manufacturing 13, 15, 74, 92
high-rise, multi-family structures 121
high-rise timber buildings 28
hingeing 65, 70
holistic approach 105
home amenities experience studio 117
Home Delivery exhibition, MoMA, New York, 2008 110, *127*
Home Delivery: Fabricating the Modern Dwelling (Bergdoll and Christensen) 31–2
Hong Kong 145
horizontal integration *124*
hot water, domestic 141
House 55 competition 94
housing: shortage 121, 122; Swedish *120*
housing affordability 42, 93, 118, 127–9
Housing and Urban Development Code (HUD Code)/ US 66
Housing and Urban Development, Department of (HUD)/US 29
housing estate development 140–1
housing markets, volatility 91
housing pods *14*
Houston, Texas 129
How Buildings Learn (Brand) 109
Huf Haus system 27, *28*

Hurricane Katrina *127*
Husqvarna 121
hybrids 27
HYBRID-Z 140

IBC Type II 40
IBC Type V 40
IKEA 121, 133, 134, 135–6
indoor construction 15
industrial designers 92
industrialised construction 57–60, 145
industrialised house building: 24–8, 31, 58–9, 60, 136
industrialiserat byggande 63
Industriellt byggande 63
Industriellt Husbyggande 24
Industry 4.0 *131*, 131, 132, 136–7
Industry Lite 131–2, 136–7
in-line production platforms 40–1
in-line technique 67
innovation 62, 70, 72, 81, 82, 120, 138, 147;
    disruptive 106, 110–11, 119, 125; in Japan 95;
    at Sekisui House 115; at Simplex Homes 69;
    in Sweden 121, 123
innovation accounting 104, 105
The Innovator's Dilemma (Christensen) 110
in-situ casting 122
'Instant House' 76
integrated building performance 84–6
integrated platforms 136
integrated solutions 138
integration mechanisms 60
Intellectual Property (IP) 90–1
internal spaces 65
invention 15, 70, 72, 147
iPhone 119

Japan 24, 29, 33, 63, 74, 78, 93–6;
    environmental systems 139–42;
    Sekisui House 50, 74, 78, 115–17
Japanese Lightweight Iron Construction Association 93
jidoka 78
Jobs, Steve 51, 138
Jonsson, Henric 99
JPA (Japanese Prefabricated Construction Suppliers
    and Manufacturers Association) 94, 95
Junghanns, Kurt 24

Kafka's Castle 76, *76*, 77
Kamprad, Ingvar 133
Kaufmann, Michelle 65
Kelly, Burnham 16, 29, 32, 63, 82, 102, 113, 125
key worker housing 133
Kieran, Stephen 29, 32, 110
Kieran Timberlake Architects 109–10
Kings Road House 75

kit 15
Knapp, Chris 16
knowledge 97–8, 132
knowledge-based engineering (KBE) 77
knowledge production 102–3
Kobe 140
kogyo-ka jutaku 63
komponent 63
Komponenttillverkning 63
konkurito 63
konkurito-kei purehabu jutaku 63
Koones, Sheri 29
Kronenburg, Robert 29
Kubota House 141
Kvillebäcken, Gothenburg, Sweden 26

labour: costs 136; displacement of 35; nature of 83;
    skilled 37
lamella 87
landmark studies 28–9, 31–2
'layered' design strategy 109
layers, shearing 109, *110*
lean production 63, 74, 93, 138
*The Lean Startup: How Constant Innovation Creates
    Radically Successful Businesses* (Ries) 104
Le Corbusier 25, 44, 45
Lendlease 124
Lessing, Jerker 134
Levy, Jared 41–2
life cycle analysis (LCA) 143–6
Lindbäcks Bygg AB 27, 28, 118; factory *26*
load-bearing walls 26
loans for houses with PV systems 139–40
Loblolly House 109
location 89
logistics 98–101
Long Island, NY 12
loose fit 80–1
Los Angeles 146; Star Apartments *42*, *146*
Low-Income Housing Tax Credit (LIHTC) 129
low-rise, multi-family houses 121
Lucas Valley, California 47
Lustron company 54, 55–6
Lustron Home/House *54*, 55
Lynn, Greg 33

Maison Metropole 43
Maison Tropicale 43
'Man Camps' 38
Manning, John 22
Manning Portable Colonial Cottage 22
Mansfield University of Pennsylvania 69
manufactured housing industry *39*, 39–42
manufacturer-direct 41
manufacturers 41

margins 125
marketing and sales strategy 96
market knowledge 59
market position 58, 59
markets, new 110, 111
Mars *14*, 14, 38
Martin, Roger L. 103
Marywood University 69
mass customisation 13, 16, 94, 140–1
mass housing 38, 133
mass production 16, 133
materials: reuse 108, 109; shortages of 37
materials science 137
MBHA (Modular Home Builders Association) 41
MBI (Modular Building Institute) 40, 41
MB platform *79*
McCarthy, Maura 41
the 'means' 64, 90, 104, 113, 114
means and ends 64–5, 70, 72, 97, 104
medium-rise buildings 28
Melbourne 73
Melbourne, bishop 14
meta-structure 111–13, 114, 147
Michael Maltzan Architecture 146
Midget House 93, *93*
mid-rise construction 42, 66, 69
Miljonprogrammet (The Million Homes Program) 24, 63, 88, 121–2
Minimum Viable Product (MVP) 138
mining 38
mining company site 37
mining village *38*
Misawa Homes 94, 140
Misawa House *96*
MIT *127*
Mitchell, William 33
Mitsui Home 94
mobile/manufactured home industry 16, *30*, 37, 40, 55, 111, 118–19; and Bernhardt 29–31; US 39, 41, 88
Mode 1 102
Mode 2 102–3
Modernism 24–5, 52, 121, 122
Modern Modular 41, 68
'mod-pod' *128*, 129
Modular Construction Code, draft (Australia) 88
Modularer Baukasten (MB, or Modular Building Block System) *48*, 48–9, 100
modular housing 18, 39–42, 66–9, 75, 129
modularisation 15, 79
modular service pods *128*
modular volumetric system 94
mokushitsu-kei purehabu jutaku 63
MoMA 31, *127*
montage 63
monteringsbyggande 63

motion tracking 35
mottainai 63
Muji: 'Vertical House' *10*; website *126*
multi-criteria optimisation 77
multi-family housing 28, 121–2, 123
multi-residential housing 27, 28, 115, *118*, 128
multi-storey timber building system 77
multi-unit mid-rise construction 42, 66, 69
MVP (Minimum Viable Product) 104, 105
My Micro, New York *42*, 42

NADAA 35
Nagoya, Japan 96
nARCHITECTS 42
'Nattoku Kobo' 117
natural resources 106–7
NCC 26
Nehemiah Housing Development Fund Company Inc. 42
neighbourhood cohesion 127, 129
Nest 142
Netflix 111
net zero-energy buildings 145
net zero-energy housing 140, 142
Neutra, Richard 53
New Orleans *127*
New South Wales 38
New York 12, 18, 35, 78, 79; My Micro and The Stack *42*
Nobs, Madeleine 134
North America 38, 39–42, 64–5, 66–9, 70
Norway 122
Notes on the Synthesis of Form (Alexander) 75–6

object-oriented programming 76
offering 58
off-site assembly/construction/manufacturing/ production 15, 63, 88, 100, 101, 145
Ohio 55
Olsson, Inger 134
online platforms *126*, 126
on-site assembly/construction/manufacturing/ production 27–8, 63, 100, 101
on-site installation of volumetric modules *42*
open building systems 28, 90–1
operational platform 58, 59
Operation Breakthrough 39–40
The Opposable Mind: Winning Through Integrative Thinking (Martin) 103
overheads 91, 132

packaged homes 15
the Packaged House 31, 51, *51*, 52–3, *53*, 56, 81–2
PanaHome 94, 140–1; City Seishin-Minami *140*
Panasonic Group 140
panelised system 94

'Parametricism' 76–7
parametric modelling 77
Parfait AE 139
partial solutions 81–2, 92, 138
Parvin, Alistair 70, 132
path dependency 25, 126
pattern of operations 29
patterns 111–14, 147
Patterson, Daryl 152
Pavillon de l'Esprit Nouveau 44, *45*
Peab PGS 100, 101
Pennsylvania 41
Pennsylvania State University 69
performance 95
permanent modular construction (PMC) 40
Peter Gluck Architects 42
Philadelphia 42
*Pioneers of Prefabrication: The British Contribution in the
    Nineteenth Century* (Herbert) 31
Pipe House 93
Piteå, Sweden *26, 28*
planelement 63
planelementtillverkning 63
planets 38
planning regulations 88–9
plasterboard 72, 119
plasterers 36
'Platform Manager' 50
platforms 48–51, 126, 134, *135*, 136
platform-thinking 48, 50, 126
Poing, Germany 28
pollution 109
popular literature 20–2
Porsche 49
portable housing 15–16
'A Portable Town for Australia' *14*
post and beam system 94
post-war mass-housing schemes 88
pre-built housing 15
precast concrete building systems 88
precast concrete technology 121
precedents 106
predictability 86, 136
*Prefab Architecture: A Guide to Modular Design and
    Construction* (Smith) 16, 32
Prefab Architecture (Loft Publications) 22
Prefab (Arieff) 16
Prefab Houses (Cobbers, Jahn and Gössel) 22
'Prefab Lives!' (Arieff) 16
The Prefabricated Home (Davies) 31
Prefabrication and Pre-assembly (PF&PA) 100
Prefabrication and Sub-assembly (PF&SA) 100
The Prefabrication of Houses (Kelly) 29, 32
pre-made housing 15
price points 90, 91, 92, 118

problem-oriented approach 45
problem solving 92, 103, 104–6, 110–11
process-based approach 83
process domain 58
process-driven approach 80, 138
'Process Owner' 50
procurement capabilities 59
product-centric business model 135
product development model/platform 134, 136
product domain 58, *59*
product-driven approach 80, 138
production efficiency 136
*The Production of New Knowledge: The Dynamics of
    Science and Research in Contemporary Societies*
    (Gibbons et al.) 102
production/process platform 58
production systems 132
product-oriented business model 134
product/production platform 58, 59
product quality 95
product standardisation 100, *101*
professions 92, 119
profitability 25
project management systems 83
project managers 87
project production 57
project-to-project approach 83
proprietary building system 90–1
prototyping 103
Prouvé, Jean 43, 106, 110
public safety 83
pure customisation 100
purehabu jutaku 63
pure standardisation 100
PV integrated roof systems 140
PV mass-customised homes 139–42

quality 93, 95, 124, 125
quality control accreditations 116
quality standards 116

R&D 91, 104, 138; Blu Homes 65, 70; General Panel
    Company 54; Japan 24, 139; Problem A 110;
    Sekisui House 116; and vertical integration 124
'R4' project 2
Rathenau, Emil 14
recycling 109, 110, 116
Red Hook, Brooklyn 77
reductive approach 105
Refabricating Architecture (Kieran and Timberlake) 29,
    110
regulation 88–9
rehabilitation 129
reliability 95
relocatable modular construction 40

renewable-energy technologies 139–40, 142
renovation 129
rental housing units *128*
repetition 25, 86
reports 29
reputation 88, 93, 95
research: architectural 121; and industry 123;
    see also R&D
Resolution: 4 Architecture (RES 4) 18, 23, 41, 68
resource deployment 57
resource environmental profile analyses (REPAs) 143
resources, natural 106–7
reuse of materials 108
revolution 61–2
R.HOUSE 2
Rice Building Workshop 128, 129
Ries, Eric 104
risks 82–3, 91
Rittel, Horst 98, 102
robotics 33, 34, 36, 94
roof cassettes 122
roof forms 135
roof systems, PV integrated 140, 142
Rudberg, Martin 99
rural areas 122

SAAB 121
safety risks 82, 83
sales experience 135–6
sales strategy 96
Sandvik 121
San Francisco 79
SANYO HIT solar cells 141
Sanyo Homes 141
Sass, Larry 76, 127
scaling 79, 91, 92, 132
Scandinavia 23; *see also* Sweden
Scania 121
Schindler, Rudolph 75
school classrooms, demountable 38
Schörling, Melker 133
Schumacher, Patrik 76–7
Scotland 2
SCRA Oversize/Overweight Permit Manual 40
scripting 34
Seat 49
second-home market 68
Segal, Walter 76
Seishin Minami 140–1
Sekisui Chemical Co. Ltd 115
Sekisui House/Heim 50, 74, *80*, 93, 94, *94*, 115–17, 139–40,
    141–2; display home *115*; factory 95; 'Slow and
    Smart' 78, 91, 130; zero emission house 116, *141*,
    141–2
service pods 27

settings 113, *114*
shape grammars 76
Shawood timber construction system *117*
shearing layers 109, *110*
sheet material 34
Sheetrock 72
Shimizu SMART system 33
Shizuoka factory 115
SHoP Architects 35, 42, 77, 78, 119
'show villages' *137*
similarity 80, 136
Simplex Homes 41, 66–9, *69*
Simplex Solar 68
single-family homes 27–8, 41, 66, 117, 122
single-pour concrete house *44*
sites 88, 89, 127, 136
in situ building 16
Skanska 42, 133, 134, 135, 136
'Sketchpad' 75, *75*
Skid Row Housing Trust 146
skills 35, 127, 129
Skoda 49
Skye, Isle of 2
Slovakia 43
'Slow and Smart' philosophy 78, 91, 115, 130
smart homes 135
Smith, Ryan E. 16, 32, 78
Snøhetta 35
social benefits 129
solar cells, SANYO HIT 141
solar energy 68
solar homes 139–40
solar photovoltaic (PV) power-generating systems 139
solar PV glass units *142*
solar water-heating panels 141
solutions-in-search-of-problems 19, *21*, 45, 64
solutions-oriented approach 43, 45
Southern California, university 36
space colonisation 14, 38
Spain 76
specialist works 23–4, 29
'spiral plug-in' concept 76
The Stack, New York 42
standardisation 25, 79, 80, 92, 94, *101*, 108; and BoKlok
    homes 134, 136; product 100; tailored 116
'Standard Separation' delivery model 50
Star Apartments, Los Angeles *42*, *146*
stationary production platforms 40–1
Stavna timber block system 109
steel 55, 65, 80, 115, 121, 141; all-steel home 54
steel-framed detached houses 115
steel-framed systems 95
steel-frame panels 140
Stehn, Lars 126
Stiny, George 76

Stott, Gordon 41–2
Strandlund, Carl 54
'Strategy on the Sustainable Use of Natural Resources used in Europe' (European Commission) 106–7
structural engineers 86
subcontracting 83
subfloor climate control system *141*
subsidies, construction 122
subtractive manufacturing 137
Sullivan, Louis 24–5
Sumitomo Forestry 94
Sumitomo Trust and Banking 139
supply chain *59*, 59, *125*, 134
supply chain management (SCM) 98–101
supply + product domain *58*
sustainability 86, 135, 139
Sutherland, Ivan 75, *75*
Suuronen, Matti 43
Sweden *26*, *27*, 28, 33, 58, 63–4, 74, 120–3; BoKlok 50, 133–6; Mediaeval Church buildings 109; Million Homes Program 23–4, 88; 'Show villages' 137; Tyréns AB 77

Tafuri, Manfredo 45
'tailored standardisation' 116
Taisei Corporation's Technology Centre *142*
taxis 110, 111
Taylors Island, Maryland 109
technical platform *135*
technology 78, 137
tekko-kei purehabu jutaku 63
temporary mass housing 38
tendering 59
terrace houses 134
Terzidis, Kostas 76
Tesla electric car 119
Texas 129
'Theory of Constraints' 106
thermal measurement and analysis *86*
thermal performance 86
thermo-acoustic performance 145
Third Way 37, 46–7, 51–6
tilt-panel walls 75
timber 27–8, 65, 80, 87, 115; house 95
timber block system 109
timber building system 77
timber-framed construction 39, 122; detached houses 115; house, Long Island, NY *12*; multi-family housing 123; single-family homes 41, 122
timber-framed curtain walls 121
timber-framed volumetric construction *27*, *39*, *118*, *133*
timber jointing techniques *109*
Timberlake, James 29, 32, 110
Timberlake, Kieran 33
timeframes 128, 129, 133

toaster, Dualit *107*
'Total Architecture' 85–6, 87
'total system' 55, 56, 102, 111, 113
Toyota 74, 78
Toyota Camry *73*
trade-offs 105–6, 147
trailer park, American *119*
transportable housing 16
transportation 37
triple bottom line benefits 129
trucking, dimensional limitations of 40
trust 95
Tyréns AB 77

Uber 50, 110, 111
UK 88
unit system 94
University of Southern California 36
uptake 110
USA 31, 39–42, 88; Blu Homes 64–5, 70; Home Delivery exhibition 110, *127*; LIHTC 129; and the Packaged House 52–3; Simplex Homes 66–9
use phase 145
user groups 110, 111
utilitarian prefab *37*, 37–8, 56, 88, 137, 138, 147

value 119, 137
value-adding activities 99, 100
value chain 57, 58, 134
value creation 57
Value Engineering (VE) 138
vanity metrics 104
Veidekke 50
VeidekkeMAX *25*, *27*, 50
vernacular buildings 16
vertical circulation 76
'Vertical House' 10
vertical integration 88, 124–5, 130
Veterans Emergency Housing Program 52
villages, show *137*
Villemard 33, *34*
visual programming languages (VPL) 77
Volkswagen 48–9, 79
volume 132
volumetric construction 15, 26, 27, 65, 82, 129, 146; B2 tower 78; off-site fabrication of modules 100; on-site installation of modules *42*, 63
volumetric house builders *40*
volumetric timber-frame construction *118*, 134
Volvo 121
volymbyggande 63
volymelement 63
volymelementtillverkning 63
VW 49